"Barb is a committed lover of J
using the gift of biblical dream i
ies, you can learn how to unders
may direct you, encourage you a.
.... or your true self
for divine healing. Our Father longs to speak to us and often He does that
through our dreams. I believe this book can help you better understand
His voice and the plans He has for your life."

Rev. Cindy Strickle*r* | Director of Presbyterian Reformed Ministries International
(PRMI), & Co-Author of *Let Jesus Heal Your Hidden Wounds*

Barb does an incredible job of unraveling the mysteries of dream interpretation while applying God-given insights. This eye-opening beginner's
guide will help you discover patterns and rhythms of God's nighttime
parables and provide fresh motivation to hear God's voice in unique and
compelling ways.

Rev. Bryan Finley | Foursquare Senior Pastor of Hope Chapel Apex

"Barbara Koob is a woman who seeks fervently after God's own heart. In
her longing to be made whole and to know the God who created and loves
her, she has embraced the reality that God is for her, and not just for her,
but for you, the reader, as well. Barb has produced this wonderful volume
that explores a topic many would shy away from, and she does so within
the confines of a grounded biblical witness. Let the reader beware, if you
do not believe that God longs to communicate with you as you begin reading *Dream Discoveries*, be prepared to have your thinking adjusted. The same
God who spoke to Joseph and Daniel through dreams still speaks today,
and he is speaking to you as well. To step into *Dream Discoveries* is to begin
to know God at work in your life in a whole new way."

Rev. Becki Neumann | Rector, Christ Church, South Riding, VA
Anglican Church in North America

"I've known Barb for over a decade and have watched her carry this message and now birth it into this insightful book. With so many "spiritual"
voices resounding today Barb Koob offers a solid approach for hearing
the true and living God speak to us in ways that will not only change your
own life; but also, change the course of history. I am thankful for Barb's
message and her willingness to share it with such transparency and clarity."

Dr. Kristina L. Chalfin | Adjunct Professor of Spiritual Formation,
Regent University, School of Divinity.

"It is a privilege to endorse Barbara Koob. She is a strong woman of God whose heart is to serve with purpose and her goal is to impact all she encounters with the good news of the Kingdom. Barb has a longing to see others come to Christ and to experience the healing and freedom that only He can offer. She listens closely and intently for God's voice and that powerful discipline has led to the writing of *Dream Discoveries*. This resource, full of Biblical knowledge, personal experience and practical instruction, will be an impactful teacher for individuals and groups seeking God's direction through their dreams.

Stephanie K. Moore | MSW, LCSW,
Therapist, Center for Psychological and Family Services

"Barb is a woman of uncompromising faith and her tenacious belief that God speaks to His children through dreams and visions has set many free to dream once again. Barb has led many small groups into a deeper understanding of God's voice through listening techniques as well as through the interpretation of dreams. Barb has such a heart to see the prophetic voice of God released through dreams."

Melissa Bolden | Prophetic Ministry Team Pastor,
Hope Chapel Apex, MBolden Ministries

"I was thrilled to find so close a friend writing for others and encouraging people how to go about understanding the God given meaning behind their dreams. I know Barb has given grave consideration to where such information stands in relation to the Word of God and the Holy Spirit.

You will enjoy not just the information but the way Barb seems to address you personally. You will be blessed to invest time in this information. Enjoy the humor as Barb laughs at herself on her own training program with the Lord. Understand the intimate insights into our loving God and how He will choose to use whatever means to get our attention, speak to our very being and draw us closer to Him, to our destiny, and how to live life on the way."

Lindy Bravo | Founder of WheresoEver Ministries, Missionary/Pastor

"The heart of a true follower of Christ shines through in this fascinating take on how God speaks to us through our dreams. Barb's insight and experience lead the reader through an amazing journey into the night world that we all experience within our dreams. With extensive research and development, Barb guides the dreamer lovingly toward answers to their most curious questions: those of a dreamer. With personal examples, she shows how to unravel the complex world of dreams and imparts with confidence the encouragement necessary to launch them on a dream quest. I loved this book, and look forward to putting into practice all of the unique facets learned within it."

Lisa Evola | Founder of A Beautiful Life Ministry, Writer/Speaker

"Behind every book is the one who wrote the words. The words in this book come from a heart seeking to know the True God...the God who delights to speak to His children, the God who heals the brokenhearted. I know. The one who wrote this book has prayed with me, has cried with me, has spoken Good words into my soul. And she has blessed me with the gift of dreaming.

The day had been filled with healing prayer sessions. . .six, seven, eight. Barb and I, praying together, were tired. A woman came into the room and asked us to interpret a dream. I nodded to Barb, her realm, her forte. I half-listened as the dream was described; my heart woke a bit as Barb asked questions, inviting the woman into conversation with the God who gives dreams. No interpretations, no imperatives...simply wisdom and encouragement to quest. That night, this dream skeptic, believed. A woman encountered the True Jesus and was healed...and the three of us together were able to see Father-God communicate truth to His children...through a dream.

So come, sit with Barb for a bit, and listen. Bring your dreams and let Jesus explain them...bring your heart and be healed."

Susan Ramsey | Founder of The Connecting Point

Dream Discoveries

Dream Discoveries

Learn to Hope and Dream with Purpose

Barbara Koob

Fedd Books
P.O. Box 341973
Austin, TX 78734
www.thefeddagency.com

Published in association with The Fedd Agency, Inc., a literary agency.

ISBN: 978-1-943217-27-4
eISBN: 978-1-943217-28-1

Printed in the United States of America
First Edition 15 14 13 10 09 / 10 9 8 7 6 5 4 3 2 1

*This book is lovingly dedicated to my darling husband, Jim.
I thank you for being my greatest supporter throughout this writing and speaking
journey. God has used you mightily to encourage me to keep writing about my dreams.
I will forever love you for this and all the God adventures that we have walked together
in making a beautiful story for His Glory.*

Contents

Awake Beautiful Dreamer

Part 1 of the Dream Process: The Revelation

Part 2 of the Dream Process: The Interpretation

Part 3 of the Dream Process: The Application

Dream Discoveries

APPENDICES

Awake
Beautiful
Dreamer

"Who looks outside, dreams;
who looks inside, awakes."

-Carl Jung

1

Are You Lost in Your Dreams?

"Every great dream begins with a dreamer. Always remember, you have within you the strength, the patience, and the passion to reach for the stars to change the world."
–Harriet Tubman

I Was Lost

So many people think *it is just indigestion* when they awake with a strange dream. They erroneously attribute the presence of their dreams to acid reflux and last night's pizza, but I have come to believe differently. One day I could no longer ignore the voice of God in my dreams, but there was no one who could help me navigate through the maze of these nighttime mysteries.

I was lost, yet, in the midst of my search I discovered that there is a Creator who desired to personally speak to me.

Am I crazy?

This vivid dream caught my attention, but like so many of my dreams, I was rather naïve in my understanding.

Scene 1:

I am at a friend's house waiting for some food that she is preparing; however, I believe that this food is not for me. Noticing that my friend is extremely thin and weak, I wonder if she will be OK. I can see her china cabinet filled with many beautiful wedding gifts, but I take the food and leave.

Scene 2:

Next, I am at my house with my husband, and my baby daughter is sleeping upstairs. We have a small steady stream of water running through our backyard. It begins to rain and the ceilings start to leak. The rain grows heavier, developing into torrential falls like Niagara. It breaks through the roof, sopping through the windows and walls. I think we cannot stand under this waterfall and remain alive.

Suddenly my house starts to shake. It appears that it is built on top of this stream which becomes a raging river flowing right through the foundation, rocking the house back and forth. I feel frightened.

Scene 3:

My husband wakes my daughter from her sleep and brings her downstairs due to the storm and raging river. For some reason, I wash my baby girl in the kitchen sink. Then, he brings our yellow Labrador retriever who is covered with mud inside our kitchen.

I am so upset that I scream, "Why are you letting that dirty dog into our house?"

He answers, "So she can be saved." Ugh. I allow my husband to do this, but I let him know that he absolutely must wash that dog's feet before her grimy tracks tarnish our floors and soil our home interiors.

I was fearful of all the mighty waters, but couldn't leave the house.

I woke up

My emotions were a mixture of excitement and fear as I ruminated on those mighty waters flowing above and beneath. Certain that this dream was important, I wrote it down as various questions floated through my foggy brain.

- Could my friend really be sick?
- All those beautiful gifts in my friend's china cabinet must be from God, but what were they?
- The food my friend offered me was for someone else, but who?
- The backyard stream, the powerful waterfall and the raging river intrigued me. Could God's Spirit be falling on me so that I could minister to others?
- Why was I bathing my daughter in the kitchen sink? Was this a symbol of young ones being washed in God's word?
- Who would want a muddy mutt to dash through their clean house? My heart softened as I considered all the people who needed their lives untangled from various circumstances.

Overtime I learned that I was wrong about many of these initial conclusions. The only thing that I rightly understood was that God's Spirit was definitely being poured out, but not for the reasons I thought.

This dream was about *me*—not others. It was the beginning of my dream journey. I wanted answers and set out on a quest to find out.

Are you confused about that dream you just had? Do your emotions and reflections beg further exploration? What will be your next steps to figure out what is really happening?

My Discovery Developments

Today I am confident of this dream's meaning because I lived it and learned from it. It's a miracle that I discovered the truth, but it didn't happen all at once.

During my search, I found many dream interpretation books that contained great information and even good answers, but when it came to unraveling my own mysteries, I often struggled.

That's why I started reading, journaling, praying, blogging and eventually writing this book. Using my mathematics and engineering background, I set out to take the materials that I read and define my own methods of working through my dreams. This book contains my developments and discoveries, but from a biblical perspective. For those of you who are Christians, this book will be exciting as you will see how someone who shares your faith found answers.

But what if you do not share this belief system, or this viewpoint is a turnoff?

I want you to know that I, too, had many feeling and questions about religion and church…of offense, of hypocrisy, of doubt and skepticism, and truth.

I want you to know that I believe that everyone must make their own decision when it comes to faith, and not by force or coercion.

With regard to offense, I encourage you not to allow past injuries to cloud your assessment. Wounded people are often blinded by their offenses and cannot see truth.

With regards to hypocrisy, did you know that Jesus despised duplicity, especially religious leaders who loved to put on pretenses? Don't let the stumbling blocks of man's organized religion and traditions turn you off. God is a loving Father and He grieves when the actions of His so-called followers are contrary to His nature.

With regards to doubt and skepticism, I encourage you to exercise a degree of doubt. A healthy skeptic is open to belief, but thoroughly checks things out. An unhealthy skeptic wants to doubt, gladly accepting a mole hill of evidence that confirms their doubts while rejecting a mountain of evidence to the contrary.[1] I challenge you to test everything in this book for yourself.[2]

If you are sincere in your search, I am confident that God will reveal truth to you.[3]

And so, without further delay, I'd like to introduce my Three-Part Dream Process which you will use in this book and throughout your personal dream journey:

1. **The Revelation:** The revelation is what you see in your dream. It can contain people, places, colors, numbers and more. You will learn about the different types of dream revelations, their purpose, how to journal them, and why you need to do this.

2. **The Interpretation:** The interpretation takes what you see

and tries to make sense of it. Here you need to become skilled in understanding God's voice in your dreams. You will want divine assistance to consider your dream's source, decipher various dream symbols and clues, as well as define the dream message and test it. Other considerations are to practice with a pure heart for we all have blind spots where we cannot see truth and need God's healing touch.[4]

3. **The Application:** The third and last part is the application process—what you do and how you do it. Actually, this is much harder than it appears, for it is dependent on whether you arrived at the correct interpretation. Allow God to gently guide you on how to respond using ways that will spring forth encouragement, hope and a bright future.

As you read through this book, I hope my stories and examples will aid you with your own epiphanies and that they will compel you to rethink your interpretations where appropriate. My intent is that by the time you finish this book you will have a working knowledge of dreams and be well on your way to using this new alternative approach.

An Alternative to Contemporary Dream Interpretation

Today all sorts of dream interpretation books abound, especially in Western civilization. The most famous book is Sigmund Freud's *The Interpretation of Dreams* because it was one of the first to substantiate the science of dream psychoanalysis by validating people's feelings and emotions. As a result, many books were spawned as more people attempted to understand the unconscious mental process.

New Age dream interpretation is also prevalent. It employs the idea that your dreams talk about your life, lovers, health, and your future. Requiring little more than your imaginations, people think it's interesting and even fun to dream, yet rarely are real answers found that reveal the meaning of the dream.

And do you know how old these methods are? Sigmund Freud's book was published in 1899. That's over one hundred years ago. He may be considered the father of modern day psychiatry, but these practices are considerably older than that. Thousands of years ago, ancient Egyptians used the messages in their dreams in order to cure illnesses, make important state decisions, and even decide where to build a temple or when to wage a war. Dreams were considered to be divine predictions of the future—messages from the gods to foretell events. Seems surreal, but the bottom line is that contemporary dream interpretation isn't so modern.

It also isn't accurate. You may receive insight into the meaning of your dreams, but you will never attain full illumination. It's like trying to learn a language without knowing the cultural experience from which the language originates. Just as you can't translate one-to-one words from one language to another, you can't create a dream interpretation method without learning the basics of this heavenly language and the culture of its creator.

It's time for an alternative, a new approach, one that is not preachy or judgmental, but one that opens the door to biblical truth so that ordinary people like yourself may personally discover God and find out exactly what He wants to do in your life. It's my desire that anyone who uses this book will be able to make their own observations, findings and choices using biblical truths regardless of their background and their beliefs.

But before you embark on your self-discovery dream journey, I recommend the following steps as a general outline:

1. **Read and Study:** Examine and analyze the material in this book including the biblical references with an open mind. For some of you these ideas may be new. Try not to discount them until you see the bigger picture, and as I said before, test with a healthy skepticism.

2. **Interpret, Understand and Learn:** Practice how to translate your dream's heavenly language into a meaningful message from God's perspective. This step means that you need to know how to recognize the types of revelations in your dreams. Plus, you need to know how to identify the source and purpose of your dream, along with how to define a meaningful message for your life, and you need to position yourself to keep learning. Practice and Pray: Once you know the basics of interpreting and understanding, realize that dream interpretation can take considerable time, so practice to get good at it. Pray and ask God for His help. Don't give up. And make a point to learn from your mistakes.

3. **Live Your Life:** Serious dreamers are notorious for getting stuck on a dream and even stuck on a life issue. Live your life well while you are awake. Love, laugh, and give yourself a healthy dose of common sense. Celebrate the diversity of friends and family with a conscious commitment to promote good influences in your life.

4. **Respond with a Healthy Choice:** The messages in a dream can be wonderfully revealing or even frightening. It's important to remember that our lives are never determined by a dream, but are determined by our choices. Respond by making good life choices

and reap the benefits.

Understand that even with this approach, it sometimes takes months or even longer for you to discover the meaning of your dream, and sometimes you never comprehend what it fully means.

Try to walk in faith that God will give you the interpretation as you listen, interpret, and understand. I know that may be a stretch for some of you, but trust me that testing this approach can't hurt.

Are You Listening?

Did you know that the Bible is filled with numerous stories of how God used dreams to speak to people?

From the Old Testament, God gave Abimelek a dream to stop him from pursuing Abraham's wife, Sarah.[5] Jacob had several dreams from God. One was about a stairway reaching to heaven and another was about wisely breeding flocks of goats and sheep.[6] God also spoke to Jacob's father-in-law, Laban, warning him not to say anything bad or good to Jacob.[7]

The great biblical dreamer Joseph had experienced two double dreams of how his brothers would one day bow down to him.[8] After being sold into slavery and unjustly sent to the Pharaoh's prison, God used Joseph to correctly interpret the King's Cupbearer's dream and his Baker's dream.[9] All this was to prepare Joseph for his destiny. It started with Joseph successfully interpreting Pharaoh's double dreams regarding a forthcoming famine, and it ended with Joseph applying wisdom about what to do.[10]

Gideon overheard a Midianite's dream that foretold of Israel's victory.[11] The Lord appeared to King Solomon in a dream declaring that he could ask for whatever he wanted, and Solomon chose to ask for wisdom.[12]

Nebuchadnezzar, the King of Babylon had a few dreams from God too. One was about the kingdoms of the world.[13] The other was about his life being cut down like a stump on a tree until he acknowledged the King of Heaven.[14] Fortunately, God had bestowed great wisdom upon another great biblical dreamer named Daniel to interpret these dreams and visions.[15]

From the New Testament, Joseph received a dream to not be afraid to marry Mary because what was conceived in her was from the Holy Spirit.[16] Joseph was also warned in a dream to quickly get up and take Mary and the baby Jesus to Egypt, bypassing Herod's decree to kill all the baby boys under the age of two.[17] God even directed Joseph on when to return to Israel and where to settle.[18]

After the three wise men visited the baby Jesus, they were warned in a dream to return home using a different route thus avoiding King Herod's wrath.[19]

And after Jesus grew up in wisdom and in stature fulfilling his three-year ministry on earth, He was in prison awaiting the cross, and Pilate's wife dreamt that Jesus was an innocent man. She suffered so much regarding this dream that she sent a message to her husband to have nothing to do with crucifying Him.[20]

Clearly, God used dreams to speak to mankind. Did you notice that some of the people He spoke to didn't believe in Him? I used to think that He only spoke to a privileged few. Not true. God says that in the last days that He will pour out His Spirit on all flesh.[21] That means He wants to speak to you and me.

Yet, sometimes our dreams can have false messages.[22] It is not God speaking, which is why we must test them.[23]

Years ago, a good missionary friend urged me to speak to her supporters about how I unravel my dreams using the Bible. Ever since my first presentation, I realized how much I learned and how great the need was to help people discover what God might be saying. From that initial speaking engagement, I saw an amazing phenomenon the next day: When we asked God to speak to us, He did.

Afterward so many people told me that God spoke to them that I found it rather unnerving. They wanted to know what it meant. I was ill equipped to handle the deluge of people who would seek me out to find answers. All the while I proceeded to rework my material with the intentions of teaching people this skill, discovering more about myself and my own dreams.

I began to see an interesting correlation between the people who dream frequently and their need for inner healing. Like me, these people were captivated by their dreams. Like me, they wanted to understand these cryptic codes, but were unable to see clearly until God opened their eyes.

I admit it took a long time to understand what God was telling me. I was not purposely missing the point; I was just wounded, confused and deceived. Having experienced trauma, anxiety, fear, control, lack of self-worth, and rejection, I learned there was an enemy that existed in my soul. Unfortunately, the survival skills I adopted became the obstacles to my moving forward.

Sadly, many of us trash our dreams like unwanted junk emails, but God wants us to understand our predicaments. He wants to help us. He rewards those who diligently seek Him.[24] As God began to reveal truth in my dreams, I gladly surrendered to His amazing grace and extravagant love.

Please accept my invitation to join me on this journey of dream discoveries. I promise God will speak to you… just as He did during biblical times. But there are two conditions you must meet. First, you must want to hear from God from the depths of your heart, even if He's saying what you don't want to hear or do. Second, you must be listening.

The choice is yours.

Do you have within you the strength, the patience and the passion to reach for the stars to change the world? It begins with you.

The Bible tells us that the glory of God conceals a matter, but the glory of kings searches it out.[25] Choose to search out the real meanings of your dreams, and allow God to awaken your senses to hear His voice. Only you and God can find His secrets.

Will you start your journey by praying?

Dear God,
I open my heart to You throughout this dream journey. Please give me dreams that I may know for sure that it is You. Forgive me when I have not paid attention and didn't do what you asked. God, I am listening now. I want to hear whatever you may say to me. Thanks so much! Amen.

Review

1. What is your dreaming experience? Do you know what it means?
2. Have you ever had a dream you thought was significant? What did you do about it?
3. Name the three parts of the Dream Process. Describe the functions of each part.
4. How do you think God speaks to the world today? How might God use dreams to communicate to you?
5. Name two things you must do to hear God speak.

P.S. I hope you will try this prayer stuff as that's part of the test, but don't forget those two conditions. By the way, do you want to know the interpretation of my dream? That dream is a complex one with no simple answer. So please be patient with me and read on.

2

Awake to God's Whispers

"Listen for the whispers"
– Esther Kerr Rusthoi

Who is that Beautiful Dreamer?

Have you ever turned up the volume to your favorite song? There is a mystical quality to music that touches the depths of your soul. You can tune into the melody, the words, and the accompanying instruments while tuning out the world. This experience is one of our natural escape mechanisms, and it is similar to dreams. We listen to the pleasant sounds we want to hear, and if possible, we tune out the ones we don't.

I love listening to various types of music that inspire my imagination, and then try playing those tunes on the piano by ear. As a young girl, I remember this one particular song, "Beautiful Dreamer." Poetic and melodic, this song perfectly describes the alluring quality of dreams that woo in the night:

> *Beautiful dreamer, wake unto me,*
> *Starlight and dewdrops are waiting for thee,*
> *Sounds of the rude world heard in the day,*
> *Lulled by the moonlight, have all passed away.*
> *Beautiful dreamer, queen of my song,*
> *List while I woo thee with soft melody;*
> *Gone are the cares of life's busy throng.*
> *Beautiful dreamer, awake unto me,*
> *Beautiful dreamer, awake unto me.*[26]

Like starlight, dreams shed light in your life. Like dewdrops, dreams refresh. Dreams bypass the cares of your life's song like magic. These revelations disclose your true self; they depict what is really happening in your life, and it's not necessarily what you think.

You are this beautiful dreamer to whom God wants to speak. It's not because of your outward appearance. You are beautiful because God made you in His image.[27] It is God who uniquely created you, loves you and wants to communicate with you.

Are you willing to awake to God's voice and do whatever He may ask? If so, He will transform you into something absolutely beautiful for His glory, but you must have a heart that wants to hear.

God is Whispering

I dreamt I was flying with roller skates. An absurd dream, it was from my early childhood recollections. Struggling to stay airborne, I was moving too fast and out of control. As I soared in the sky, I kept bumping into the tree-tops and it hurt. When my body would descend, I was afraid that I could not land safely. I suppose it reflected my life as a kid, but as the years went by, that dream faded, and new ones emerged.

In my adult years, I often dreamt that my husband and I were moving back into my childhood home. I was excited about all the wonderful restorations. It was as if God knew deep down inside of me that I desired for all my childhood memories to be beautifully transformed. Do you think that God can use the natural dream process to kindly whisper to our subconscious mind and heart?

God is the amazing Creator, an infinite being of love, full of knowledge and wisdom. For the longest time I totally dismissed the fact that God might be speaking in my dreams, but He will speak in any number of ways to get His point across, including the use of dreams. Here are just a few of the ways He speaks today:

- God speaks through His Word. You can find all kinds of divine revelations in His Word, if you'll take the time to start reading it. One of my favorite revelations is that I can be God's friend.[28]
- God speaks through other people. I chuckle when I think of how many times God spoke through my mother. So keep an open mind to hear what God might be saying through others.
- God speaks in His creation. For example, whenever I see a butterfly I sense God speaking glorious freedom. This method isn't as tangibly understood as a clear spoken word, but it can be very powerful.
- God speaks in life's circumstances. He uses your personal experiences like having children, job problems, financial woes and even family strife to mold you. Rather than steam rolling ahead with your plans, you might want to pause to hear His plan. (P.S. I've learned this the hard way.)

- God speaks in songs. Sometimes the words of a musical phrase speak to my heart as they replay in my head. One of my favorite examples is the song *Everything's Alright*, from Jesus Christ Superstar, as He was cautioning me not to worry. Since I love music, He seems to speak to me a lot using this method.
- God speaks through dreams and visions.[29]

Don't ever think that God speaks in just one way. While all these methods are valid, He will speak whatever way best fits how He has created you. For example, I love music, and often He uses songs to speak to me. I am also a visual learner, which is why He frequently speaks to me through dreams.

I've found that God will speak the same thing but often confirms it using different methods. I'm so glad because if I miss something, I have another chance to find out.

Nonetheless, we must open our hearts to hear His whispers regardless of how He speaks.

Matters of Our Heart

One reason that God uses dreams is to reveal matters of our heart. Most people don't know the deep thoughts and intentions within their hearts, but God knows everything and delights to show you without getting in your face.[30]

God also speaks in dreams because when you sleep, you are quiet. In today's world there are so many voices competing for your attention. God takes advantage of this opportunity when He knows you'll be attentive, and of course, too tired to talk back.

God also uses dreams to bypass your walls of self-defense and pride. Dreams can catch you off guard appealing to your natural mind (soul), yet speaking to your inner man (spirit). Dreams can be weird, funny, sexy, or even inspiring. If you look beyond the surface, God is opening your ears to hear instructions.[31]

Many times you don't recognize your own heart issues or incorrect belief systems. These wrong beliefs, sometimes called strongholds, are lies that come against the knowledge of God. Dreams are God's way of gently tapping you on the shoulder and saying, "Hi there. You might want to look here. If you'll let me, I'd like to help you."

One of my favorite dream examples is what I call "Bikini Babe." Here, I enjoyed seeing myself in this very cute bikini. It sure pleased my senses as I felt fabulous about my great little figure. Yet, when I looked deeper, I saw my problem.

My carnal nature, my flesh was showing and I needed to cover up. Yikes!

It was God's gentle tap on the shoulder to shift my focus from outward appearances to an inside makeover of my character flaws.

This example is also a great one on how dream symbolism and interpretation works. Images are not always what they appear to be and need a deeper interpretation if they are to reveal our true unconscious state.[32] I suspect a number of people could have told me, but I had a blind spot.

Thankfully, God is a gentleman and His purposes are always good. He never pushes His opinion, but sweetly guides to wholeness. He knows I am sensitive and He is unfailingly kind when speaking correction. Somehow I know what He's talking about, yet I am never shamed when He reveals my insecurities, my fears, and all kinds of wrong thinking.

While these taps are not pleasant, I have learned to welcome His insight. Will you?

Wake Up and Start Listening

It was an unforgettable encounter.

When I was about twenty-two years old, Jesus appeared at my bedpost. Petrified, I purposely kept my eyes tightly shut, but somehow I continued to see Him as He repeatedly spoke, "Wake up and start listening!"

Regretfully, I answered with an excuse and did not respond to His call that night. "I'm so tired. Can you come back in the morning?"

I can't believe I actually said that to the Lord; however, that is the truth. Immediately He left me. Suddenly I felt alone with haunting thoughts of what I had done.

Although I didn't grasp it at the time, I sensed that His presence left me. For years I contemplated the meaning, but today it stares me in the face. All He wanted was for me to wake up and start listening.

There is a story in the Bible of how God spoke to a young boy named Samuel one night. At first he didn't recognize God speaking. In fact, it took three times before Samuel responded, "Speak Lord, your servant is listening," and that was with the help of an older high priest.[33] This story is dear to my heart because it reminds me of my experience.

Could it be that God wants to speak, but like Samuel, you are not recognizing it? Or like me, you choose not to answer? Notice that God spoke to a child, not the high priest. Being childlike is definitely a characteristic that touches God's heart.[34] Even people with feeble faith can learn to hope like a child.

Dream revelation is one of the best ways God can download His thoughts, intentions and divine plans to earth. Even when my daughter was little, she would tell me how she heard God speak to her. God was one of her best friends. Sometimes she even told me about their conversations. If it's possible for me and my daughter, I know it's possible for you. So go ahead and ask, my friend.[35m] We can ask for anything in His name and He will do it.[36] Sometimes all you need is a little faith, and you can ask God to increase that, too.[37]

It's been my experience that whenever we sincerely ask God to speak, He does.

Just spend time with God and relax. No need to struggle. With childlike simplicity, expect an answer. After all, you are God's beloved child, and if you choose, you can prepare yourself to receive, and keep seeking until you find.[38]

Beautiful dreamer, God is whispering. Awake and start listening.

Dear God,
Please help me to relax in the knowledge that I am Your beloved beautiful dreamer to whom You desire to speak. I ask You to increase my faith with a childlike quality of expectation. Lord, I ask you to come tap me on the shoulder today for I am listening to your whispers. Thanks God! Amen.

Review

1. Who is that beautiful dreamer and what does that mean to you?
2. Why does God use dreams to speak to our heart?
3. Has God ever tapped you on the shoulder? What was it about?
4. Do you have childlike faith to expect God to speak? If not, will you ask Him to increase your faith?

Part 1 of the Dream Process:

The Revelation

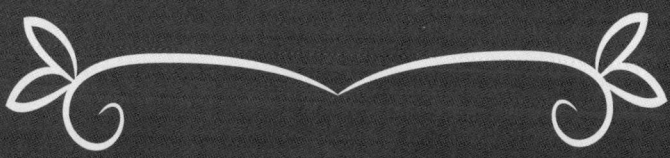

"The future belongs to those who see the beauty in their dreams."

–Eleanor Roosevelt

3

Start a Journal and Write

*"I am a little pencil in the hand of a writing God who
is sending a love letter to the world."*
-Mother Teresa

Dream Science

On August 26, 1910 a rosebud was born in Albania. Inside this little flower was a passion to help the poor, the sick, the orphaned and the dying.[39] As a matter of fact, the lives of missionaries and their service in Bengal, India absolutely fascinated this young girl. Her name was Agnes Gonxha Bojaxhi, but we respectfully know her as Mother Teresa.[40] I wonder how this simple Roman Catholic nun bloomed into an international humanitarian and advocate for the poorest of the poor. I wonder what she dreamed and how her passion became so much more than a dream.

It is a medical fact that we all dream. Science tells us that dreams are expressions of thoughts and feelings that are represented through the creation of sensory environments in our minds. Dreams occur naturally during REM sleep about every ninety minutes throughout the night for progressively longer periods.[41] This is the science of dreams, but why don't we remember our dreams?

I blame those dream snatchers, dream drainers, and dream busters.[42] Dream snatchers are lies used to convince you that your dreams are meaningless. Dream drainers are poor environments, poor attitudes, and bad circumstances. Dream busters are distractions, misinformation, disbelief, and depression.[43] These dream thieves can subtly sift through your conscious thoughts tempting you to think that God isn't real, that He doesn't speak in dreams, and that He isn't there to help you.

So be on-guard. Be proactive. Here's how I recommend that you begin your dream process.

Start a Journal

Journaling is one of the best tools to help you retain your dreams accurately. I can't tell you how many times I thought I would remember, and then didn't. I recommend a separate dream journal, exclusively set aside for recording your dreams.

A dream journal allows you to keep all your dreams in a single place. No need to scour the house looking for that piece of paper or fall back on your unreliable memory. You'll find everything right there ready for your personal reference. You will recognize recurring themes more easily, and you can record visions and prophetic words, too.

When you have a dream, write it down as soon as you can. Write when the dream is fresh in your mind. I once had a very complex dream where the source was God. I call these dreams my God dreams. As I gazed upon what I saw, processing the content, the Lord had me return to my written words. I was so happy that I had transcribed the dream exactly as I saw it because I noticed that my thought process had automatically predetermined a dream element incorrectly. The dream clearly revealed that it was I who needed help, but I erroneously thought I was the one called to help. It was a good word for me.

Have you had a complex God dream cross your path? Resist the temptation to wait to record it. Delays can fool your memory into a false remembrance. You could be deluded to write what you think you saw. Don't be tempted to fill in the missing blanks.

Go ahead and keep your journal and pen by your bed. Or if you prefer, use a tape recorder, but make sure you transcribe it to paper later. Once you have a permanent record, you can always refer back to what you wrote. This exact record will prove extremely useful for future use, for you'll know for certain what you really dreamt and not what you thought.

After you have written your dream, I recommend leaving extra space that can be used later as you write your impressions, your thoughts and your possible interpretation.

Dream Details

There are many aspects of a dream's details that might be recorded. I like to think of it as taking good notes for a class. While you may not use all of these dream details, here are a few things for consideration in your journaling entry:

- The date and time when you had this dream could be noteworthy as numbers can have symbolic meanings. The date and time can also relate to a key event, either past or present.
- Landscapes and scenes, especially at the beginning of your dream,

provide the context of your dream. These settings should be used to determine what your dream is about. So make note of these in your journal.

- Feelings and emotions can speak loudly in your dreams. Don't be apprehensive to note them especially if they appeared real.
- Colors and numbers can have symbolic significance.
- People, places, and things have symbolic importance, too.
- Current circumstances or activities going on in your life could be directly related to your dream. Although they may appear unrelated, sometimes your dream is the exact answer to your life situation.
- The actual physical location of where you were sleeping could have meaning. Being in a strange hotel room or someone else's house can certainly influence the atmosphere of your dreamscapes as well. These things are noteworthy.

You will see the details of your dream crystallizing as you start writing your dream down. That's a good thing for you'll have some excellent records to work with later on.

I have one last caution. Never attempt to interpret your dream while you are recording it. It causes confusion and incorrect results! You may find yourself writing what you think you dreamt and not what you actually did or you may also find yourself writing your interpretation without realizing it. And so, always keep your dream and the interpretation separate.

The Out-of-Bed Factor

As I talk with people about dreams, I often hear comments about being too tired to get out of bed. I certainly understand; however, I have to ask you. If a loved one in desperate need called you in the night, would you take the call? If waiting for an important word from your doctor, would you roll over and go back to sleep? God is calling you. Will you take His call?

Sorrowfully, I hung up the phone on God when I received my first vivid spiritual dream. Jesus stood at my bedpost and repeated these words over and over to me, "Wake up and start listening!"

I groggily replied, "I'm so tired. Would you come back in the morning?"

At my response, He left and I awoke startled with a great sadness. Oh my God! I can't believe I did that, but alas—it's true! Because of that experience, I promised myself that I will never miss another phone call from God again. Many times we ask the Lord for help, and He answers. However, He does not do it on our timetable. So often God speaks, but we ignore His promptings, His words. After a time, I think He does go away just like He left me that night.

If you are not already convinced, I must tell you that my best revelations have come in the middle of the night for He spoke when I was quiet. Even if I have to get out of bed, I quickly write down my dream, pray for understanding, and then ask the Lord to help me go back to sleep.

Are you persuaded yet to journal? If you are serious, go to the store and buy yourself a dream journal and a tape recorder if that's what you think you'll use. You can even use the recording apps on your cell phone, but whatever you choose, when that dream appears, you will be ready to write.

So you decide. What's it worth to you?

Something Beautiful

In one very small way, Mother Teresa and I are alike. We were both raised Roman Catholic. While I was never captivated with missionaries and the people of Bengal, I did aspire to be a nun as a young child. Spellbound with a religious vocation and yearning to be good enough, I dreamt of what it might be like to live that lifestyle of sisterhood.

Undeniably I am no Mother Teresa, but for a little fun I dressed as a nun for Halloween one year. My mother brilliantly used black and white crepe paper along with white paper streamers to transform me into a Sister of St. Joseph. It was a wonderful costume except for one problem. It rained.

My costume worsened as the night progressed. As I trudged door to door, my outer clothing deteriorated into pieces of wet black and white paper. Reminiscing, I can't forget this one comment from a neighborhood gentleman before he dropped candy in my bag.

"Now exactly *what* are you?"

By the end of the night no one could tell what I was supposed to be. Tired of telling people, I eventually gave up and went home.

Just as my costume faded as the night went on, so too will your dream memories disappear if you do not write them down right away. This is why journaling is important. It helps us clear our thoughts to define who we are and what we are doing with our life. It documents where we are in our self-discovery process. It aids us to stop and think about the problems we face. When we invite God into the process, journaling allows us to dream for our future. Even Mother Teresa journaled and we know from her writings that she continually asked God to come, to be her light.[44] Although she struggled like many of us, journaling was one of the tools she employed as she lived her dreams.

God made Mother Teresa into something beautiful for Him.[45] She took steps of obedience to love people, and miraculously others started following her. It wasn't her; it was God. Indeed, she loved God so much she continued pursuing Him even when it hurt. While we may not be called into formal ministry, I think we can learn from her example.

We can be little pencils writing our dreams, our visions, our deepest personal thoughts and desires, asking God to come and be our light. If we let Him, He will write our unique life story.

So write, my friend, write. Do it anyway.[46] When that divine revelation comes, make sure you write it down. Write down all those details including your thoughts and emotions. As the morning light of daybreak appears, you will be so excited to read your dream revelation—God's special present for you.

He waits for you to seek Him. It's His love letter.

Dear God,
I need Your help to pull the plug on all my dream snatchers, dream drainers, and dream busters. Should You call me in the middle of the night, I promise to answer by writing it down. Because I love you, I desire to be a little pencil in Your handwriting of my life story. Please come and be my light. Thanks God! Amen.

Review

- Name some dream thieves that might be hindering God speaking to you, and think about how you might remove them.
- What details should you record about your dreams? Why might they be important?
- Will you commit to journal your dreams? If not, what is stopping you?
- How do you feel about being God's little pencil? Do you believe He will help you write your life story? Why or why not?
- Have you asked God to come and shine His light on your life?

4

The Dream Revelation

"Never lose an opportunity of seeing anything beautiful,
for beauty is God's handwriting."
–Ralph Waldo Emerson

All About Dreams

Do you realize that all kinds of revelation experiences surround you every day? Similar to reading between the lines, these experiences often do not use words. Every time you devour a dessert, cuddle your child, sniff a fresh rosemary twig, dance to your favorite song, or gaze upon the crashing ocean waves, you receive revelatory gems through your five senses.

These gems disclose valuable information about you, other people, the world, and God. But revelations can come in other ways, like from a premonition, a word, a vision, and of course, a dream.

Dream revelations are one of easiest to receive because you don't have to do anything. They are similar to visions, but just happen while you sleep. Your own little intelligence report is downloaded with an important news flash. Could it get any easier?

Dream revelations are also the first part of the dream process. There are different types of dream revelations too, and I refer to these various revelations as dream types. As you learn to process your dream, choose one of each of these possibilities:

- **Simple or Complex:** A simple dream is obvious; it means exactly what you think it does. On the other hand, complex dreams are difficult to discern and require more thought and time to understand.
- **Symbolic or Literal:** Symbolic dreams use a strange dream language, which requires unmasking the codes, while literal dreams can come true exactly as you see them. In order to determine if your dream is symbolic or literal, look for anything that appears symbolic. If you find a dream symbol, then the entire dream must

be considered symbolic. For example, if I dreamt that I took my Bible on a roller coaster ride, something that I would never do, that entire dream must be treated symbolically.

However, if your dream does not appear to be symbolic, you can probably assume it is literal. Literal dreams have the potential to happen the way you dreamed it. You need to watch closely as the events could unfold before your eyes. They could provide directions or even a warning.

A girlfriend once told me of a dream where the sun blocked her vision as she was driving her car. In the dream she kept driving and accidentally hit a child playing in the street. The next day she found herself living that dream, but stopped her car beforehand only to discover that she avoided a terrible tragedy. I've also heard of a man who dreamt his young son drowned in a nearby pool. He took precautions and nothing happened. All I know is that sometimes we should pay attention and use wisdom.[47]

- **Visual and Maybe Actual:** All dreams are visual, but only some are actual.[48] In a visual dream you see things, but with an actual dream there is some type of impartation. You can physically receive an extra dose of faith. There could be angels present, or even heavenly instructions to transform your circumstance.[49] It might not make sense, but you know in your heart that something happened. It was more than a dream.

- **Natural or Supernatural:** Natural dreams are derived from your own psyche including the world around you, but supernatural dreams originate from an outside source, either God or Satan. The world often defines the supernatural as a type of sixth sense; however, did you know that God also has a name for it? We believers call it prophetic. Always consider the source of your dream for it is the key to correctly applying the interpretation, but we'll talk about that more in the next chapter.

- **Prophetic or False:** Your dreams can be either prophetic or false. Prophetic dreams refer to the Lord speaking and can even have a futuristic dimension to them. False dreams, which can come from your own natural mind or from the enemy, carry lies and deceptions. This is another reason to ask God to help you understand your dreams.

Prophetic Dreams and the Future

One day a local storeowner relayed his bizarre dream to me and took me by surprise by asking, "Barb, is this a prophetic dream?" I didn't know what to say, but if God was speaking, then it was certainly prophetic.

And so, my definition of a prophetic dream is simply *God speaking in a dream*. From a biblical perspective, the prophetic means God speaking, which can use any holy method of communication as long as the source is Godly.

Around 350 B.C. the western worldview of dreams drastically changed because of a philosopher named Aristotle. He thought the five senses and the reasons of the mind were the only valid means to obtain true knowledge.[50] Sorry to say, this mindset has endured through the centuries for many people today continue to equate dream information with one's imagination.

When people do ask me about a prophetic dream, I often hear about a catastrophe forecasted for the future, a doom and gloom scenario. They wonder if it's destined to come true.

Honestly, no one can know the future but God Himself. However, I do know that God uses a prophetic dream in the same way He uses a prophetic word—to strengthen, encourage and comfort.[51] His purposes are always to point people to Him.

He wants to warn you of things that may come and offer the opportunity for constructive change. Two examples in the Bible that foretell of disaster are that of Ninevah and Israel. In each case, God directed a prophet to speak for Him.

Jonah was sent to Nineveh, calling the people to repent to avoid judgment and they did. Jeremiah was sent to His own people, the Israelites. He beckoned them to circumcise their hearts and change their evil ways, but they did not.

History tells us that Nineveh was spared, but that Israel was invaded by the Babylonians and the people taken captive. Notice both examples were a clarion call to penitence, but with different outcomes based upon the people's response.

Don't worry about that frightening dream. You can take comfort that dream revelations are always conditional based on the choices we make. Altering your course of action can change an outcome. The consequences of a poor decision can also be lessened with prayer. So while a prophetic dream can be a powerful catalyst, its message is never cast in concrete.

God's Purposes for Dreams

As a kid, I often amused myself and my friends on the piano with a song entitled, "Heart and Soul."[52] With a great set of four simple chords we played this melody over again with great delight. Usually a parent's screech to stop would temporarily halt those sounds, but it fully never stopped until someone finally decided that that was the end.

Nowadays I think of that song as both a comedy and tragedy. Like replaying that tune in your head, we replay the same issues of our heart and soul unless we consciously choose otherwise. That's why God's purposes for dreams are to reveal your true self, to encourage you, and to direct you. I believe these purposes can come in the form of three unique dream types that I've listed below:

1. Heart and Soul Dreams: These dreams reveal your innermost self, the condition of your heart and your soul. Your heart could be broken, wounded, or hard towards certain people and circumstances. Your soul could be captive by your past and other problems lurking in your thought life. Nightmares fall into this category as bad dreams often reoccur until the root problem is solved. Here are some other reasons for Heart and Soul dreams:
   - Disclosing the true motives of your heart.
   - Exposing the deep thoughts you carry in your soul, both negative and positive.
   - Uncovering the offenses you still lug around.
   - Illuminating the need for forgiveness.
   - Shedding light on areas of erroneous thinking and wrongdoing.
   - Highlighting the stumbling blocks to healing.
   - Making urgent appeals to your heart.
   - Helping pave the way to repair relationships.

2. Encouragement Dreams: These dreams provide comfort and God uses them by:
   - Revealing His love.
   - Producing hope.
   - Inspiring faith.
   - Filling you with joy.
   - Calming you with peace.
   - Easing your grief and sorrow.
   - Cheering you on your journey.
   - Satisfying you with His Spirit.

3. Directional Dreams: God uses these types of dreams to keep you on His straight path. Prayer alerts, which reveal the

need for spiritual warfare, are also included here. Directional dreams help you chart your life's course by:

- Foretelling or preventing an event.
- Defining your destiny.
- Warning of impending danger.
- Appealing to your senses for prayer and intercession.
- Giving advice, wisdom and counsel.
- Offering important instructions as to where to go or not go.
- Providing discernment.
- Stirring up your God-given calling.
- Helping you grow spiritually.

As He opens your ears and gives instructions, never forget that God can say so much more with a picture.[53] So while focusing on a single purpose may be sufficient for a simple dream, do not overlook that complex dreams may have more than one purpose.

Yet, sometimes even the simplest of dreams are not understood. One example occurred soon after I married my wonderful husband. I dreamt that I was tightly bound by a thick rope, and someone came and cut me loose. Often I wondered what this could mean, for a type of darkness habitually clouded my emotions.

Born to strong-willed teenage parents who were unprepared for parenthood and its responsibilities, I had a sense of freedom when I was no longer under their roof. Haunted by a few bitter memories that I was forced to suppress, it was the first time that I felt safe to allow my true feelings to surface. Crippled in my present because of lack of knowledge from my past, I did not understand the underpinnings of my emotions, but God visited. My answers didn't come overnight, but He loved me through it releasing me into His good purposes.

Beautiful one, God gave you these emotions for a reason. Your emotions explain what is going on in your life, which is why they often spill over into your dreams. You need to process these emotions, for He desires to kindly guide you as your loving Heavenly Father.[54] His heart aches for you to see the truth about yourself and your situation. He longs for you to know who He is, and He is eager to encourage with good plans for your life. Yearning to help direct your next steps, He desires relationship.

It's About Relationship

Our omniscient God is not hard of hearing. A great example is that of a parent and child. My daughter may not be open to what I'd like to say, but I still want to communicate with her. One day as I was speaking to my three-year-old darling, I tested her listening and obedience skills.

"Don't go in the pool," I firmly reiterated several times. "You need your floaties." I watched closely; and of course, she ignored her mother and tromped right into the deep water.

While I spared not a second, I was stunned that she wasn't upset after almost drowning. Didn't she understand what I said and why? I suspect that our Father God has rescued you and me many a time, too, and often without our knowledge.

Anyway, now that my daughter has grown, I often talk to her, but not necessarily about life and death situations. Defining moments exist, however, the reason I speak to my child is not to tell her what to do, but to develop a relationship. Don't you think it's the same with God?

When I first began my dream journey, I wondered if one dream and its message were more important than another. Struggling to discern the natural from the supernatural, and the significance of each dream, I practiced on all my dreams. While my soulish dreams provided revelation, I focused on my God-inspired dreams to learn what God was saying and why.

Like words that are not understood, dreams without an interpretation are meaningless, lost forever.[55] Open those deaf ears to understand God's purposes that you may see His beautiful plans.[56]

Seeing Beauty

After I married, I had the most unusual recurring dream where my husband and I owned a small used popup camper which parked right outside our home. I fantasized about where we would go camping, as I had such great memories of camping with my family. Every time I awoke from this dream I felt so happy. Yet, I purposely ignored the deeper meaning. I suspect it was because I was relatively happy with where I was.

Today, I clearly see how God was using this dream metaphor to reveal that I was held captive. I was not openly trapped in an awful place, but I was in my own little world not wanting to settle down and grow up. Enjoying the prospect of camping was a sign of deliberately avoiding motherhood because I couldn't face some things from my younger years.

God wanted to heal that dark place.

Having lived through some verbal and physical abuse from my childhood, God knew that a fearful little girl hid deep inside. While others judged me as a selfish career woman who enjoyed the world and all it offered, He saw my desire to be a mother. The real reason I was camping out wasn't because I didn't want to change. It was because I was terrified of repeating a generational curse that plagued the women in my family.

How lovely that God desires to give beauty for those ashes.[57] He perfectly orchestrated my circumstances using infertility treatments to change my fear to faith.

In the days of the Old Testament, there was a man named Daniel who was also held captive. Exiled to Babylon, Daniel became a prisoner placed in training for service to their King Nebuchadnezzar. During that time, God gave him supernatural knowledge to understand visions and dreams of all kinds. He studied and made himself approved by God, and in turn, was recognized by the king for his skill that was found ten times better than all the others he worked with, for God was with him.

One day this skill proved exceedingly valuable as the king had a very troublesome dream, which he could not remember when he awoke. In an effort to have his dream resurrected from his memory and interpreted, the king ordered that the wise men, astrologers, magicians and soothsayers declare the dream and its meaning. Relentless to receive an answer, the king threatened them with death, but no one on earth could give the king what he sought.

But Daniel knew that there is a God in heaven who reveals mysteries.[58] Miraculously Daniel received not just the dream but its interpretation, and God saved those lives.

God is willing to travel with you on your dream journey just as he did with Daniel, but you must look to Him to see His beauty. He wants to give you hope and plans for your future.[59]

Sometimes it's hard to have faith, but don't give up. Even if you don't agree with everything I'm explaining biblically, you can start where you are and use what you do learn to behold His beautiful handwriting for your life. So dreamers, let's move on to next part of the dream process – the interpretation.

Dear God,
I want to behold Your handwriting for my life. Help me to start seeing Your beautiful purpose for dreams is having a relationship with You. Thank You God! Amen.

Review

1. Name some facts about dream revelations.
2. How can you determine if your dream is literal or symbolic?

3. What is a prophetic dream? Do prophetic dreams always come true? Why or why not?
4. What are the three main purposes that God speaks to in a dream?
5. How does God speaking in our dreams compare with a parent speaking to a child?
6. How can you see God's beautiful handwriting in your life?

The Interpretation

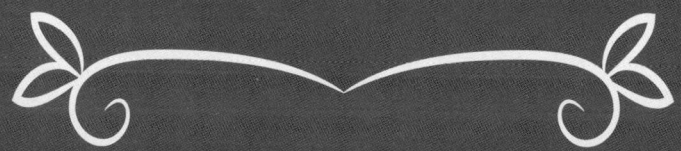

"Out of intense complexities
intense simplicities emerge."

–Winston Churchill

5

Get God's Understanding and Interpretation

"Any intelligent fool can make things bigger and more complex...It takes a touch of genius—and a lot of courage to move in the opposite direction."
– Albert Einstein

What is this Get GUI Process?

The interpretation, understanding what you see in your dreams, is the second part of the dream process. Dreamers often get shipwrecked here, which is why I'm going to explain my unique process for dream interpretation here. But first, let me explain the Get GUI name.

Many decades ago I worked in software development. At that time, the information technology industry began developing a graphical user interface called GUI (pronounced gooey) for their software applications. Today many know this front-end interface as Windows.

Like using your TV, DVRs, iPhones and every other technical device, customers can now utilize these intricate applications with these cool dashboards that use pictures to cue the user into what functionality is underneath so that users can be totally unaware of the cutting edge technology seamlessly running behind the scenes. Well, just as an application GUI provides a window into a program's functions, God uses dreams as a window into your life.

Dreams are like windows into your true self, revealing all the things going on around you and inside. If you commit to some deep soul searching, you will be able to see what's really going on. Still, we often don't understand why things work the way they do.

For this reason, I use this same GUI acronym to coin my dream interpretation process, but to me, it means *Get **G**od's **U**nderstanding and **I**nterpretation*. Incidentally, I love this GUI abbreviation because when God gives you something, it's like eating a caramel apple—tasty, fun, and sweet. In fact, He purposely makes it good and gooey, so you will want to stick with it; however, it can get messy.

No matter. Just Get GUI in four relatively simple steps and enjoy.

Step 1: Consider Your Dream and Its Source

One day it dawned on me that I must always consider the source of my dreams. Funny that the importance of who might be speaking in my dreams never occurred to me earlier in my journey, but it sure is critical.

I believe there are three sources for dreams: God, your own true self and Satan. God speaks for the purposes of edification and comfort. Satan speaks to steal, kill, and destroy. Your true self speaks whatever resides within your being.[60] You can never accurately critique your dream message unless you understand the true motives behind your dream.

Contemplate on the characteristics of your dream revelation for you will need this info in your final analysis. What type of dream was it? Was it a supernatural dream or a natural one? Was it symbolic or literal? Simple or complex? What was the purpose of your dream? Do you know what fueled your dream and why? Write down what you think. Then, consider its source.

Below is a description of these possible sources of your dream, and how to determine which is which:

- **God:** God dreams contain a calming presence, a holy atmosphere, and a profound impact on our psyche the morning after. I have found that most of my God dreams occur in the early hours of the morning. They contain a sense of His peace flooding over me. This manifestation is important to recognize because natural dreams don't carry His presence.

  Have you ever noticed that you can pray while asleep? God's spirit appears to intercede with yours while you dream and the messages flow both ways. In God dreams, He communicates with you, and your spirit can communicate back.

  Saint Peter had such a dream. A devout Jew who ate only kosher foods, he had a vision to rise, kill and eat whatever God had cleansed.[61] Here in his sleep, Peter finds himself talking back to God and saying no. Can you imagine telling God no? This vision is an excellent example of a spiritual source because it clearly shows how God can speak to us and we can speak back.

- **Natural (You):** Natural dreams spring from the thoughts you carry in your mind. Often these thoughts are driven by the day's activities where your subconscious mind takes over. I can't tell you how many times I dreamt about software bugs I found in the programs that I wrote. Regrettably, I was never paid for all the work I did in my sleep.

Have you ever had to use the bathroom in the middle of the night and you were too tired to get up? When this happens to me, I've found myself dreaming about it. Natural dreams can also be stimulated by your body's physical needs. Studies have shown certain foods, medications, or even your body's physical needs can inspire a dream.

In addition, natural dreams can be stimulated by the thoughts you meditate on and the feelings and emotions you carry in your heart. If you are under extreme stress, fearful about a situation,or watching a scary movie, these circumstances can have an effect over your dreams. Meditating on God's word can also guide your dreams. If your mind is flooded with negative thoughts, your dreams can unfortunately be induced by that evil. Often natural dreams are difficult to discern because we don't recognize how much we are being influenced by an outside source.

- **Satan:** Dreams from Satan reflect his influence. I don't know of satanic dreams in the Bible; however, I do believe that this is possible from a personal experience.

One Halloween evening I had an evil dream at about four in the morning which spoke of a horrible ending to a poor relationship between me and my mother. During part of the dream I shook with fear.

When I awoke and composed myself, I realized that this dream revealed the enemy's destructive plans. I knew not to receive this message. The next morning, I made a conscious choice to walk in love and forgiveness regardless.

Another example is from a friend who had a terrible nightmare that foretold her husband's death. In this case, my friend's husband was seriously hospitalized for forty days because of a brain aneurysm. Numerous surgeries were performed as he clung to life. This dream was from the pits of hell to torment. Fortunately, my friend believed God, and her husband was healed.

How absolutely awful are these occultic dreams! I pray that you are not deceived into believing these lies and acting on the enemy's schemes. Ask for God's protection and guard your heart.

Step 1 may sound simple, but it is very tricky because your own body, your will and your spirit can influence your dreams, and there is often a battle within. Look at Figure 1 and that big cloud depicting your dreams and you. Only with God's help can you correctly discern the origin of your dream. See all those arrows pointing to and from? It is super easy to make a source mistake because you must rely on your own discernment of what the origin of your dream might be.

barbarakoob.com

Figure 1: You and the Source of Your Dreams

One reason a dreamer can mistake the source of their dream is because God can reveal things they don't want to see. Our first inclination is that the enemy is giving such a dream, but actually it could be God warning us. Often we have difficulty with our dream source because of our own selfish thoughts. Determining the source requires good perception coupled with hands-on practice. You must be steadfastly committed to rightly discern, recognize and learn from your blunders.

Step 2: List and Decipher Your Dream Symbols

If your dream is literal, skip to the next step. Otherwise, make a list of all the possible symbols in your dream. Dream symbols can be persons, places or things.

People symbols refer to persons you know in real life, like your mom, your sister, your child, your boss, the president, or a famous actor. Fictional characters like Snoopy or James Bond could also be a people symbol. I find people symbols the most common to miss, as I personally know these people, and often forget that they are a symbol about myself. And so, don't omit your people symbols.

Places can be symbols too, such as your childhood house, a city or country, a factory, church, or school. And of course, any "thing" in your wildest imagination could be a symbol. Your dream world has no limitations as to the types of things that can be contained in your dreams. Just go for it when you make your list.

Next, decipher each symbol through research using any of these methods listed below:[62]

- **Scripture:** Scripture should be the first basis for interpreting the meaning of every symbol for God really does use biblical symbols and their meanings in our dreams. Two great examples of biblical symbols are that of a house and food.

  Using 2 Corinthians 5:1, a house represents a person's life.[63] Here, God refers to our earthly house as our body, but the building made by God is our real life. For years, I intrinsically knew that my house dreams were about my life but didn't know why. In John 4:34, Jesus said that His food was doing God's will.[64]

  By reading my Bible, I have been able to discover the meanings of many dream symbols, and I believe you can, too.

- **Inherent Character:** For symbols not listed in the Bible, you can decipher the meaning by looking up the inherent characteristics in a dictionary or on the internet. Obviously electricity didn't exist in biblical times, but it does represent power. I once saw a turtle in my dream. Knowing that animal is known for moving slow, I determined that God was cautioning me not to quickly walk away from a business we started. However, do jump into researching the meanings of your dream symbols for that's how you learn.

- **Personal Experience:** Because God is so personal, He frequently uses your own experiences about a symbol and its meaning. Often this is exactly why no one can unlock the key to your dream but you, and it's why you need to chew on your own cud.

  In one of my favorite examples He used a plastic grocery bag in my dream. I dreamt that I could not take a shower because of a clog in the pipes. Apparently, the clog was caused because someone had shoved a plastic bag and an empty orange juice carton down the commode. For years, I couldn't figure out this strange picture until one day while I emptying the trash in my kitchen.

This symbol was a trash bag. Only God and I knew that I used those types of plastic bags for trash. Immediately I returned to my dream to research that symbol again. Since trash is always discarded, I recognized that God was showing me the reason why I had so much trouble with getting the water to flow. I was dealing with a spirit of rejection from my past. I was having trouble forgiving because I felt the sting of rejection. The OJ container indicated that I had no more energy left to fight these feelings. Fortunately, God had also shown me how to get free from that thing in my dream. I had to realize that was God will never reject me. I needed to receive total acceptance from God so that I no longer needed to look for that person's approval. It was then that I was able to forgive. And that forgiveness would start the faucet water running again. Yea God!

- **Society:** This last method is one I have rarely used, but I will mention it. A symbol can have a meaning based on the country and culture where a person lives. For example, if I said, "The force be with you," most everyone in America would think of the movie *Star Wars*. God knows the cultural significance of all of our surroundings, and He does use this in our dreams.

  Always remember that a symbol can be either good or bad and that you have to seek out the proper meaning.

I'll never forget a very detailed dream about a friend with multiple sclerosis. I dreamt she had a terminal inside her house. I woke up crying thinking the terminal represented the deadly disease; however, I later learned that MS is a chronic disease. People don't die of MS; they die of complications due to MS. This error meant I deciphered that symbol incorrectly. With more research, I uncovered the true meaning of this symbol from the definition in my dictionary… to make smooth, easy connections, like an airport terminal.

I sensed God saying He was going to help my friend make smooth, easy connections from her brain to her central nervous system. Years later, that friend confided in me that she also dreamt about seeing herself well standing in her kitchen washing dishes, something she has been unable to do. Both dreams brought great encouragement during difficult times. I still pray and believe for my friend's miracle, but only God knows the day and the time.

Step 3: Write Your Dream Message

Meditate on your dream and oblige yourself to write your thoughts. Attempt to create a concise understanding of your dream. Sound easy? With simple dreams it is, but with complex ones this will take considerable effort. That's why I started writing a comprehensive interpretation with all my complex dreams. I call this a GUI Dream Script, and it helped me learn dream interpretation, especially with my complex dreams.

Utilizing the symbols deciphered in the prior step, write all of the details of your interpretation, scene by scene, line by line as you understand it thus far. If you are unable to grasp some aspect of your dream, write what you think or simply write that you don't know. Sometimes I have devised several GUI Dream Scripts for the same complex dream as I travailed to discern the hidden message. Writing a GUI Dream Script is a great tool to help you learn and improve your skills, especially if you go back and check your findings. After I have finished my GUI Dream script, I work on crystalizing my dream message.

Here are some suggestions on how to help you do this:

- **Re-inspect the first scene of your dream.** Make sure you know what your dream is about by carefully inspecting the first scene of your dream. Often the subject of your dream is revealed in the first part of that scene.
- **Re-visit your dream's details.** Knowing why God is speaking can help you determine what He is saying. Study the outcome of your dream by looking at the big picture. The outcome, whether good or bad, may help you define your message. Examine your dream's details, for they might reveal inner heart and soul issues. The feelings and emotions you experienced in your dream are also significant, and they can point to a hidden message.
- **Re-view your current life situation.** What thoughts or questions have been buzzing in your head lately?

At one time in my life, I waited so long for God to hand me my assignment on a silver platter that I decided to change directions and work as a real estate agent. My plans were to sign on with a particular firm the next morning, but the night before I had the most strange and sensual dream that made me feel so good. While I didn't understand it, God was teaching me his dream language and cautioning me not to work in real estate.

Not recognizing God's understanding, I went ahead with my realtor plans. Mind you, there is nothing wrong with being a realtor. It was pleasurable for a moment, but that was not what the

Lord had for me at that time in my life. Ultimately, I was miserable for about six months until I quit. That dream was straight from the Lord, perfectly timed the night before to train me on how to understand His voice in my dreams. While I misinterpreted the message; and of course, did what I reasoned best, I sure did learn from this experience.

Review your present life situations and ask God. He loves to answer your questions and concerns, but you must seek Him. Often your dream will be a direct word from God about your current situation.

- **Skip the superficial and go deeper.** Since dreams entertain your natural senses, your inner true self is the only one who can discover the subconscious message. One time a woman told me of a dream where she and her husband were driving a blue convertible, but they stopped at a house where there was a sign "Beware of Dogs!" As I reflected on her dream story, I was invigorated at the thought of cruising in that cool car with the top down; however, when I delved deeper with her, it became clear that the Lord was cautioning her about not fostering a particular relationship. Apparently, this lady was already serving with that person, and God was revealing that she would get hurt. Unfortunately, she did not heed the message, but hopefully she'll know for the next time should something like this happen in the future.

  Did you realize that God can use current events to stimulate conversations with you? Let's say there's some big happening in our world, like a presidential election, a declining day in the stock market, or some other full-size bulletin. Most of us will totally ignore that dream because we think it's related to the world's news; however, these are frequently news flashes from God about us. We need eyes to perceive and then go deeper learning from our dream experiences.

Through all these suggestions, remember that God desires to dispatch His message to you more than you want to know it. More than ninety percent of your dreams are about you. Even with all my experience, I can't tell you how many times I have made this mistake thinking *I am so glad that's not me.* But God was lovingly making known my true self that I may turn to Him for help. I suppose my heart doesn't want to see the truth as it applied to me? Therefore, always go back and apply the dream to yourself. It's a great practice that will serve you well.

And so, after all this exploring, rummaging and inquiring into your dream, your heart and your life, seek God to compose His understanding and endeavor to write your dream's message. Remember real life has snags and difficulties. While we may desire to only write beautiful messages, make sure you write honestly about your dream messages and know that we'll deal with those awkward, and sometimes unpleasant, images in the application process.

Also recognize that with complex dreams you may have more than one message, but journal all of them with your GUI Dream Script and look again at the original dream that you wrote when you awoke. Then, move to the final step.

Step 4: Test and Go

Testing your dreams involves carefully analyzing the results of each Get GUI step correctly. Did you accurately consider your dream and its source? Rightly list and decipher all those symbols? Properly determine your dream's message? In the beginning stages of your dream journey, you may find this step cumbersome. Yet, if you never tested your dream's interpretation and your personal understanding, you will never know if you got shipwrecked. You will not be developing your skills either. Go back, examine your analysis of your dream's understanding and test yourself.

If you are regularly examining your dreams, don't be surprised if you catch a recurring theme. Most likely a problem has taken root in your life and this is God's way of showing you what you are struggling with. Thankfully, He desires to help you.

Once in a while a double dream will occur. These dreams appear simultaneously one right after the other with the same theme, usually in one night, and they are very significant. Joseph had a double dream which foretold of a great future, but his test and go process sorely lacked as he proudly shared it with all his family. In his first dream, he and his brothers were binding sheaves of grain. All of a sudden Joseph's brother's sheaves bowed down to Joseph's sheaf.[65] The second dream told of the sun and moon and eleven stars bowing down to Joseph.[66] Joseph and everyone around him knew the meaning of those dreams, but sorrowfully Joseph's response was foolish. It never occurred to him how his brothers would feel about his dream, nor what their response would eventually lead them to do. We can learn much from this example.

Even when we have a great message, we need to respond with prudence. Unquestionably Joseph should have noticed his brother's jealousy and not provoked them.[67] His insensitive pride led him into slavery, and then, the lies of Potiphar's wife sent him into the Pharaoh's prison.[68]

Interestingly, God knew Joseph's personality flaws, yet He purposely omitted those difficult parts of Joseph's future. God used those hardships to redefine and strengthen Joseph's character so that he would save a nation, the surrounding areas, and even his family from a severe famine.

For that reason, never blindly follow your dream. You may sense the outcome, but only God knows the future. God may give a prophetic dream, reveal the finale, and thrust you into His plans, but He usually does not enlighten you on His character building path. Only our daily decisions coupled with God's sovereignty will produce His triumphant ending.

Years later, after Joseph's nature was cleansed and shaped for his destiny, God used him to wisely interpret Pharaoh's double dreams. In Pharaoh's first dream, seven gaunt cows ate up seven fat cows.[69] The second dream followed with seven thin heads of grain swallowed up seven healthy full heads.[70] But this time, I believe we can learn even more lessons from Joseph and Pharaoh.

While Pharaoh did not understand, he recognized when Joseph successfully unraveled the mystery of his dreams, and he acted wisely with the recommendations Joseph suggested. You and I need to do the same. If you don't understand something, find a trustworthy mentor who does and listen.

Every time I read Joseph's reply when he was called before Pharaoh to interpret his dream, I get goose bumps.[71] Joseph didn't spout off his mouth with arrogance. He did not declare that he could interpret dreams. He didn't use his skill to manipulate Pharaoh in an effort to be released from prison.

He humbly stated, "It is not in me; God will give Pharaoh an answer of peace."[72] Don't you think that was the answer that catapulted him into God's ultimate plan?

You and I need to learn to be like this transformed Joseph. We must walk in meekness to pass God's test. We must know that the interpretation of our dream is not in us, but it is in God. We must test our dream message with God's word, knowing that He would never lead us astray. It is only then that we can go with God.

Do you realize how seductive dream interpretation can be without God? This is what the world calls fortune telling and it is vastly different from biblical dream interpretation. Fortune telling speaks of the future, but it does not give an answer of peace, nor does it lend itself to righteousness. We are to believe that God will guide us working all things out for good because we love Him.[73]

Take those dream messages and respond to them with His love, goodness, compassion, forgiveness, and restoration for both you and others.

Go with a response that will strengthen your character, inspire others and move you forward with positive steps for your life.

Even if a dream has a disturbing message, seek God's answer of peace as you test and go. If a dream message happens to reveal negative aspects of your true self, humbly ask God to change you into a better you. Acknowledge your limitations before God and refuse to carry out your self-improvements plans on your own. Go ahead and ask God for His help, and He will give you an answer of peace.

Nevertheless, sometimes you just don't know what God is saying, especially with complex dreams. Look how long ago Saint John the Apostle wrote the book of Revelation and still we don't understand. Sometimes things are revealed later, but always in His perfect time, and sometimes we never know.

The point is to follow the Lord, not a dream. When you do not understand your dream, tuck your interpretation away and choose to live the abundant life that He has for you, with family, and friends, with good goals for yourself and others.[74] This philosophy is consistent with what the Bible tells us. It is not an ill-fated destiny, but one that heartens hope. Just invite God to awaken you when the time is right.

Now imagine that caramel apple from the beginning of this chapter and let's get sticky with dream symbols and healing.

Dear God,
Please help me to understand that the interpretation of my dream is not in me. No matter what I understand so far, I invite You to come and transform my life just like You did for Joseph, and I thank You for Your good plans for my life, to give me hope and a future. Please give me an answer of peace. Thanks God! You are the best! Amen.

Review

1. What does the Get GUI acronym stand for?
2. What are the three possible sources of your dreams? How do you determine the source of your dream?
3. Name the various methods that you can use to decipher the symbols in your dream.
4. What is a GUI Dream Script? Why would you write one?
5. Name various methods you can use to create a concise dream message.

6. How might you test and go with God regarding your dream?
7. What do you do when you can't understand your dream?

6

Deciphering Dream Symbols

"Symbols are the imaginative signposts of life."
–Margot Asquith

The Category Approach

Wouldn't you like to know how to accurately decipher dream symbols without all the research and rigorous memorization? Well, you can by learning what I have coined as *The Category Approach*. This approach organizes symbols into various categories. The theory behind this approach is that if you understand the definition of the category and the inherent meaning of a symbol from the Bible, you can better discern the symbol's meaning and complete the interpretation faster.

Since there are thousands of dream symbols, I have organized *The Category Approach* into three distinct groups—Basic, Clues, and Numbers/Colors. Keep in mind that some miscellaneous symbols might not fit into a category, but practice recognizing the symbols in your dreams according to a category if at all possible. This approach will save you time and energy as you run your race and cross the finish line with God's understanding.

Almost certainly, you will need to use a dream dictionary when you start deciphering symbols, but over time your symbol recognition will improve as you discipline yourself to memorize these categories and grow accustomed to filtering these symbols through their respective category.

And don't forget that while caramel is sticky, it can sometimes be difficult to chew. Just keep biting into the next piece of your messy but delicious apple. Now onward with the basics.

The Basic Grouping

In this chapter, I am going to introduce you to the basis grouping of most common symbols found in dreams. These symbols include houses, vehicles, people, places, animals, body parts, and clothing. In the following two chapters, I will look at the Clues Grouping of symbols and the Numbers/Colors grouping.

Are you eager to get started? Ready. Set. Let's go.

House Symbols

House Symbols are indicative of a person's life.[75] If your dream is set in your childhood house, your living room, your bathroom, or anything that pertains to your house, you can know it is about your life. That seems simple enough; however, there are a number of nuances.

When you dream about a particular house that you lived in, it usually refers to a particular time period of your life. For example, when I dream about my childhood, my dream takes place in the house I lived in as a kid. When I dream about moving into a new house, it is often about an upcoming life change in my future.

The rooms in your house also have various meanings as they reflect what you actually do in that room of your house. For instance, your living room is normally the place where others come and hang out. And so, living room refers to your life revealed to others. Your bedroom is typically a place of rest and relaxation where only your most intimate friends are invited. In my house no one is permitted upstairs unless they are a guest staying in our home. That's because I normally don't clean as well upstairs as I do downstairs. In my dream language, the entire upstairs refers to my private life, as in real life, it is usually off limits to most people who visit me.

Now the basement is quite a different place. Living space there is usually dark, sometimes wet and considered sub-standard. Typically, you store things in the basement that you no longer use and have not gotten rid of yet. So in dream language, basements are representative of hidden behaviors or sins that may still exist in your life. The attic is another place where items are stowed. It can refer to memories and thoughts and possibly a treasure tucked away for safe keeping.

In addition, bathrooms have great importance for everyone must go there at some point. It's the place where you soak in the tub, take a shower, and use the commode. In essence, this room symbolizes your need to relieve yourself or to be washed clean.

Both the kitchen and dining room relate to food. Biblically speaking, spiritual food refers to doing the will of your Heavenly Father.[76] The kitchen is where food is stored and prepared, while the dining room is where folks serve and are being served. Consider those rooms in your dream and take the time to explore what is the will of your heavenly Father for you, and if you are walking in obedience to it.

Apartments are for renters. They are like a house, but not owned. According to my real estate training, they actually termed non-freehold estates. In the dream world, they can indicate a type of captivity for you are not free to make changes unless approved by the owner. In other words, someone or something else is controlling your life. As a tenant you have access to the premises because the owner has given you the keys, but you are not free to do as you please with the property.

Sometimes I've dreamt that someone else is living in my house. While my first pass at the interpretation is usually that my dream was about that person, I have discovered that the Lord was speaking to me about my own life in areas that resembled that other person. In one of my dreams, a couple that I considered to be legalistic once showed up on my house dream. On the outset, I thought the dream was about them, but God kindly divulged the dream's secret. He was revealing my own black and white opinions, and His desire to transform my thinking.

Apparently, the mistake of assuming your dream is about that other person is extremely common even with my experience as a skilled dream interpreter. So keep a watchful eye.

Vehicle Symbols

Vehicle Symbols represent your life's journey. They are similar to the *House Symbols*, but reveal where you are going with your life and how. Do you know your destination? Is it a smooth and easy ride? Or are you struggling along a dirt path? Vehicle symbols are all part of your transportation system, and they describe who you are traveling with, who is in control and by what power you are moving.

Here, you'll see yourself traveling on a road, the water, or through the air. Road vehicles can include a car, a motorcycle, a bus, a van, or train. Water vehicles could be rafts, speed boats, cruise or cargo ships, or wartime and submarine vessels. Obviously, planes travel through the air, but some of my dreams include flying on the craziest contraptions, like a sky ride or a flying motorbike. And of course, you could walk or ride a bicycle using your own personal horsepower.

In America, the most common type of vehicle is a car, which is why I often dream about it. The person who is sitting in the driver's seat is also important. If you are the sitting in the driver's seat, it probably means that you have control of where you are going. If someone else is driving, you are probably not in charge. Is that good? It depends.

When I dream symbolically and my husband is the one driving, it usually means that the Lord is directing my journey, as my husband symbolizes Jesus, my bridegroom. However, if I am the one driving, it usually refers to me directing my ways and not God. Is that good? Probably not.

I will never forget when a friend told me about a dream she had where her ten-year-old son was driving their car. She understood it as she was teaching her son how to drive. I saw it as her son was the one in charge. I think several of her girlfriends might agree with my interpretation, but who was right? Normally, we don't let our minor children drive a car as that would be against the law, however, my feeling is that it was her dream, and she had the right to see it as she pleased. Ironically, I might also add that I too have dreamt of my teenage daughter driving, but she was of legal age to do so.

In addition, you might think about where you are sitting in the vehicle. Is it the front seat or the back seat? Sitting in the front allows me to participate with the driver. Conversely, being in the back seat implies that I am being taken for a ride. Is that good or bad? Well, are you supposed to be in the front seat? Like most dream symbols, it depends. These types of clues reveal little hints of how you are traveling on your life's journey.

Since boats are agents that float on the water, in my dream language, these vehicles describe my support system on the waters of the spirit. For example, if I am on a raft, I am drifting with no direction. If on a canoe, I am powered by my own strength. If on a cruise ship, I am engaging in missions, stopping at various foreign ports of call. For a battleship, I am involved in spiritual warfare.

A plane usually refers to your work, your employment or even your ministry. And if you are perceptive, you'll notice the size of your plane. A two-seater plane refers to a small ministry, while a large jet refers to a bigger ministry, one that travels faster, has more power and carries many people.

Also notice that some of these vehicles have the ability to carry many persons, which implies working in a group, such as a classroom of students, a missions trip, a Bible Study course, a business office and so on.

There are many other vehicles that I won't detail here such as an elevator, a tractor, a hot air balloon, a roller coaster, etc. An elevator indicates whether you are moving up or down. A tractor reveals farm work, or sowing gospel seed, and a roller coaster is fast, fun and thrilling, but is unstable and doesn't go anywhere.

Years ago, the great biblical dreamer Joseph was sent against his will on a caravan to Egypt as a slave. However, he was eventually promoted to riding on the second of Pharaoh's chariots.[77] This image represented the powerful journey of Joseph's life. The next time you dream about a vehicle remember that all you need think about is where are you going and how, and take this info to the Lord and ask Him.

People Symbols

I can't tell you how many times I have been deceived regarding the people I see in my dreams. Initially, it never occurred to me that I might be seeing a reflection of a part of my self. Yet, ninety percent or more of the time, the people you see in your dreams symbolize you. In fact, all people in your symbolic dreams should be treated as a symbol first.

Think about what that person symbolizes to you. In one of my dreams, I have a girlfriend who tends to worry more than she should. Whenever she appears in my dream, I have learned that this is not about that girl-friend for God is speaking about my own tendency to worry.

Here are some other personal examples:

- The baby sleeping in my dream represented me. It wasn't the grown up me; it was the innocent baby, totally unaware of what was going on.
- My daughter, frightened and alone, characterized me as a little girl.
- My mother represented an aspect of myself where I am called to be a nurturer and caregiver.
- A sibling and a friend in my dreams revealed aspects of my personality that I didn't otherwise notice.

I've even heard of a lady who often dreamt about her brother. Although she didn't know about people symbols, her instincts told her that those dreams were about her because she and her brother were so much alike.

Often our human nature does not like to see ourselves in a certain light, but that is exactly why God uses dreams, especially when the symbol is of a baby, a child, a sibling, a parent, or a friend. Isn't it odd how we will see things in other people, yet discount it in ourselves when they reveal our own unflattering characteristics?

My husband is a good example of a people symbol. Since we've been married for quite some time, I know this man loves me. He's seen me at my best, and sadly, at my worst, and yet when I dream of my darling man, I instinctively know that my husband and bridegroom is a symbol of Jesus.[78] If you are not a Christian, this connection may sound strange, but we believers are called the Bride of Christ in the Bible.

Once I met a sweet gal at a prophetic conference who was grieving the sudden loss of her husband. She confided in me about a tormenting dream where her husband kept coming back from the dead. When I suggested that her alive husband could symbolize the Lord, it seemed to help her view this dream in a different light. Whether or not I was correct, I do not know, however, there is one thing of which I am sure. The Lord would never give a disturbing dream for the purposes of tormenting for He is our Prince of Peace.[79]

Occasionally, you can dream about a generic type of person, one that you don't know, like a doctor, lawyer, a clown, a thief, or something else. In these cases, the person type has a symbolic meaning. For example, a doctor may represent healing. A lawyer could symbolize your defense and personal advocate. A clown can indicate foolishness and a thief might reveal that something valuable has been stolen. Simply take the time to ponder the person symbol and ask the Lord. It's really not that difficult once you understand what you are looking at, and I'm sure He will help you discover the meaning.

Nonetheless, sometimes the person in your dream is both a symbol and a real person. It's fascinating when your dream symbols overlap with your real life. This dilemma is a natural anomaly of the dream process. Just keep practicing, for God is training you how to discern.

Place Symbols

Similar to the people symbols, the places in your symbolic dream do not refer to the real location. You need to treat each place as a symbol, which is why I am listing them as a unique category. Think of what a place personally means to you. Reflect on those characteristics.

There's a place that I dream of that is special to my heart. It's the place where I began my life with my bridegroom and best friend, my darling husband. Don't be disappointed when I tell you where this place is. Just listen with love and imagine a romantic rendezvous in the most unlikely spot.

It's Poughkeepsie, New York—the place where we first lived as husband and wife.

When we first married, we rented the ugliest second floor apartment in a dilapidated three-family house within walking distance of the mighty Hudson River. Covered with multicolored gray asbestos shingles and trimmed in Pepto-Bismol pink, the exterior of the house was hideous. The interior was also in desperate need of repair. The walls were lined with cheap dark paneling. The bathroom and kitchen were functional, but severely outdated, but all of this bargain housing cost us only two hundred dollars a month.

While the rent was cheap even for those times, I have the most wonderful memories on the inside of this apartment house. It was our first home. There was love in that place. Whenever I dream of 172 South Avenue Apt. B, I sense the Lord reminding me to return to the place of my first love—

Him. He uses this place to romance me back into His arms.

Here are some other examples of places where their natural descriptions can infer a symbolic interpretation:

- The USA could symbolize freedom to some people, or it could mean decadence.
- The city of Las Vegas could represent a place of sin, or anonymous fun. (P.S. I have a dear friend who grew up in Las Vegas and takes exception to my definition—to her it means home. Keep in mind that dream symbols can always be personal, and that is perfectly acceptable.)
- Paris may represent love or lights. It just depends on your personal thoughts of that city.

Places don't have to be a country, city or town; they can be buildings like a hospital, school, or park. In these cases, the places are actual buildings and they represent a particular purpose. A hospital could symbolize a place where people receive healing. A school specifies a place of learning and a park can symbolize leisure and relaxation.

Every now and then, I will research a particular place to learn more about the history and famous characteristics regarding that location to give me more insight. And just like people symbols, sometimes that place represents the actual place. You have to discern its meaning as you work out the dream interpretation prayerfully.

Animal Symbols

Have you ever had an animal symbol strangely appear in your dream? The most peculiar animal I ever saw in my dreams was a penguin. I can almost guarantee you that you won't find a penguin in a standard dream symbol dictionary, but you, like me, can figure out its meaning.

So what is the dream definition of a penguin?

Well, I gleaned that penguins are birds from the South Pole who are black and white and love to swim. It took me about six months to figure this out, but I was looking at myself. Yep, I was the penguin. I'm left-handed and I love the water. I am also a black and white opinionated bird, and I bet the Lord revealed this self-truth so that I would see my true self and surrender to His ways.

Animals are a category all their own in dream language. Ecclesiastes 3:18 says, "I also said to myself, 'As for humans, God tests them so that they may see that they are like the animals.'"

To find the symbolic meaning of an animal, look at the inherent characteristics of that animal and then take a good look at yourself. In some cases, it's probably a symbolic revelation about an aspect of your unredeemed nature. Don't be surprised if this revelation comes to light. It happens to me all the time, and I just take it to the Lord for more of His transformational grace.

Remember the dog in my dream that I referenced in the first chapter? My husband had opened the door and allowed our stinky, dirty yellow lab into our house. I was so upset because I didn't want that dog tracking mud in our house. Isn't it funny how the Lord used my own dog to show me a reflection of myself? Gretchen was her name, and she represented my wicked perfectionism. That dream revealed my unwillingness to openly accept a part of my life that needed cleansing. I actually thought I could keep my house clean, or should I say my life spotless from sin, by controlling each and every situation around me. What a joke!

I know of a dear lady who told me that she kept dreaming of cats. If you think about it, cats have a mind of their own and are untrainable. Where most dogs will do anything for a piece of meat, cats will never obey a simple command even for an indulgent small snack. But offer a dog a delectable treat and they will shamelessly beg. Unfortunately, that was me as I would have done anything to receive a pat on the back that meant, "You're good."[80]

Ouch.

I never dream of cats. But if you have a cat or if you have dreamed of one, could the Lord be speaking to you about not being teachable? Or perhaps the Lord is showing you as His pet?

Another way to determine the meaning of an animal symbol is to research it in your Bible. Fish can refer to men as Jesus said He would make Peter a fisher of men.[81] Birds represent a spirit, which can be either good or bad.[82] A dove would indicate the Holy Spirit while a hawk or vulture indicates a predator.[83] Frogs can refer to a plague as frogs were used as a curse to come upon Egypt because Pharaoh would not let the Israelites go.[84]

Like the animals, we can't hide our deep instincts that reflect our corrupted humanity.[85] I take one look at my cute little cockapoo, who we affectionately named Sunshine, and know this is true. Sunshine may try to act like one of the family. On occasion, we treat her like royalty by allowing her table food and a nice bed to snuggle into with us, but she is still a dog. She licks her behind (big yuck!!) and brazenly pleads for more scraps. God has used Sunshine in my dreams many a time to speak to me about my cute little self.

Surely God can use any animal He likes to reveal the real you on the inside. I once had a woman tell me of a yak that consistently emerged in her dreams and spoke to her. "What does it mean?" she asked. She would have to research this animal and go to God, for only He knows.

Nevertheless, in some cases, an animal may not reflect you. It could indicate an action toward you that could be either uplifting or destructive. For example, a white dove descending on your shoulder could indicate the presence of God resting on you while a ferocious black panther could point towards a spiritual attack. Keep conscious of the fact that the animal is just a symbol of the action that will more than likely flow through a person. For example, a lady who attended one of my dream workshops told me about a bobcat who attacked her in this dream. It turned out to be one of her family members during a weekend visit. Now that she knows this possible interpretation, she can better prepare in advance by knowing how to pray for protection and peace and for a right response to the attack.

Body Parts and Clothing Symbols

The body parts symbols figuratively describe a characteristic or function of the body using a biblical reference. You can find many body parts listed in the Word of God. For instance, a head refers to authority, a neck to your will and feet to your walk. Without doubt, God will use these symbols in your dreams to reflect various functions within His body and yours.

One illuminating dream I'll share included my pastor's wife and me. I had this dream when our church was in the middle of a major building project. Almost everyone in the congregation was helping with all kinds of skills, from painting to electrical, to you-name-it. Take a look at the numerous body parts used here like legs, feet and shoulders along with a happy face. At first I was tempted to think that this dream was actually about my pastor's wife. Silly me. Have you any idea of what this dream might mean?

I saw my pastor's wife sitting in a chair across from me. She was barefooted and suddenly spread her legs. Although it seemed awkward, I allowed her to rest her feet on top of my shoulder. When she did, I felt her pain. It hurt but I allowed her to do this as I wanted to help her, and she was relieved. Suddenly, I saw her smiling face morph into the face of her husband, my pastor.

In most dream languages, the pastor and his wife are indicative of Christ, the good shepherd and His lady, the church. Seeing a person's *face* in your dreams has a special meaning too, for face indicates a reflection of the heart. Proverbs 27:19 says, "As water reflects the face, so one's life reflects the heart."

I can't tell you how long it has taken me to finally understand this dream, for this dream revealed deep elements of my true self. At that time, scores of church members were running around doing all sorts of odd jobs to get our new building ready for Sunday Services. I however, was not working that hard.

In fact, I'd call myself a slacker. I'd prance over to a do few things, and then slog on home. I suppose I was feeling a little remorseful about not doing my fair-share.

But physically and emotionally, I knew I needed to rest. Things were busy with my family, and I couldn't continue to push through a to-do list, even for a church that I loved, as it was just too stressful.

I suppose these feelings of guilt stem from my childhood, as my mom would forcefully insist that I pitch in when others in my family were not required to do so. It's probably because I was the oldest child and a girl, and because it was easier for her to get help from me than from the other younger children. However, it left me feeling like I never had time-off to be a kid like my other siblings.

I believe my inner self was confirming my need to sit still, and I think God was smiling that I gave myself the grace to do so.

Upon further inspection of this dream, you can see the bare feet, which represented an unprotected walk from self-condemnation, legs and shoulders to provide support for my decision to rest, and a smiling face, which reveals God's heart of love for me.

Similar to the body parts symbols are the clothing symbols. These symbols can be a hat, shoes, dress, socks, coat, etc. and they are worth mentioning because many of us completely overlook our clothing symbols and the clues associated with them. Take notice of the clothing you wear in your dreams They can be dirty or clean and even colorful and great.

For example, the prophet Elijah wore a powerful mantle—a robe, which anointed him to accomplish many miracles in Israel.[86] One dream example I had was that of wearing blue socks, which were symbolic of my spiritual walk with God. Another illustration is wearing a scarf on your head; it reveals that you are covered under an authority.

I recommend that you look at the clothing that you are wearing in your dream. Like certain clothes often reflect aspects of your personality, they can also reveal the spiritual anointing on your life. In other words, it's a deeper snapshot of your true self.

For example, my blue shoes could indicate my spiritual walk with God. A black dress could reveal a dark covering, while a beautiful white wedding dress would say beautiful and pure. A red bikini probably spells flaunting your flesh. A crown could symbolize a king's authority. Just take notice of what you see and ask God.

Remember though, whatever you may be wearing, that if you are a

Christian, that your good works are as filthy rags. Only Christ's righteousness is perfect.[87]

Check out the dream dictionary in the appendix for further details of various symbol definitions. Now let's move on to another unique set of symbols. These symbols are unequivocally helpful in solving the mystery of your dream and they are part of the *Clue Grouping.*

Review

1. Explain the category approach and why it is useful for deciphering dream symbols.
2. Name the basic categories of dream symbols and give their definition.
3. What is the difference between the house symbols and the vehicle symbols?
4. Why are people and place symbols more difficult to recognize and process in your dreams?
5. Have you ever seen an animal in your dream? What did you think it meant?
6. Explain some figurative uses of body parts in the Bible and how they can be used as a dream symbols.
7. Name some ways that a clothing symbol can act as a clue to explain the meaning of your dream.

7

Clues to Unlock Your Dream

"Inside every human being there are treasures to unlock."
—Mike Huckabee

The Clues Grouping

Every dream has hidden treasures within. Somewhere in my compulsive nature to ascertain the meaning of a dream mystery, I have discovered buried treasure in certain symbolic clues. They are like a signpost on the door. If you are paying attention, you can learn to spot them for yourself.

But before I reveal these treasures, I'd like to share one of my outlandish dream stories that used a few of these clues. This dream, straight from His throne room, occurred at a time in my life when I had just passed my real estate test and planned to sign a contract to work as a sales agent for a local firm. God's timing was impeccable, and like so many of my follies, I proceeded with my plans and ignored His. (Sigh.)

Scene 1: (It's nighttime.)

I am married to Tim Allen and we are in bed together.[88] *We are having so much fun enjoying our marital bliss. I see myself as this gorgeous babe who is being loved by her man. It feels so good to my senses. Almost like…I am in heaven! Not really, but you get the picture.*

Scene 2: (It's daytime.)

Morning has come and I'm in this shoe store. There are huge stacks of shoe boxes piled high and wide. I find myself selling shoes and fitting all kinds of people for the right shoes for them. This job sure isn't what I planned for my life, working with people's prickly personalities and their smelly feet.

Suddenly, my lover boy, Tim Allen, enters the shoe store and pleads, "Hey honey, why don't you quit your day job? Then, we can spend all day together, too."

I was being lured away by my own lust.

I woke up.

This dream contained classic clues that are absolutely hysterical, for God is also a great comedian. This dream felt so good to my carnal senses, and it was flattering, too, yet I instinctively knew that something was amiss.

Surely the timing of this dream message was not a coincidence. The clues are in the night and day symbols as well as in the marriage symbols.[89]

Night and Day

Night and Day symbols are revelation symbols. Night means darkness referring to your ignorance and inability to see your true self. Day suggests light and your capacity to perceive the real you that God wants you to see. Both symbols expose secrets, but one wishes to cover it up, while the other shines a spotlight on it.

God was both testing me and teaching me with this dream. He was enlightening me regarding my desire to work outside the home and how good it would feel to my natural senses. Who wouldn't enjoy a relationship with that successful "Tool Man" celebrity?

However, God was also revealing that He had a different plan for my life as indicated during the daytime hours. His wish was that I would help people with their walk with Him. Remember the feet symbol referring to a person's walk?

Obviously, I was sorely tempted to work outside the home, but God was challenging me to listen and obey. He wasn't mad that I became a real estate agent; he just had other things planned as presented by the daytime job fitting others with shoes. And so, the next time you are in the dark regarding your dream, think about what revelations are exposed using the night and day symbols.

Covenants of Agreement

Another clue in my dream was the person depicted as my husband. After all, I am not married to Tim Allen, the hugely successful "Home Improvement" TV Star, who happens to also have a history of criminal charges before his fame. This clue should have been a big bright red flag for me as it reflected the marriage symbol, one of the *covenant of agreement symbols*.

A covenant is a solemn agreement that is binding to all parties. In the Bible, covenant refers to the promises that were made between God and His people, the Israelites. Part of the agreement was that they would not worship other gods. If they obeyed, God would bless them. If they didn't, they would not receive His promises.

Covenants of agreement symbols include dating, kissing, marriage, and sex. They indicate that you are contractually obliged by a particular thing in your life. For example, if I dream of being married to my real husband, it reveals that I am faithful to the vow I made on my wedding day. In other words, I am staying true in my heart, my soul, and actions to my first love, God. Conversely, if I am kissing my old boyfriend, or married to someone I shouldn't be, it could indicate that I am unknowingly tied to an old love in my life. This symbol is not about a literal old flame or a new love in my life; it reflects a form of idolatry, a love for something other than God.

Use the people symbol, mentioned in the last chapter, to assist you in determining what you have unconsciously agreed with and examine your true self.

It was not a coincidence that the Lord gave me this dream on the exact night that I planned to sign a contract for employment. Because I made the wrong decision sailing ahead with my real estate plans, I quickly discovered that this job wasn't working for me. It consumed my time, cost me business expenses that were not reimbursed without additional income, and it seriously interrupted my family time. Thank God the Holy Spirit would not allow me to overlook that dream.

While I tried to erase it from my mind, this dream message persisted to plaque me regarding what I was doing and what God wanted me to do. Although working in real estate isn't a sin, it was not God's best for me. Finally, I quit and started selling shoes, figuratively speaking, of course. And when I did—I had peace again. Plus, I learned a great deal from this dream experience.

At times, these convents of agreement symbols and their implications can be R-rated. Often we reject that God would give such risqué dreams; however, they can, indeed, come straight from heaven. Never forget that God is the brilliant creator of romance and intercourse. So naturally, He would use such dreams to intimately speak to us as it's His way of revealing truth without getting in our face.

Unlike many human beings, God would never manipulate or control you to obtain what He wants. After all, He is God and He doesn't have to. If you have ever had these alarming dreams and you wonder where in the world they originated, especially if you are not struggling with pornography, I hope you now know that you can relax.

And so, if you know you are not engaged in sexual sin, just consider the symbolic reference and closely examine your life. Search your heart and ask God if you have possibly agreed to something that truly is not in your best interest.

The level of your agreement is also revealed in your covenant action. Dating is just seeing a person, while a kiss good night takes it to the next level. I probably should mention that marriage used to come before sex. God created kissing, marriage, and sex, and they are beautiful when used correctly in accordance to His design.

Perchance, if you are not married, or deliberately not dating for what-ever reason, you may not have these covenants of agreement symbols in your dreams used in the same way that I have described. However, God can speak this same principle in a slightly different way. For example, I know of a single lady with two teenagers, and she told me of a dream where another girlfriend and her were on an outing together. She also shared how she was being tempted to date this perfect guy in her real world. I really believe God was using this dream to confirm to her what she already knew—it wasn't time to start dating again.

Someone once told me of an unsettling and recurring dream with her old boyfriend, yet she was happily married. Using this same clue, my speculation was that this old boyfriend was only a symbol, and that this gal needed to seriously search her life asking the Lord what struggle He is trying to reveal. God allows such dreams to help us release our sinful hindrances, but we have to want to see truth and desire to be set free. That's just another reason why I believe we can do nothing without Him.[90] For He is our only hope.

Covenant of agreement symbols can be very powerful. Over the years, I have learned when I dream of someone other than my husband, some-thing is off course. For me, these symbols are huge indicators to confirm if I am on track with the Lord and following His lead, and I believe you can use them to do the same with your life.

Dream "Words"

Sometimes the words we speak in our dreams are not an accident. They could be words from the Lord, or they could be words from your own spir-it, something your carnal mind won't grasp, but it needs to. In my funny shoe dream where I was married to Tim the Tool Man, I heard the words, "Honey, why don't you quit your day job?"

Don't you think it's possible that those words were the message of my dream? God knew that I had already planned to start working outside the home, and He knew that wasn't the best choice for me for that season of my life. He even called me "Honey" when He made His suggestion. Now isn't that sweet? God loved me so much that He was warning me not to proceed with my plans, but He was OK if I did it anyway. What a great guy (God)!

This dream wasn't the first or only time I've experienced that the words I heard spoken in my dream were the actual message. One time I dreamt that I was working at my old engineering job in an industrial park called Regency. Out to lunch at a restaurant, I was waiting and waiting for the server to take my order. I became very impatient and frustrated, but when he finally arrived, I surprisingly remarked, "I am not ready yet." When I declared those words, I couldn't believe what came out of mouth.

This dream revealed that I was not ready to begin my ministry, although I was shocked when I discovered that fact. Now that was the message God wanted me to hear. Remember when I told you that food was symbolic of doing the spiritual will of my Father? Apparently, He had more lessons for me to learn. I was not ready until He said go.

Beautiful dreamers, use your dream "words" as hints to solve your mystery. You may be stunned at what you discover.

Directional Indicators

You can be confident that God knows exactly how to give directions when you need them. In fact, God will show you in your dreams even when you are not looking, for He loves to direct our path.[91] That is exactly why God uses biblical *directional symbols*, which are similar to routing your course on a map.

First, there are the four directions on a compass—north, south, east and west. Normally people think of north as pointing upward to heaven, and that would be a correct interpretation. So south would denote the opposite. There's even an expression that a particular situation is "going south." Everyone in my family knows what I mean. As for east, we know that sun rises in the east. In the Bible the glory of God will enter the temple from the east gate.[92] Therefore, east means beginning, entering in a new day, and west indicates the end, exiting the last day.[93] Actually, those compass signs are rather obvious, but other directional signs are not.

Right and left are definitely contrary to what you might normally think. Usually people think of the right side as the one that is not wrong. Right is precise and proper, true and approved. For most persons, their right arm and hand are stronger with and better skills. And of course, if the right side is superior, then the left is the opposite; the lesser.

But in dream language, the meanings of right and left are a little reversed. Right is no longer the better side. The reason is because right refers to the natural strength of man or man's power revealed through the flesh.[94] Left becomes the excellent side because it refers to the spiritual realm and the strength of God. Left also refers to man's weakness.[95]

I know these meanings may seem odd, but the biblical truth is that man cannot make himself righteous in his own power.[96] Always remember that God's strength is seen when we are weak, not when we are strong. That's why you can remember that the left side refers to our weaknesses and His strength.[97] Hopefully, this revelation should cause some of you to rethink some things.

By way of illustration, a lady who I knew was held captive to a particular problem, told this dream to me. She dreamt that a rope bound her around her left arm as she was trying to free herself. She conveyed to me that she knew that the symbol of her left arm was significant. Do you think God might have been saying that it is by His strength that she would be set free—not in her own ability?

Front and back also have directional connotations. Front refers to the future and back refers to the past. When I have a dream that includes a symbol of a front porch, I usually infer that I am seeing a revealed part of my future. Whenever I see a back door or my backyard, I know this refers to my past.[98]

Personally, I have found these simple directional signposts to be extremely helpful once I learned their definitions, and I hope you will, too.

Travel Ways

Travel ways suggest your journey whether it is a dirt road, an icy driveway, a highway, an elevator, a river, or some other passageway. To receive insight into this clue, couple it with your vehicle symbol and the destination that you are heading toward as this will shed light on your life's journey.

A dirt trail implies an arduous path that is no clearly not defined while a rocky road is bumpy and difficult. Highways and railways allow for faster travel that is definitely easier, but you need to make sure you exit at the proper place and make the right connections. Just like in real life, a dirt trail or rocky road may signify a road less traveled. These paths are usually traveled on by pioneers who create more established routes, like highways and railways for others to follow.

Traveling on the water has a special connotation. Like the whispering waves of the ocean, a surge of flooding storm water, or cascading waterfalls and rushing rapids, water reveals the spirit which can whisk you away to an unseen world for either good purposes or bad. But how can you discern?

Water is an astounding substance essential for life here on earth. In its natural state, water is clean, colorless, odorless, and tasteless, but it can be polluted. I always test the type of spirit based on the nature and quality of the water. When the water is crystal clear, I am confident that I am walking on His waters; however, when it's muddy, I know something is not right.[99] Also, salt water might be fun to swim in, but I definitely can't drink it.[100] Interesting that the ocean represents the sea of humanity, while the spirit of God is symbolized as rivers of living water.[101]

The characteristics surrounding the water can also have implications. Water can be peaceful or full of power, shallow or deep. These attributes have the potential to divulge the type of spirit that you could be carrying, either an angelic spirit or a demonic one. They can also disclose the need for wise navigation to ensure safe arrival. Be careful if you see the water symbol in your dreams and perceive with God's understanding.

Although mankind could travel in a balloon ride by the eighteenth century, it wasn't until the twentieth century that man could man travel through the air via plane. So I don't think of air travel in quite the same way as waterways. However, air definitely characterizes the atmosphere where we live and breathe, and it is crucial for sustaining life.

Like water, air references spirit and can be expressed as a wind whether it is a light puff of air, a gust, a tailwind, or a tornado.[102] Ask God to reveal the type of spirit behind your sail, whether it is from Him, from Satan or from your own natural spirit. Then, ask God what He wants you to do about that.

In summary, I recommend that you combine your vehicle symbol with these travel ways to assist in effectively deciphering the message that God is presenting about your journey. Often, the clue is staring you in the face.

Spiritual Elements

Spiritual elements like earth, wind, water, and fire can play an important role in unlocking your dream mystery. These four elements are considered by many philosophers and scientists to be the purest form of a substance; they make up all the matter on the earth. Yet, there is also a spiritual component to each and that reference could be a key in your dream.

Clearly the earth is the Lord's creation; He owns it all.[103] Earth, in its original form, started out void and dark, but God chose to bless the earth with all kinds of beautiful things so that mankind could be fruitful and multiply.[104]

Without water and sun, without good nutrients in the soil, the earth is barren and dry, yet it has the capacity for seed to sprout and life to grow.[105] Think of the earth symbol as containing the dormant promises that God has for you, but you must allow God's Spirit to hover over you so that your promised land will reap blessings.[106]

As I've already discussed in the prior section, air (i.e. wind), and water can be traveling clues on your life's journey. That's because both of them can symbolize spirit, but it is worth mentioning them again as these symbols have very powerful meanings in the spirit realm.

Wind is symbolic of the spirit, either the Holy Spirit or another spirit.[107]

It can also include doctrines that may be able to erroneously blow us away if we are not grounded in the gospel truth.[108] Strange that you cannot see the wind, but you can feel it whether it is a gentle breeze, a gust of energy, or a foreboding storm. You can also see its effects; therefore, look beyond the physical.

And last, there is fire, that all-consuming element that can overtake and utterly destroy if not handled properly.[109] Fire can represent power and passion of the heart. It can also refer to destruction.

Even smoke, which usually accompanies fire, can represent the presence of the Lord. I once dreamt that there was a fire in my house, and I actually jumped out of bed afterwards to double check. In the dream, I darted into the kitchen, as I thought I had accidentally left my oven on. However, I soon discovered hundreds of white Christmas lights all laying on the ground floor of my house, tangled in all kinds of ways, but connected and plugged it. Apparently, these lights were smoking so much that it set the alarm off.

After I woke up, I scurried downstairs to my living room just to see if anything had happened. Thank God there wasn't an actual fire. Perhaps this is what you'd call an "actual dream" for the Lord's presence seemed so strong that this dream appeared real. But seriously, I have been known to leave the oven on after using it way too many times. (Yikes!)

I'm not exactly sure what that dream was all about, but when you have one of these experiences, you'll know how I feel. I know that something happened, but I can't fully explain it. Here is what I think. God was just letting me know that He sees me and all my imperfections. He sees my worries and fears about making a mistake, but He was reminding me that His presence is all around me. My life may look like a bunch of tangled Christmas lights, but everything I do is brightly shining for His glory. I am smoking hot with His presence because He loves me. How's that for an interpretation?

Dear readers, God will use these spiritual elements to speak to you in your dreams. These symbols may not appear plainly as earth, wind, water or fire, but you need to recognize their various forms when you see them and ask the Lord what He is saying.

And I'm sure that as you and God process your dreams, you will discover more clues that shed light on your dream revelations.

Have you had enough of that caramel apple? Is it sticking to your teeth and the roof of your mouth yet? Are you ready to move on? Part 2, the interpretation is the biggest and hardest part of biblical dream interpretation, and it requires a long time to acquire all the aspects and get it right.

So slowly chew on each bite while enjoying your dream journey, for there are still more symbols to cover and lessons to learn.

Review

- Names some symbols that can be used as clues to solve your dream mystery.
- Can God give an R-rated dream? Why might He do such a thing?
- Why are the symbolic meaning of left and right contrary to what we might naturally think?
- Have you ever had specific "words" spoken to you in your dreams? Was it God speaking?
- Name some travel symbols and the clues they suggest regarding your life's journey.
- Explain the symbolism of these four spiritual elements; earth, wind, water, and fire. Which of these symbols have appeared in your dreams? And what do you think it meant?

8

Numbers, Colors, and More

"Fatigue is the best pillow."
—Benjamin Franklin

Numbers

One Christmas morning I awoke from an amazing God dream and saw that the time on my digital clock read 2:52 am. Another time I dreamt that my husband purchased a house for us costing exactly $395,000. Strangely, this house was not the one I longed for in my dreams. In yet a different dream, I learned that my purse was stolen, and when it was found, I was surprised that it contained only $6. As a young woman I earnestly prayed to receive the gift of God's Holy Spirit, and when I did, it was on the date August 1st. I once met a gal at a prayer meeting who had the most peculiar experience with regard to loose change. She kept finding lots of dimes and quarters all around her house. Well, do any of the numbers in these dreams and circumstances mean anything?

Ever since I was a young girl I adored math. I loved playing games with numbers, like with dice, dominoes, or cards. Evidently God loves using numeric symbols and mathematical patterns, too, and He does so repeatedly in His word. It's just another fascinating way of hearing God speak, and all you have to do is take notice.

Let's look at some of His examples in the Bible:

- After God created the earth, He rested on the seventh day.[110]
- God told Abraham to circumcise all the males born in his household on the eighth day.[111]
- The kingdom of heaven is compared to ten virgins who take their lamps and went out to meet the bridegroom.[112]
- When God told Noah to build an ark, He allowed it to rain for forty days and forty nights.[113]
- Before Jesus started His ministry, He fasted in the wilderness forty days.

I could go on with more illustrations; however, my point is that God unquestionably used numbers and gave them specific meanings. No number is used haphazardly. The numbers seven, eight, ten, and forty have specific meanings.

I've learned the symbolic meanings of numbers in the same way I learned the other biblical symbols—by reading my Bible and researching through various Christian dream books and their dictionaries. Because I am such a visual learner, the secret to remembering these symbols lies in seeing pictures in my head. For the numbers one through ten, here are some visual reminders that I use along with some biblical definitions.

1. When I think of the number one, I harken my heart to the fact that there is only one God and the importance of unity in the one body of Christ.[114] I also think of new beginnings (one ~ unity, first, beginnings).

2. For number two, I imagine a scale weighing two separate items. I see a judge who decides between two sides of a story and issues a verdict (two ~ scale, separation, decision).[115]

3. With number three, I think of the Trinity, three persons in one God all revealed in the obedience of Jesus Christ (three ~ obedience to Christ).[116]

4. Number four strikes a chord with me in regard to the earthly elements and directions. There are four elements (earth, wind, water and fire) and four directions (north, south, east and west).[117] I am reminded of the kingdoms of the earth, the one who rules and reigns these nations, and how it affects the people in the world (four ~ rule, reign).[118]

5. I love number five and its significance as I picture the miracle of multiplication. Jesus started with just five loaves and two fish, yet He fed five thousand (five ~ abundant grace).[119]

6. The number six refers to mankind, his carnal and fleshly nature for it was on the sixth day that God created man.[120] And don't forget the Antichrist, the prideful epitome of a supreme world leader sold out to Satan. He is represented in the book of Revelations as the number 666 (six ~ man, carnal, fleshly).[121]

7. The number seven represents rest, completion of God's work as indicated in the fact that God rested on the seventh day after He finished His work (seven ~ completion, rest).[122]

8. Male Jewish children were circumcised on the eighth day of their life.[123] The number eight signifies a cutting away of the old covenant, putting off the sinful flesh and the beginnings of new life

(eight ~ putting off the old man, a new beginning).[124]

9. There are nine fruits of the Holy Spirit.[125] Fruit is ready during the harvest and the number nine refers to harvest and fruition. It can also refer to judgment because all people will be judged when God's harvest time arrives (nine ~ harvest, fruition, selflessness, judgment).[126]

10. As for the Number Ten, the best example that comes to mind is the parable of the Ten Virgins who were waiting for the coming of the Lord. Five had prepared, collected oil and were accepted. The other five were not ready; and thus, rejected.[127] I've always found the number ten difficult to discern especially when I was first learning biblical symbolism. So, I'll say it this way. Ten refers to a time of testing for the purposes of accepting or rejecting (ten ~ trial, test, accepted or rejected)

As you probably can tell by now, I could go on about each number, as I tend to view the world through my symbolic "Son" glasses.[128] Nevertheless, I have just a few more things to tell you about number symbols.

One golden nugget of special significance is information about the numbers eleven through nineteen. They are sometimes the exact opposite of the numbers from one to nine. For example, the number eleven has the opposite meaning to the number one. While one signifies unity and a new beginning, eleven refers to chaos, destruction, and the end, or judgment. The number twelve is opposite to the number two. While two denotes to judge, to separate and divide, twelve symbolizes a perfect small group which is able to easily govern itself. Do you think that's why Jesus picked only twelve disciples? Or maybe this is why God laid plans for the twelve tribes of Israel to each be ruled by a leading judge, with other smaller groups within each tribe. This model became an early form of a government, so that order could be established and maintained.[129]

Another example is the numbers thirteen and three. Three symbolizes the Trinity and obedience to Christ, while thirteen refers to rebellion against God. For example, the number thirteen means the opposite of the number three—rebellion to God. We often see the number thirteen used during Halloween. Even hotels purposely mark the 13th floor as the 14th floor to avoid potential problems. Are you one of those superstitious people who think the number thirteen is haunted? Never forget that God created everything and that the earth and all its fullness belongs to the Lord.[130]

Also, the Lord might have you separate a number by using a mathematical equation. The number thirteen could be interpreted as good, if listed as twelve plus one, meaning beginnings (one) of government (twelve). Additionally, the number twenty could represent "holiness" by multiplying two and ten. Two infers that you are separated from the world and ten suggests that you are accepted in the beloved regardless of your failed tests.[131] Forty is another such number which could be broken into ten times four. The ten could symbolize a time of trials with four signifying a reign after your wilderness experience. Thus, forty refers to a testing period, which is closing in on either victory or defeat. The number fourteen suggests seven plus seven, or a double completion and rest. In these cases, you need to pray and ask God for how to arrive at specific interpretation of that number.

The meanings of a hundred and a thousand when attached to a number also have importance. Hundred indicates fullness and thousand refers to maturity. Therefore, 300 might signify fullness in obedience to God. The number 7000 may point towards maturity where you can completely rest in God.

Now for some tips on how to use this cool information about number symbols, as I'd like to explain the scenarios I posed earlier in this section. It's true that God uses numbers in our dreams, but He also uses them in dates, times, and in real life, for He will use whatever is necessary to get your attention.

When I saw the time at 2:52 a.m., I immediately knew God was referencing Luke 2:52 as I have prayed that scripture many times for my daughter and other children. It says, "And Jesus increased in wisdom and stature, and in favor with God and men."

But this time I knew that God was talking to me about me, that I was to grow in His wisdom and favor like Jesus. Receiving that dream on 12/25 was like a sweet Christmas present from God. Another date where God spoke was 8/1.This date appeared like a signpost, a divine appointment of baptism with fire.[132] It signified a putting off my old self and beginning a new life in the Spirit.[133]

As for the house dream, the cost of $395,000 could be broken down into 395 times 1000. After prayer, my interpretation is that this number indicated that I would grow in maturity (thousand) in the areas of full obedience to Christ (three), fruitfulness (nine) and grace (five). Regarding the dream where my purse was stolen, the amount of $6 revealed my perceived value. Much to my dismay, the Lord revealed to me that I had a very low sense of self-worth, which had been wrongly based on my accomplishments and the approval of men. But praise God! Jesus paid the ransom. My stolen sense of worth was restored when I placed my true value in what God thinks of me.[134]

Even the large amounts of loose change found in that gal's house turned out to be God speaking. Shortly after this strange seemingly insignificant phenomena, that girl's husband suddenly died. She lost the love of her life and their income drastically changed, not to mention that she still had two teenage boys to raise. The hidden message was that big change was coming to her house. While tough days lay ahead, God was with her. I had the honor of walking with her through part of this storm, and I can tell you that He was faithful.

Always remember that God can use any "number" of ways to get your attention. Pun intended.

Colors

Beautiful dreamers, God delights to use color to convey His purposes, either within a dream or not.

One day my mother slipped a yellow dress on my young small frame and that color made me shine. I don't get whether it was my skin tone or the shade of my hair, but yellow remains one of my personal favorites. Every time I wear it, people remark how well I wear that color.

If you are an artist, you know exactly what I am talking about. Color sets a mood and compliments. It either makes or breaks your masterpiece.

Most of the times we don't dream in color, but when we do, you can know it's significant. Here's how I remember the meanings of some basic colors along with their biblical definitions.

- Blue – The blue sky reminds me of the heavens and the God who lives there.[135] Blue can also refer to a baby boy or being depressed as in "singing the blues" (blue ~ spiritual, heavenly, healing, blessings, or depression).
- Green – The natural color for almost all plant life is green.[136] When grass is healthy, it is green and full of life. And so, green refers to life, either eternal or mortal. It can also refer to being green with envy or unripe (green ~ life).
- Orange – This color reminds me of fire.[137] Scripture tells us that our God is a consuming fire. Fire can be wonderful when used properly, but deadly if uncontrolled (orange ~ powerful energy force).
- Red – This color signifies Christ's perfect sacrifice on the cross.[138] When you think of red, it can also mean anger or emotion as you can turn red when enraged. The color red is also used on Valentine's Day and it denotes, love, zeal, and enthusiasm (red ~

passion, love).

- Purple – I like to think about *The Purple Princess* storybook to remind me that this color signifies royalty. In ancient days, kings, nobles, priests, and magistrates all around the Mediterranean used purple as it signified majestic and noble (purple ~ royalty).[139]
- Yellow – Remember the old song, "Tie a Yellow Ribbon Round the Ole Oak Tree"? Yellow can have several meanings. One is a trial of waiting for your beloved to return. Another military meaning is to signify that we are waiting for our troops to come home.[140] Usually yellow refers to marriage, family and honor. Yellow can also symbolize the glory of God (yellow ~ gift of God, welcome home, marriage).
- White – A bride's dress is white symbolizing her purity.[141] White signifies spotless, without blemish, righteous, true, and innocent (white ~ pure).
- Brown – Brown is the color of dust.[142] It is also the color of dead grass that is without life (brown ~ dead).[143]
- Gray – Gray refers to those areas that are in between white and black; and so, it symbolizes not defined, vague, and deceived with false doctrine. It can also denote wisdom, age, or weakness as in gray hair (gray ~ not defined).
- Black – The scientific explanation for the color black is the absence of color. Black means lack. Just remember it rhymes. Also, black can refer to sin, evil, grief, and mourning (black ~ lack, sin, grief, mourning).[144]

Another fact about colors in our dreams is that when these colors are dark or muted, they often give a sense of unease and discomfort. Sometimes these dreams can have a demonic source due to involvement in witchcraft or use of illegal drugs.[145] However, if you sincerely ask God to rescue from these dark dreams, and if you are willing to repent, He will set you free.

Metals

Many metals are extracted from the earth by means of mining.[146] This arduous process symbolically refers to digging deep to pull out the requisite precious element. Have you ever dreamed of gold or silver? Surely the Lord wants us to extract these precious ores for His objectives.[147]

To find the symbolic definition, look up the characteristic of each metal and check the references in your Bible. Here are a few examples:

- Gold, one of the most expensive metals that exists on the earth, was used to cover the Ark of the Covenant.[148] It refers to God's glory, wisdom, and His precious truth (gold ~ glory, wisdom, truth).[149]
- Silver is also a valuable commodity, as Jesus was betrayed for thirty pieces of silver.[150] Because Jesus perfectly revealed our Heavenly Father, we can know God. Silver indicates the knowledge of God or revelatory knowledge (silver ~ knowledge).[151]
- Iron signifies strength or power, but often reveals stubbornness (iron ~ strength, power, stubborn stronghold).[152]
- Lead refers to weight, usually the burdens of sin and the world (lead ~ weight of sin, burdens).[153]
- Brass refers to words or sounds, especially that of a resounding gong and clanging cymbal that makes an annoying noise (brass ~ words, sounds).[154]

Miscellaneous Dream Symbols

Have you had your fill of dream symbols yet? Seriously, how many caramel apples can you eat and still enjoy? No one can know and experience every dream symbol; there are just too many.

That's why the category approach aids in quickly processing the most common symbols for maximum ease of interpretation. When you first start out using this method, I am sure it will appear tedious, but as you grow in your interpretative skills, you will learn how to recognize groups of symbols and quickly discern how they are used.

Still, not every symbol can be categorized into a group. Sometimes a symbol is just that—a miscellaneous dream symbol. I've found that some of my symbols have the strangest meanings, too. Here are a few samples and how I found their meanings:

- I once dreamt about my house, which you should know by now clearly represents my life. Funny thing is that the back of my house faced the street and the front of my house appeared to be butt up against the intersection of two main streets in the heart of town. For days I pondered this picture until one day it occurred to me. That intersection represented my life which was backed up on the cross of Christ.
- Another time I saw a big L-shaped sofa in my living room in one of my dreams. Pondering that symbol for a few days, I decided that God was comforting me with His love. Well, that's what a big L-shaped sofa means to me.

- Jewelry is another symbol which puzzled me until I realized that jewelry is man-made and used to adorn ourselves. On the other hand, jewels are made by God. Oh how ashamed I was when I realized that my jewelry was a form of idolatry. Time to repent.
- One day I was reading a Beth Moore Bible study and she compared the walls of a room to her thought life. Well, ever since then, the Lord has used this same paradigm in my dreams. I can't tell you how many times the Lord has used a wall covering to reveal my stinking thinking and coach me to start replacing those thoughts with good ones.

If you wish to explore more dream symbols, I'd recommend a good biblical dream dictionary. I've even included a small one in the appendix of this book. Truly, God will use all kinds of ways to get His message across to you for He is the master of all creation. And I know, if I can learn how to find God's voice, you can too. In fact, you can start now and develop your own dream dictionary.

For example, God often uses skiing metaphors in my dreams as He knows it's one of my favorite sports. When I dream about skiing, He is usually chatting to me about my faith using the quality of snow and how well I'm skiing. Instinctively I know that when the snow is not perfectly packed powder that I'm having trouble with my faith. How do I know this?

He uses a mountain symbol to represent my struggle and the snow conditions to represent Him. Snow is a form of crystalized water which can represent God's Spirit and His Word. If you don't know, slushy snow is difficult to ski. As you traverse through all those hefty soggy snowflakes, you'll find it harder to make those turns because it will require lots of effort. Here, the Lord revealed that my faith is faltering. It was based on me carrying those heavy burdens – and not Him. When the snow is icy, I know that treacherous times are ahead. In each case, I see myself with God when I am skiing, believing that He is there and acting on the faith that He is helping me arrive safely to the base lodge.

I know it sounds crazy, but that's how it works for me. It's like I can have my own personal cell number to chat with God.

You know, He knows your name and your personal cell number, too. Don't be surprised if He calls you up in your dreams, for He would love to have a heart-to-heart. You can encounter God. You can see the mystery of your dream unlocked. It could happen suddenly and when it does… WOW, GOD!

So don't miss His voice. Start listening and asking God and begin to build your own dream dictionary today by learning these categories, their symbols and the personal significance to you and your life.

One last reminder—always keep in mind that as you define the interpretation for every dream symbol that Satan is bad and God is good. While the meaning of a symbol could indicate a bad thing, it is always to be interpreted and processed in the light of God's love. God is good. He has good plans for your life. He desires to give life abundantly. It's who He is—the giver of all life.

In the next chapter, let's look closely at a topic that is often omitted with regard to dream interpretation—healing. It's something that we all need, but often overlook due to our pride and stubborn self-will. Normally we don't see it and we won't hear it either because we've neglected to turn our hearts to God. So how about if we stop and pray?

Dear God,

As I learn about biblical dream interpretation and dream symbols, please reveal Your loving kindness to me. I want to believe with my whole heart that You are good and that You have good plans for my life. Help me to process every dream revelation with healing truth at the forefront of my understanding. Thank you, Lord! Amen.

Review

1. Explain how God can use a number to speak.
2. How does God use colors in your dreams? What could a dark or muted color represent?
3. What does a colorful life mean to you?
4. Name some metal symbols and their definitions.
5. What miscellaneous dream symbols have you seen in your dreams? Were you able to figure out their meanings? Have you ever considered building your own dream dictionary?
6. Do you believe that God is good? Why or why not?

9

Healing and Dreams

"The best and most beautiful things in the world cannot be seen or even touched—they must be felt with the heart."
–Helen Keller

Look at Your Self-Portrait

Ever since my early adult years, I have always enjoyed the artwork of Norman Rockwell. A twentieth century painter and illustrator, he captured real life scenarios in truthful and humorous ways. It's funny how that reminds me of dreams and healing.

In 1960, Normal Rockwell's *Triple Self Portrait* was displayed on the cover of the Saturday Evening Post. He comically painted himself looking into a mirror but drawing the picture of a different man. Through his tinted lens, he saw a handsome man that was significantly younger, no glasses, fewer wrinkles and definitely more distinguished. Like our dreams, he saw what he wanted to see, what he hoped for—not his real self.

Over the years God has revealed many healing clues in my dreams, but honestly I was habitually blind to truth. I've already mentioned my dream about a stolen purse in the last chapter. That dream spoke of my lost identity suggesting a poor self-esteem and low self-worth.

Another time in a dream, the Lord asked me to remove all the fences. Suddenly the words "all the fences" turned into "offenses." Regrettably, I didn't think I carried those offenses, and I sure didn't know how to rid myself of them.

And so, understanding your dreams is just like Rockwell's self-portrait. You won't see your true self and your own need for inner healing unless you want to.

Will you recognize these healing clues when they appear in your dreams?

Healing Clues

I love it when God taps me on the shoulder and personally speaks truth. I didn't always, but I have grown to welcome His insight because it proves His love for me.[155] His eye-opening revelations are always kind, too. They reveal my secret self without shame.[156]

In order to appreciate what I am talking about, take a look at the healing dream symbols below for they could indicate a hidden problem, a hole in your heart:

- *Stolen goods* can refer to something that has been robbed from your life.
- *Prison* can indicate that an enemy holds you captive.
- *Rope* is used to tie things up and denotes that you could be bound.
- *Baggage* can depict a heavy load of lies that you may be carrying.
- *House issues* can reveal problems with your life. Specifically, a back door break-in could indicate a disturbance from your past that stole your sense of safety.
- *A trip to the bathroom* may indicate your need to eliminate or wash off a sin or offense.
- *Sickness/Hospital* could be a signpost that there is a spiritual illness.
- *Rape* implies that you have been violated against your will.
- *Intruders or burglars* can point to an infringement of your personal space, or a theft.

These healing clues are just a morsel of God's big imagination when it comes to revealing truth. Additional clues regarding the need for healing are found in the negative emotions that you experience in your dreams. And of course, nightmares reveal problems. My experience is that when you properly deal with the root problem, the nightmares disappear.

Here's an excellent example of an intriguing dream which will show you what I mean. It occurred when my daughter was a toddler. Although I chose to leave my job after nineteen years and made the decision to become a full-time mom, I found myself wresting with my identity. See if you can recognize some of the healing clues that I mentioned.

Scene 1:

For some reason, two demons broke into my house. I was frightened as they threatened me with these words, "We are going to steal everything we can from you. Don't bother casting us out because the predator will just send more reinforcements."

When I heard the word "predator," I shook with terrible fear but responded, "You can't steal from me because everything I own already belongs to Jesus."

Scene 2:

My husband and I are sitting sweetly together on our bed. He was carefully removing a tiny blackhead from my back.

Apparently, I could not see it. I allowed him to do this. It only took a second, but it sure did hurt.

I woke up.

This dream was so awful. I knew I wasn't possessed, but I sure wondered where this dream originated and what it meant. Searching for answers, I shared with one of the pastors I knew at my local church. She emphatically told me that this dream was not from God. I can certainly understand her comment, but she never answered my questions and I didn't receive a resolution in my spirit.

Yet, this dream had several of the healing clues I listed. There was the fear factor, a forced entry, two intruders and some stolen goods. I sensed this dream was from heaven, but why would a loving God give such a dream?

As I prayed, I knew God wasn't saying that He was allowing two demons to rob me; however, He was revealing that somehow I had opened the door for the enemy. Apparently, I had unknowingly embraced two lies and had given Satan a legal entry into my life. Yikes!

But what were these lies? And what should I do about it?

This revelation is exactly how healing dreams work. Even though you may not consciously be aware of lies that you believe, God will reveal the root problem. He will show you your cheating, wounded heart.[157]

A Wounded Heart

Although many of us don't like to admit it, the truth is that often our hearts are fractured with holes and cracks where we are unable to completely trust God. Often, these holes contain the lies of the enemy. They will haunt you and cripple your present. Usually, these holes don't exist everywhere in our life—just certain areas where we are tossed about with unbelief in who our God really is.[158] And it is these holes that are divulged in our dreams that disclose our need for inner healing.

In particular, Mother's Day was a difficult time. Afraid of repeating the same mistakes as my teenage parents, I ran from motherhood rather than open my "hole-ly" heart to God. Of course, I made every effort to take my thoughts captive.[159] Sometimes that worked, but there were those "other moments." Has that ever happened to you?

Do you know the holes that may exist in your heart? Were you born on the other side of the tracks? Perhaps abandoned or rejected? Were you poor, neglected, abused, betrayed, or bullied? Raised in an alcoholic home? Raped or sexually molested? Trapped in a bad situation. The list goes on.

Make no mistake, you and I live in a broken world. Either someone has hurt you or you have hurt them. When this happens, and we know it will, you and I can become angry, offended and bitter. Sadly, these poor choices will open the door to additional pain. Our hearts may harden, too, as we try to protect ourselves from being hurt again. God is so grieved when this happens, as it often results in people turning their hearts away from Him. This reason is exactly why the Satan works so hard to hinder the flow of the Lord's healing balm. He doesn't want people to look to God for help.

A wounded heart, even one that has accepted Christ as Savior, is a key target for Satan and his lies. It is he who has come to steal and destroy God's purpose for your life, not God.[160] Without a doubt, the devil loves to hit you exactly where it will hurt, right in the center of that hole, to cause the most damage. Therefore, recognize the source of your hurt.

Figure 2: A Wounded Broken Heart - Saved but not Whole

Emotional damage can be derived from many places, genealogical and ancestral influences, pre-natal and childhood hurts, adult offenses and sufferings, and even from evil spirits. Symptoms of deeper hurts can include a sense of inferiority, anger, hostility and self-hate. Other disturbing signs can include unreasonable fear and anxiety, a perfectionist nature, and a performance mentality. Still more indicators can be depression, hopelessness, and super sensitivity.

Do any of these symptoms sound familiar to you? I suffered with many of them, but I didn't see the everyday life clues because I had carefully masked them with my pride to avoid feeling shame. For example, I covered up my low self-worth by striving for a successful career. I carried offenses but camouflaged them with reasons of how I was right. When I was stressed and anxious, I leaked with tantrums and tears behind closed doors.

Masquerading as the American dream girl, I was constantly striving to improve and impress, and incessantly controlling my situations. Yet, I wasn't true to myself, and then I wondered why I couldn't get free.

The good news is that God always desires for us to be made whole! Acts 28:27 says, "For this people's heart has become calloused; they hardly hear with their ears, and they have closed their eyes. Otherwise they might see with their eyes, hear with their ears, understand with their hearts and turn, and I would heal them" (NIV).

These problems and their roots continued to present themselves in my dreams because God wanted me to see and hear truth, however, I had to discover the root of my problem and have the courage to change.

Sound simple?

Alas, when it comes to inner healing, many of us are tangled and out of tune. Often we can't see the "real" us. When the prospect of true transformation comes, normally from a hindering obstacle in our life or a major crisis, we choose to adjust our surroundings rather than reflect on changing ourselves within.

Nevertheless, these entanglements come with a big price tag and a high interest rate. Over the long haul of your life, they *will* cost you.

Will you allow God to untangle your mess?

Untangled and Tuned

For me, inner healing required going back to my younger days, uncovering the lies that I believed and replacing them with truth.

My situation was like a tiny seedling planted in the ground where some nasty weeds decided to plant themselves alongside of me. Sadly, those weeds grew around little me and their root systems became intertwined with mine. And as I matured into adulthood, I came to believe that those wretched weeds were actually part of who I was. After all, it was all I had ever known. (UGH!)

Thankfully, as I assumed my new role as a stay-at-home mom and deliberately laid down my performance based priorities, the Lord began to help me perceive how much I struggled with my identity and the emotions surrounding it.

In some cases, I had too many adverse feelings to which I was overreacting. Why was I so irritated when a store clerk asked for my work number? Why did I feel utterly abandoned when someone didn't return a phone call? Why was I not accepted by certain people no matter what I did? My life was just fine. That shouldn't have been so important.

In other circumstances, I had no feelings when I should have. I noticed when certain ladies from my Bible Study would shed tears concerning their children who were bullied. I knew I loved my child and would protect her at all costs, but why couldn't I relate. Why did I feel empty regarding all those mothering emotions when others went on and on about it?

Did you know that God uses emotions to reveal the deep lodgings of your innermost heart? In fact, the need for inner healing is often revealed when emotions are either disproportional to a particular situation or non-existent.

One day as I was crying out to the Lord regarding my dilemma. He brought me back to a childhood memory regarding a used upright piano that my mom and dad had purchased for me to take lessons. That instrument was extremely broken and out of tune, yet that piano was all I had. It was even stored in a detached unheated garage with a dirt floor and no electricity.

I can't tell you how frustrated I was when I practiced. During the freezing winter months, I had to keep the door open so that there would be enough light to read the music. Sometimes I even wore gloves as I practiced. Then, no matter how much I labored at my lesson, everything sounded awful.

If I hit the wrong keys when I played a song, it sounded bad, but if I played the right keys, the sounds were just as off. One week I practiced my entire assignment forgetting to play the sharps and flats, and never heard the mistakes. I remember my teacher, a strict Catholic nun scolding me, "Can't you hear that you are off key?" If the truth be told, it all sounded the same.

Unfortunately, I was used to that severely out-of-tune instrument. This memory exemplified the story of my life—broken. And this experience is exactly what happens to some people when they grow up in dysfunctional families with unhealthy boundaries. Like me, they are unable to see or hear truth even if it hit them straight in the face.

So how can we become whole?

We must allow the Lord to dig deep. It is not enough to pull the weeds from above the soil and leave the roots. You may temporarily have a beautiful manicured garden, but I promise you…those weeds will resurface. The roots of every weed must be carefully and totally pulled. Beloved child of God, He wants to untangle you and I more than we want it. He desires to finely tune us so we can hear His voice.

However, just as a plant may become distressed when the soil all around it is turned upside down, you can also experience an upheaval while your garden is being tilled. And just like gardening, inner healing of your heart can be a tedious and difficult process, even painful to a poor little plant who feels like it is being unjustly plucked. But as I look back on my life it was necessary to be healed and made whole, and it's an on-going journey.

Are you willing to dance through the night? Figurative speaking, that's what I refer to when we walk through those dark places of our heart with the God who extravagantly loves us. Like Eliza Doolittle singing, "I Could Have Danced All Night," we can become exhilarated, but it's more than just the excitement of a dance with a lover.[161] We are invited to dance with the supreme King of Kings, the lavish lover of our souls who desires to heal us body, soul and spirit.

How should we begin? Step by step.

Dancing through the Night

The first step is to turn your heart towards the Lord and give Him the reins.[162] He removed the scales from Saint Paul's eyes, and He will do the same for you.[163]

Next, God will breathe His Spirit into your life speaking through His Word and a still small voice.[164] And I promise He will give you God dreams regarding your true self along with words of encouragement and directions. So allow God to soften your heart as it will prepare you for healing.

In my case, my deep wounds remained unhealed until I was ready to deal with them. God was so kindhearted that He did not force me into doing something even if it was for my own good. He allowed me to make my own choice, but when I did call for help, I discovered that He was already at work on my behalf.

Through a divine connection, I met a lady from my church who taught about inner healing. I also received some awesome inner healing through a formal prayer team. Like the woman at the well who met her Messiah, Jesus spoke powerful words of affirmations to help me combat the enemy's lies.[165] In one healing prayer session where I was dealing with a spirit of rejection, He declared, "You are mine. You belong to Me." That powerful Holy Spirit truth went inside me and changed me from the inside out.

In other situations, Jesus and I dealt with some issues. I had to learn to forgive. Giving up my right to be right was all part of God's plan to set me free.[166] He gently challenged me to rid myself of offenses so that I could be released from all my debts.[167]

Also, when it was appropriate, I counseled with a professional. God even used infertility issues to change my fear of motherhood into the faith to become a mom, helping me to mature, to see things as He does.

As I mentioned earlier, I had some big mother issues. My sweet mom had been abandoned by her biological father before she was born. If that wasn't enough of a tragedy, she grew up with an alcoholic step-father who abused her. Regrettably, she unknowingly passed those generational wounds down to me, for it is impossible to give what you have never received.[168] Yet, God desired to heal us both.

How wonderful it is to serve a God who turns generational curses into blessings![169] Because of His great kindness, I've been able to replace bitter memories with sweet ones, and bad patterns with good living, step by step. Rather than pout about my past, I spend Mother's Day with a fun activity, like a beach day or a dinner out at a nice restaurant. I choose to celebrate, and pour blessings on my mom, for He yearns for us to receive His love and to offer forgiveness.

Although my healing didn't happen all at once, God was faithful to culminate all things for my good.[170] But I had to believe and walk it out. And now praise God, my past no longer stings. I know that Jesus wants to set me free![171]

This is my personal dance with Jesus. Looking back, it's interesting how many of my healing revelations started with a dream and continue with dreams, for God yearns to heal the deep matters of our hearts.

Will you step out in faith? Lovingly, He bids you come.

Why not start with a healing prayer?

Dear God,

I willingly open my broken heart to You. Help me to see my true self by recognizing Your healing clues. Please untangle me from any weeds even if it is painful, as I desire to be made whole. I ask that You make me Your fine-tuned instrument so that I can truly see and hear Your voice. Thank You for directing my personal healing dance so that I can experience the fullness of Your freedom. Amen.

Review

1. Explain the concept of Normal Rockwell's *Triple Self-Portrait* and how it relates to how you see yourself in your dreams.
2. Name some healing clues that you might recognize in your dreams.
3. Why are some tangled and out-of-tune folks unable to hear God's truth about themselves? How can God use a dream to reveal truth?
4. How does God use your emotions to signal a need for healing?
5. Describe some possible steps that you could use to "Dance through the Night" into your healing.

10

Deep Healing of the Heart

"Love unlocks doors and opens windows that weren't even there before."
-Mignon McLaughlin

Stuck on Band-Aids

One day I had the most exciting news to share with my husband when he arrived home from work.

"Honey, guess what the Lord told me?"

As I relayed my deep self-revelation, he dotingly replied, "Barb, I've been telling you that for over twenty-five years."

"Well, darling," I beamed with joy, "today, I got it."

Why is it that someone can tell you, and even tell you the truth numerous times in love, but you won't get it until you get it? Such are the deep matters of your heart.

Your heart comprises the core personality and belief systems of who you really are on the inside. It contains your selfish desires and holy passions, your conscious feelings and hidden emotions, your fears and your faith. Created in the image of God, your heart was designed to flourish in a loving relationship.[172] However, your heart also has the innate ability to be shattered with deep wounds that can leave you with a fragmented life.

Luckily, God has purposely fashioned you and me with defense mechanisms.[173] So when bad stuff happens, and we all know it will at some point, those natural survival skills will kick-in. We start protecting our hearts in an effort to lessen or dull the pain. We dissociate. We project. We rationalize. We even regress and repress, and sadly, we fortify the hurts in our hearts with unforgiveness, anger, bitterness, and don't forget pride.

I call all these things *Band-Aids of the heart.*[174] And just like that catchy jingle you might remember, "I am stuck on Band-Aids," you can get stuck on Band-Aids because Band-Aids *will* stick on you. While Band-Aids marvelously provide temporary relief, they must be removed at some point. Otherwise, there is no long-term freedom in Christ.

This phenomenon is what happened to me regarding the pieces of my life, for I was stuck. That's where deep inner healing and deliverance came to the rescue, but I have to warn you. You may find some of the contents of this chapter debatable, but like I told you in Chapter One, the choice is yours as to what you decide to believe.

When I had that dream about two demons who broke into my house, I knew something was amiss. I speculated who that predator was and why I trembled with fear at the sound of his name.[175]

Even though there was no one who I could candidly converse with who wouldn't think I was crazy, I tucked that information away in my heart for another day. Somehow I knew that God would bring all things into the light, and so He did.[176]

I found a healing place in the mountains of North Carolina through the Presbyterian Reformed Ministries International (PRMI) called the Community of the Cross (CoC).[177] This ministry is a place of encounter with Jesus Christ for prayer, equipping Christian disciples for a life of faith so that they can be sent out into the world in the power of the Holy Spirit. It is here that I attended the Dunamis Institute and learned about how God can make broken hearts whole again.[178]

Because I was spiritually hungry for more, I enrolled in PRMI's year-long inner healing and deliverance program. Although my questions were slowly answered one at a time, I kept asking God, praying and walking out my healing journey.

And one day I had this very interesting God dream at the CoC during my training.[179] I call it "my shopping dream" because it describes in great detail the lies that I purchased from the enemy and the deep-rooted problems wedged in my heart.

My Shopping Dream

I can't tell you how cool it was when I finally unwrapped the gift of this amazing healing revelation with God's understanding. Once again, you'll notice some healing clues, but God undeniably provided the details I needed to put the puzzle pieces of my life together.

Based on the dream lessons you've already learned, I wonder if you can figure out the interpretation. Read on beautiful dreamers.

Scene 1:

I am shopping at a very nice department store and buying two items. One item is not important and the other item is something I don't want. I cannot believe I am spending the money on two such items, but that is exactly what I am doing. What's more, I slip both items in a large black suitcase and painstakingly carry that baggage throughout the store.

Scene 2:

While I wanted to shop for ladies' apparel, I unexpectedly found myself stuck in the kid's clothing section. Suddenly, I notice that my big black suitcase was missing. I am quite disturbed for I value this suitcase and my purchases, and I think I must carry them with me at all times.

Now for some reason, I believe that if I climb this steep hill, I will find my lost bag there, but as I embark upwards, I discover another big problem...there are all these people blocking my way. With all my strength, I attempt to push through the crowd.

However, as I do, I see this older woman who absolutely hates me and I am terrified of her. Fear grips me as she vehemently yells these words over and over again, "You are a bad girl, BAD girl. You are selfish, so SELFISH." I do not understand what I could have done that is so bad or selfish. All I am trying to do is get my bag, and after all, it is mine.

Finally, I arrive at the top of the hill, but much to my dismay, I discover only my brown purse. My black suitcase is still missing.

Scene 3:

I am all alone and call out to the Lord, "Jesus. JESUS!" I know He will come and help me find my bag.

I woke up.

This dream contains an enlightening clue in the black suitcase. Evidently, I am carrying around that heavy baggage everywhere thinking it has value.

I'm a dreamer and it took me a few months to uncover the secret meaning, but when I did, I knew precisely what I was struggling with as the Lord exposed the specific roots.

Take a second look in the dream and see what I bought in the store, for the contents of the suitcase disclose my problem.

Now don't peek. Go back and see what I paid good money for. Do you know what lies I purchased? Here lies the answer (another pun intended) ...I bought into the lies that I was unimportant and not wanted from my childhood.

Inner Healing

If you knew my family history, you'd know that these lies were inadvertently passed down through my mother. My grandmother, after three weeks into her marriage, left her husband due to his infidelity. At that time, she did not know she was pregnant with my mother. My poor mom was conceived and born an unwanted child and sadly fought feelings of insignificance throughout most of her life.

In fact, I have often heard my mom tell me how she is invisible. I suspect her feelings are based on the miserable facts that she was abandoned by her natural father, abused by an alcoholic stepfather, and felt unloved by her mom. Sure sounds like being unimportant to me.

So when I bought those lies, I valued my purchase rather than accepting myself as a beloved child of God. And by doing that, I gave Satan legal access to steal from me. In fact, whenever we believe Satan's lies over what God says, we operate from his deceptions rather than in the truth that God loves us and will help us with our lives. Hence, that solved one of the riddles in my prior dream as to why those two demons had permission to come into my house.

Other observations that the Lord revealed were in regard to the crowd of people, that steep hill and my brown purse. I have always assumed the role of Miss Pretty-People-Pleaser to ensure that I was loved and accepted. My aspirations to climb the world's ladder of success satisfied my need to feel valued and approved. Even the brown purse represented my identity that was smeared in muddy works. All these things were hindrances to my healing. (UGH.)

This process is exactly what happens in genuine inner healing. God unsticks you from your wounded mess. With His love, He unlocks doors and even opens windows that you didn't know existed.

God is not only the Savior of your soul; He is the healer of your heart. He will fill in those cracks and holes so that you are made whole, and He does it through evangelism to those portions of you heart where you have trouble trusting Him.[180]

His lovely words, anointed by the powerful Holy Spirit always trump the enemy's lies. Your husband doesn't have to keep saying the truth and repeating it over and over again. You don't have to psyche yourself up with self-coaching either, for God will do this for you.

And when God does it, there are no more Band-Aids. Your healing will stick!

Deliverance

Clearly my shopping dream indicated my need for inner healing with directions, but I had to rise up and replace those lies with the truth. God wanted me to stand strong with a deep conviction in my inner being, to believe that I am wanted in Him, that I am important to Him, and that I am loved by Him.[181]

However, there is still the question of that older woman in my dream. It appeared that she yielded great power over me with her malicious words. Who was she? What did she represent? Maybe she was related to that predator?

It was just a hunch, but I didn't think she was a specific person. I interpreted her as a dream symbol; yet, I sensed there was something more ominous. Do you think it is possible for a Christian to have an evil spirit?

Surely Satan loves to distress, torment and enslave the human race in a many ways, These degrees of affliction can vary from flaming arrows filled with aches and anguish outside a person, to demons actually attaching to the inside of a person (demonization), and to demons totally taking over a person's will and fully controlling him or her (full demonic possession).[182] (I told you this chapter would be controversial, and now you know why.)

Most people in the western world don't like to acknowledge that evil spirits exist. Many Christians acknowledge that the evil one's fiery darts have been discharged in their direction; however, few would ever consider that they could have a demonic attachment. However, given my experience, it can happen.

Think of how bacteria or a virus can invade your body and cause sickness, especially if your body is weak. In the same manner, if you have unconfessed or unforgiven sin, an evil spirit could enter your body if your spiritual defenses are broken.[183]

That's because demons don't play fair. They will look for unguarded ground, an opening anywhere they can find one, and use that entry point to attach themselves. Then, they love to remain hidden so that we are unaware of their wicked intentions and evil activities.

The term demonization comes from the Greek word *daimonizonmai,* which is often translated as "possessed by demons."[184] It describes various ways an evil spirit may afflict a human being. Usually, a demon can manifest itself affecting only a single area of a person's life without having complete control in the other areas. (Oh thank God.)

But that's why the English translation is misleading because possession implies ownership. Most times a person is not possessed; they are oppressed. Oppression can come from the outside in the form of those flaming arrows. And if one of those arrows hit a hole in your heart, it could trigger oppression that already exists on the inside.

A good example of this phenomena is when I have been angry at my family and couldn't restrain my emotions. While the situation was enflamed, the reason I had so much difficulty controlling my fury was not because of the present issue. It was because a repressed memory of my unconscious past that was triggered— a bitterroot.

Obviously, anytime you sin, especially with sexual sins like rape, incest, bestiality, the door to Satan can be opened for a demonic attachment. But sometimes it's not you who sinned, like a child who was unjustly molested again his will. In those cases, the point of entry occurs because someone sinned against you. (Sigh.)

These incoming satanic advances are so not fair, particularly for little children. The perpetrator deliberately devours their young, vulnerable and unprotected hearts with such devilish things as sexual abuse and satanic ritual abuse.

In these cases, a demon can easily move from the abuser into the person because of the physical act of intercourse.[185] Often these demon spirits attach to a devastating memory.[186] Then, these nasty spirits disguise themselves waiting for the perfect time to cause more mayhem. (Big sigh.)

If we are not aware of what is going on in the spirit realm, if we are not spiritually equipped, the demon can remain concealed. Miserably, it could have full reign over a particular area of a person's life. It is why we need deliverance.

When most people hear the word deliverance, they think of casting out demons and they fearfully run the other way as fast as they can. However, that is definitely not the main focus of deliverance. Moreover, there is nothing to fear if you have Christ in your life. He victoriously defeated the devil and made a public display of him.[187]And so, deliverance, my precious friends, must be viewed as a *ministry of love* to wounded people![188] The only difference between inner healing and deliverance is the level of intensity caused by the demonic. No one is ever to feel bad because they got wounded by the world and slimed by an evil spirit. Authentic inner healing and deliverance ministry must never judge or condemn the person, for God is perfect love.

My friends, condemnation is reserved only for the demonic realm.[189] Now let me explain my dream revelation in view of that hateful woman and predator symbols, along with God's healing touch.

God's Healing Touch

My mom says that I was a strong-willed child. She also told me that as a young toddler she would beat me until I obeyed. Then, I still did what I wanted.

Most of my primary memories are about being teased or punished, along with a childhood nickname that I hated. I have other memories, some normal and some happy, for not all my life was broken. I am positive that my parents loved me, and that's my story.

In those days people didn't get professional help. There were no classes on how to raise your children either. My teenage parents did the best they could with what they had. Even the best of parents make mistakes, and I, too, have made my parental snafus. Did you realize that even Adam and Eve who had the perfect parent fell from grace? (Relief.)

So what in the world was that dream about? Did anything traumatic happen to me when I was little? Maybe I purposely blocked an event in my life as a survival mechanism?

I have contemplated the symbolic interpretation of that hateful woman and that predator in my dreams for several years. Is it just my colorful imagination? Or is there something creepy lurking inside? I want to know! And so, as part of my healing journey I asked God just like I do with my dreams.

I have so many memories that stand out, but the Lord allowed this one to fortuitously resurface. This memory is muted in my mind. It appeared faded, yet it has always been strangely there. I suspect it's a repressed memory buried deep within.

I remember taking my baby doll to the basement, pulling her bottoms off and placing her plastic skin bottom next to the furnace so that she would burn. As a little girl, I felt my doll deserved to be punished. My mom has told me, "I've never seen a child so cruel to her dolls." I remember treating my baby dolls meanly, but never understood why. Still, this hateful nature didn't seem like me.

After all, I don't appear to be a mean person. Most people who know me wouldn't characterize me that way. I know I've made mistakes, but I've never purposely acted revengefully or vile to others. I've even wondered if I had a split personality. Still, I can't imagine how I could be that bad or selfish as my dream indicated.

Was that me on the inside or a sinister spirit? Did you know that there are signs that can indicate the involvement of an evil spirit? Some of these signs can include incontrollable and intense attitudes and actions, violent impulses, mental obscenities and profanity, fearful and bizarre dreams or night experiences, powers and premonitions of your mind, and strong persistent fears and doubts.[190] Still more signs can consist of a continual cloud of guilt and worthlessness, depression and doubts coupled with fear and compulsivity, confusion and restlessness, extreme medically undiagnosed fatigue, physical nervousness or sickness especially around a Spirit-filled Christian, and unreasonable rebellion against spiritual authority.[191]

How can one be sure? Pray.

And so, I prayed through my childhood past and I believe the Lord allowed another memory to reemerge.

Around three years of age, my mother's cousin unmercifully teased me about being bad. He enlisted my mom, and they pretended that they were going to call the juvenile delinquency and have me taken away.

Terrorized at the thought, I'd scream, "No. NO. NOOOOO."

Tears pouring down my face, I pleaded, "Please Mommy, I'll be good.

I promise I'll be good. Please don't send me away."

Although I had done nothing wrong, I was too young to comprehend they were playing a cruel sick joke. It petrified me! With all my heart, I believed these bad guys were coming to rip me away and I'd never be seen again.

As an adult attempting to make sense of my past, I've never understood. This incident only happened a few times in my life, but this negative memory was a powerful one that shaped my early development and personality.[192] It deeply affected my innermost heart and my belief systems.

Sometimes when a child cannot deal with trauma, they repress it into their unconscious, but their hidden memory still contains all the emotions associated with the abuse including the unforgiveness of the abuser. It's that sin which gives legal ground for the demon to torment the person.[193]

(SIGH again.)

Based on my dreams and the signs displayed in my life, I have concluded that Satan found an opening and took advantage of that opportunity. Those symbols of the hateful woman and predator were the eye-openers. Unknowingly, I had been demonized.

Upon further asking and listening to the Lord, God revealed that this was a spirit of self-hate, which attached itself to my helpless little heart. Now that I think about it, it all makes sense because I have always felt like I was bad. I have strived beyond normal to be perfect so that I would be accepted and loved by others. Of course, it was a losing battle I should have never fought, but I was truly unaware.

I could have spent years in therapy trying to wrap my confused head around all these things, but my loving Heavenly Father provided that shopping dream. I only had to seek out the interpretation and go to Him for healing.[194]

So how did I receive God's healing touch?

Well, I had to first remove the garbage through repentance and confession of sin. I forgave my mom's cousin and my mom. You will be amazed at how well healing works when the garbage is removed. Demons lose their comfy home and are forced to flee.

Next, God filled that empty space with His goodness. He showered me with a miracle at the CoC during one of the healing and deliverance training weeks. One evening while asleep, I had a divine visitation.

There was a strong presence in my bedroom as I heard these weighty words resounding in my spirit, "I made you very good. I MADE YOU VERY GOOD."[195] That was God replacing the lie that I was bad. Then, I could loudly hear singing all around me, "He makes all things glorious."[196] I bet that was God's angelic choir as He was confirming to me that He will make all my mess work together for His glory.[197]

Isn't God great to do such wondrous things as to heal and deliver?

He sure is good. He made us to be good, too, and He loves to make us whole so that we can reflect His goodness.

A Whole Heart

Dear readers, I suspect you never imagined that a book about biblical dream interpretation would reveal the possibility of a demonic attachment. I know that never in my wildest dreams would such a thought have occurred to me.

Yet, the role of deliverance played a key role in the early church. Before the sixteenth and seventeenth centuries, this practice was very common. It was during the Era of Enlightenment that deliverance from evil spirits became marginalized and considered fringe.[198]

In addition, these last few years, I have had people thank me for sharing this truth about inner healing and deliverance prayer because the Lord was able to set them free when over twenty plus years of counseling did not. That is not to say that counseling is not valuable; however, it is the reason I knew I must write about this subject...so that you could make your own decision.

Should you desire to know more, I encourage you to investigate and process this information for yourself. Honestly, I don't think I would have believed either unless I had personally experienced it, but generational sin and the oppression that results from that evil can happen to good people. The sins of your parents, and their parents before them can be passed down to the third and fourth generations.[199] Often we don't want to acknowledge its existence, but sometimes we can't get free until we work through the inner healing and deliverance process for ourselves. The good news is that when the root problems are dealt with through Christ, His blessings are passed down for a thousand generations.[200]

Initially when I learned about inner healing and deliverance, I jumped in with two right feet as I was so anxious to be healed. You might think that two right feet are better than two left, but don't forget that right refers to the natural strength of man. Inner healing and deliverance works best when God does it *with* you.

God has provided healing through His Son Jesus and His perfect sacrifice on the cross.[201] When Jesus heals, your heart will experience His healing balm of love. He will do everything perfectly, in just the right time orchestrating each lovely step. He will establish a safe place for you to be healed. He won't control or manipulate you. He won't cause you anxiety and He will never condemn you. He will take the time to answer your questions and give you peace. He will forgive all your sins, and He will help you replace every lie that you ever believed with His truth.

In fact, when you receive healing, your heart will end up being *stronger* in Him than if you never had any holes. It will be a whole heart.

barbarakoob.com

Figure 3: A Heart that Fully Trusts Jesus – Saved & Whole in Christ

Jesus will do all this for you, but you have to open your heart to Him. Do you know that He is the best heart surgeon in the world?

Just like a skilled heart surgeon who can perform a quadruple bypass, Jesus knows exactly what to do, how to do it and when. And like quadruple bypass surgery, where it takes considerable time to heal, both in the hospital and at home, your healing could take a little while.

Don't dismay if your healing doesn't happen overnight. Deep wounds and deep trauma are big stuff. No one goes home from quadruple bypass surgery the same day. You will need to give yourself time to heal. You will also need to transform your lifestyle by renewing your mind and walking out your new life with good food and exercise.

As I've taught dream workshops and talked with many dreamers, I am confident that God uses dreams to show us our true selves that we may turn our heart to Him and be made whole.

Surely, it is His deep desire to heal us, and we can recover when we cooperate with the great physician. That is why Jesus came—to proclaim the good news to the poor, to bind up the broken hearted, to declare freedom for the captives and release from darkness all those held in prison.[202]

Happily, there are countless good books, counselors and lots of other resources to help you, for God uses them all. You might even consider a healing prayer team or a healing week to spend some quality time away with God. All I can say is that the process is always faster than you think when you start cooperating.

God would love to unstick you from your mess and help you to clean up after eating that delicious caramel apple. So will you turn your heart to God today?

I pray you embark on a wonderful journey of hope, healing, and purpose, which leads us to our last part of the dream process—the application.

Dear God,
Give me the courage to work with You so that all the Band-Aids of my heart are removed. I want to replace every lie with truth so that I can completely trust you. Please come and heal my broken heart, and make it whole for Your glory, for I know that You are good all the time. Thanks, God. Amen.

Review

1. What Band-Aids have you placed on your heart? Do you believe that Jesus can unstick you?

2. Describe how inner healing can transform a person's heart and make it whole.

3. Explain the difference between inner healing and deliverance.

4. What is your opinion regarding the term "demonization"? Do you believe this can happen to a Christian?

5. What steps can you personally take to cooperate with the great physician to receive your own healing? Describe some of the resources available to you.

Part 3 of the Dream Process:

The Application

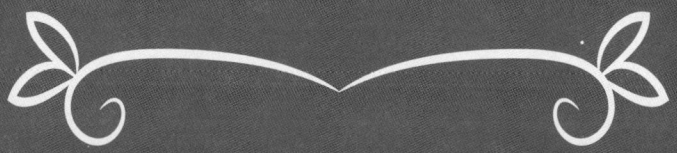

"We are what we repeatedly do.
Excellence, then is not an act,
but a habit"

-Aristotle

11

Apply God's Wisdom

"Let us diligently apply the means, never doubting that a just God, in His own good time, will give us the right result.
−Abraham Lincoln

Start with Yourself

Now that you've learned about getting God's understanding with your dreams, wouldn't you like to know what to do and how to do it? Well, that's the last part of the dream process—the application, and you should do it with the wisdom of God.

I can't tell you how many mistakes I've made with my dreams, however, it does give me lots to talk about. I used to think that God was mad when I slipped up, but that's not true. He just wanted me to learn.

One time I had this simple night vision where I saw this senior leader in our church suddenly died. I was in shock. All the church was in shock, especially his grieving wife. In the next scene, I caught a glimpse of all the rewards he was to receive in heaven, and I was so excited for him.

Nonetheless, I was quite upset with this dream revelation. I didn't want this person to die, nor did I want his spouse to be left without a husband. Of course, I constantly prayed for him and his family, but it bothered me so much that one day I shared it with him.

Fortunately for me, this mature saint was not upset. He graciously responded, "Barb, my life belongs to the Lord. My days are numbered by Him."

Oh how correct he was. How lucky for me and him that we were not blown away by this blunder.

Application blunders can happen to anyone. You may share your dream when you are not supposed to. You can have impure motives and manipulate situations without love and grace. You can puff yourself up when a cool dream revelation occurs. You may even be tempted to look to your prophetic dream and its outcome more than depending on God. However, if interpreted and applied correctly, your dreams are intended to bring hope, but that hope needs to come from God.

My recommendation is to start with yourself. Begin journaling your dreams. Learn the four steps to Get GUI as you develop your own dream language and practice mastering these skills. Overtime God will help you develop your own dream sense. He will teach you how to discern which dreams are significant and which are not. He will teach you what to do about each dream, how to test your dreams and go with God's word, His will and His ways.

With regard to God's word, He would never have you do anything contrary to His word. God never condones wrongdoing or evil as it's not part of His nature.[204] The end will never justify the means. For this reason, check yourself with your dream message and act accordingly.

Next, determine what God's will is for you because dreams do convey directions. Examine your motives, as not everyone is called to do everything. You may have the passion and even the talents, but verify if this is the right thing and right time with trustworthy friends and mentors, and allow God to confirm it.

And finally, whatever you do, do it God's way, so that it honors him. Never push your agenda, control or manipulate, especially if you will hurt another. Instead, wait on God to work through the details and obstacles, and let Him pave your path.

Let me give you an example. For years, I've had several dreams which appear to lead me in the direction of global missions. Surely God's word confirms spreading of the gospel, however, my family has not always been onboard. In addition, I had responsibilities at home to care for my child. Rather than bulldoze my plans, I have chosen to wait on God and believe that He would open the door.

That's why you need to daily go with God. Really, this process is quite similar to your spiritual formation, and it overlaps step four of the Get GUI process, Test and Go. So test your dream message and application and learn as you go.

Now remember, with dreams you only perceive a part of God's understanding and never the full picture.[205] You may know the general direction, even a preview of your God-given destiny, but don't blindly follow your dream. If you did, then you would not be building that God-relationship and relying on Him.

And as God guides your steps, keep careful watch. Satan is a master deceiver who deliberately uses pieces of twisted partial truths to derail God's purposes. I call these lies "dream pitfalls".

Dream Pitfalls

It's so easy for truth to be polluted in your dream. The enemy will use your tilted view of the world, your incorrect understanding of God's truth and the iniquity of your own heart.[206] Dreamers take heed of these three pitfalls for no one is immune.

1. **Pride:** I've nicknamed this first pitfall the "pride precipice." Don't be caught off-guard for every dreamer can be tempted to fall. Often pride is masked by self and it can come in many forms of human thinking.

   I can do this myself. I don't need anyone. I certainly don't need God. I'm the only one who sees this. And the hardest mask of all to remove...*I don't have pride.* (Did I really say that too? YIKES!)

   If you have rationalized any of the above, I hope you hear the sounding alarm and its warning. Don't be that arrogant lone ranger who has no accountability. Ensure that you stay on course by choosing people who are not necessarily like you, but have good fruit in their life to hold you accountable.

   Never think that you have arrived because of a particular talent, a man-made title, or an abundance of financial resources, for spiritual maturity is based on inward character development and true motives of love and kindness.

   In fact, I've noticed that even if I try to be humble, I become prideful of my humility. I suppose it's impossible for me to overcome this pitfall, without God's help. So beware dreamers of that unprotected ledge.

2. **Unholy Connections:** The second pitfall is what I call "unholy connections." Have you ever connected the dots in your life trying to make sense of something? There are various forms of unholy connections as they are easy to employ even without realizing it, especially when it comes to dreams.

   Over and over again, you will see a symbol and assume you know what it means, but compel yourself to go deeper. For example, I love the idea of driving a convertible corvette in the fast lane, as it appears like so much fun, but that symbol spells danger without a covering.

   When you relate one symbol to a different symbol, another unholy connection can be made. While researching symbols, I once heard a woman conclude that the porpoise had the same meaning as the dolphin because these animals seemed so much alike. Rather than researching further, she chose the dolphin meaning because that's what she knew. Yet, porpoises are dissimilar to dolphins, and this unholy connection led to a very different interpretation.

Porpoises are smaller, stouter and untrainable. Unlike the conical-shaped teeth found in dolphins, porpoises have spade-shaped teeth like a whale. And like sharp-toothed whales, porpoises can be predators using sounds to locate prey like fish, squid and crustaceans. Sometimes porpoises are even known as sea hogs.

On the other hand, dolphins are friendly intelligent animals known for protecting injured individuals in the sea. They possess keen eyesight and hearing, which explains why symbolically speaking, dolphins usually refer to a type of spiritual guidance.

Could the symbolic animal porpoise actually be a play on the word "purpose"? That's another way God can use a dream symbol—by playing with the word itself. Whatever the case, stick with the symbol God gave you in your dream and seek Him for your answer.

In addition, we sometimes make unholy connections by naturally filling in the blanks to suit our own thinking. Again, I can't tell you how many times I unconsciously did this.

I've read where that happened in the Bible, too, as people, even prophets can fail. One such case was with a respected prophet named Agabus. He warned St. Paul that if he went to Jerusalem that the Jews would bind and deliver him to the Gentiles.[207] When people heard this prophetic word, they pleaded with Paul not to go to Jerusalem as they feared for his life.[208]

Nevertheless, Paul was not persuaded; he knew his calling.[209]

As it turned out, Agabus wasn't quite right about his word. Although his motives were sincere and his overall picture was correct, his descriptive details were a little off. While the Jews did stir up tons of trouble for Paul, it was actually the Romans who bound Paul and carted him off to Caesar.[220]

Stick with the dream picture that God revealed to you and don't assume you know how the dream will unfold. Don't compromise your actions either.

Finally, sometimes you can make an unholy connection by looking to any source that is not God.[211] It might seem natural to look outside your little world using science or technology, or another person's opinion. Maybe you are even trying to find your answers within yourself? Don't be apprehensive about connecting with Godly wisdom using His Holy Word and His Holy Spirit for that is where the Spirit of Truth can be found.[212]

3. **False Truths:** False truths are one of the most difficult pitfalls to spot because they are lies covertly embedded within truthful words. Since our dreams are naturally filled with deceptions wedged within our hearts, we must be especially careful.

Let me explain this oxymoron using the story of when Satan tempted Jesus in the desert after fasting forty days.

Three times Satan tempted Jesus to act outside of God's will using scripture.[213] In other words, he used truth, but an improper application of it in an attempt to trick Jesus. Fortunately, Jesus saw through each deception because He rightly identified with God's word.

Jesus knew that He could live without impatiently satisfying His flesh through a loaf of bread.[214] He knew He didn't need the world's wealth or power for His Father already owned everything.[215] Jesus also knew that He didn't have to make himself a spectacle by jumping off some pinnacle to prove that He was God's son.[216]

Jesus showed His followers how to correctly apply scripture by recognizing the enemy's traps. At any moment, Jesus could have called on a legion of God's angels to obtain what He needed, but rather, He walked in perfect obedience.

Please understand that false truths are like saps in your dream understanding and application, but let me explain the definition of a sap. A sap is a watery fluid that circulates through a plant, carrying food and other substances to various tissues of that plant. When used properly a sap can carry the nutrients needed for the plant to flourish; however, if not pruned properly the saps can take over. They can weaken the plant by depleting its strength through diversions. That's why a good gardener will cut off all new saps that hinder healthy growth.

Well, just as a sap weakens a vine's strength through division, a false truth subverts foundational truth with confusion. That's why we must beseech God for His truth to be revealed, and we must cut off those saps that sabotage God's plans for our life.

A great story about a false truth is found in the book of Acts, where a certain slave girl spoke truth but caused trouble for Paul and Silas as they were trying to proclaim the gospel.[217]

She was possessed with a spirit of divination and constantly cried out her oracle, "These men are servants of the Most High God, who proclaim the way of salvation."[218]

Obviously, her words were true, but they distracted the people and diverted them from the true message. She did this so much that Paul became greatly annoyed. But one day Paul saw through the problem and used his authority in Christ to command that fortune-telling demon to come out.[219]

In this example, the false truth was caused by an evil spirit, but in your dreams, a false truth could also be stimulated by a spirit of self. In this case, I believe those saps most frequently come in the form of wounds and offenses.

Remember that shopping dream that I described earlier? The lies I believed were that I was unwanted and unimportant, fueled by an evil spirit of self-hate and further complicated by sinful desire to seek the love of people. Several of those lies were caused by my own self; however, the spirit of self-hate was empowered through the demonic.

Often we can see the hurt caused us in a dream as we are intimately aware of that problem in our life; however, we usually don't recognize the path to freedom such as taking a thought captive, giving up our right to be right, or just opening our heart to honest-to-goodness forgiveness.

Yet, the absolute truth is that God wants me. I am important to Him. He unconditionally loves me. As I remove the rubbish and consciously choose to walk in God's truths, I experience more of His freedom.

When it comes to false truths in your dreams, symptoms are exactly like a sap on a vine. They exhaust the energy of the person thwarting healing and moving forward with positive life steps. Usually false truths are very hard to recognize because they will appeal to your heart's belief system.

Take heed, dreamers. In regard to each of these dream pitfalls, you and I must depend on God's help to unmask our pride, to stay holy connected and to cut-off all hidden lies so that His beautiful truth can reign in our lives.

Dreams About Someone Else

So what do you do if you think your dream is about someone else? My advice is to go back and check again, for most of the time your dream is about you.

If you don't feel that your dream is about you, carefully discern and proceed with caution. And if you feel led to share, never forget that how you deliver the message is of utmost importance.

There are two main indicators that I use to decide whether or not my dream is about someone else. First, check if the setting of your dream fits your personal life landscape. Scrutinize your dream and verify if it is about you and your life. For example, the dream setting will not be in your house or you are not the main person traveling on this dream journey.

One of my dear girlfriends was going through a very nasty divorce after twenty-seven years of marriage. During this time, I had this God-dream about her and the custody of her children. I typed up the dream, interpreted some of the symbols for her so she might understand, and kindly offered it as a possible word from the Lord.

Both of us were amazed at how God revealed the details of her personal struggle, for I was completely unaware of the grueling details involving her pending situation. In addition, the Lord gave her a specific answer directing her next steps. It was a key response to her prayer request with an encouraging word that He would take care of everything.

Afterward, this gal asked me, "Barb, why didn't the Lord give me that dream?"

I suspect that she was questioning herself and that He wanted my dream to confirm the word she already held in her heart, but who can say for sure?

The other indicator that I use to determine if a dream is about someone else is by double-checking that I have no personal connection to the dream message. This method doesn't always work because sometimes your heart is deceived and you may not see the real truth, however, it's still a good check.

One time I woke up in the middle of the night in a panic due to a horrible nightmare. I heard these fearful words thundering in my throat, "He died in a car accident because I was chasing him. Now I will be blamed by the courts for his death and go to jail." The words *I am so afraid* repetitively echoed in my soul as I awoke quivering with terror.

I thought *what in the world did I do to be so petrified?*

As I gained my composure and prayed about what just happened, God revealed that it was not me who was so frightened. It was someone who had lived in an apartment that I was cleaning earlier that day.

Prior to my entering that unit, the property manager had shared some sobering news about the former renter. Her son had ventured into a risky adventure with the local drug dealer and the police were planning to arrest him. Naturally, I prayed for this young man that he would find Christ and that He would be set free.

While I can't explain it, I think my spirit somehow tapped into the evil forces that worked in that home. This sort of thing appears to happen to me relatively frequently, and I have learned to pray over places and people that I come in contact with, along with praying for protection for myself.

On one particular year, our family celebrated Thanksgiving with a big gathering of friends and family. While enjoying the festivities, I met a beautiful young lady and learned that she had two cousins who had committed suicide within a short period. Surely, it was not a coincidence that I had this strange dream that evening.

I saw an evil spirit coming to attack her life, but in the dream, I stood between the spirit and its impeding its power to destroy her life. I have no clue as to the source of this dream, and I felt led not to share that dream with her, however, I did pray, use my authority in the name of Jesus to stop it, and she appears happy and healthy today. Yea God!

When and How to Share

Everyone has a sphere of influence for God desires to include us in His great plan. But how does one know when to share? Is one way better than another?

There have been several times where I received an encouraging word through a dream for someone else, and I have loved sharing it. I have had many tell me how much it meant to them.

Nevertheless, I will never forget this gal who called me up to share her dream, but her delivery technique was severely lacking.

"Barb," she declared, "I had this dream and God told me that you need to repent. You need to repent now."

It wasn't just her words; it was her demeanor over the phone. She was hell-bent on insisting that I repent right now right over the phone, and she was going to ensure that I did what she felt I was supposed to do.

Folks, I take my relationship with the Lord seriously. I am well aware of my own transgressions. I know I have faults, however, I can't tell you how unnerving it was to receive such a call.

If there is anything I hope you remember when sharing your dream, it is this…be kind and back off if the person isn't receptive. Any type of forceful delivery which does not strengthen, encourage, lovingly instruct, comfort or edify is form of spiritual abuse which can severely damage a person.[220] Here's a warning for you and those around you…don't ever push your agenda!

You can trust that God is bigger enough to get His message across. And when the Lord does release you to share, offer your words with the understanding that the person is allowed to make their own choice as to whether they accept or reject it. Because you offered, rather than told, you will reduce the risk of a spiritual abuse.

We are not called to be the judge of people. We are called to love them no matter what their circumstances. I know how difficult this can be sometimes as life isn't perfect, but sadly many Christians feel it's their duty to straighten mankind out and put them on the right path.

And so, the bottom line is…if Jesus didn't condemn, control, or coerce others to accept Him or His message, neither should we.

Make sure you walk in love.

When I gave that dying word to that church leader, I felt awful telling him such a thing, but I was deeply grieved for what I saw and afraid for his life. It was that dream that propelled me to earnestly pray for him and his family in those months ahead. I know that my motive was love for this man even though I might have made a mistake sharing.

Even today, I have no idea if my dream message was correct or if I wrongly applied it. He never shared any personal details regarding his life; however, he did eventually step down from that ministry position.

While I knew nothing about his decision, I wonder if God had been speaking to him about leaving that role to make room for the next generation. Years have gone by, and as I think about that dream message and my application, I am so thankful that he is alive and well, and that he is thriving in a new position. Only God knows the whole situation.

As I look back, I think I could have talked to a pastor, a counselor or mentor to confirm my dream message before sharing. I could have just prayed, and I could have waited on God for it never hurts to wait on God. Yet, because I was walking in love and kindness, and probably because he knew to go to God for himself, the situation did not blow up.

I may never know if I applied that dream correctly. I may never know for sure until I get to heaven and ask God for myself, but then sometimes you know and sometimes you don't, and it's OK.

When sharing your dream, pray first, walk in love and don't be afraid to wait on God. If possible, check in with a trusted pastor, counselor or mentor. Certainly, we all need to practice this, for that is applying the wisdom of God.

Now will you join me in a prayer to apply and practice God's wisdom in your dreams? I' hope you are starting to get onboard with this prayer stuff; it really works.

Dear God,
Please help me to apply the interpretation of my dreams

so that I know what to do and how to do it according to Your word, Your will and Your way. I ask for Your divine assistance to deliver me from all those pitfalls, too. Teach me how to discern when I dream about someone else and show me when and how to properly share such that You are honored. Thanks God. Amen.

Review

1. What is the application part of the dream process and why is it important to start with yourself? What is the application key if you made a mistake?
2. Describe the three dream pitfalls and how they can affect your dream understanding and application.
3. How can you discern if your dream is about someone else?
4. Describe when it might be appropriate for you to share a dream interpretation about someone else? Are there times when you should not share?
5. What roles do prayer, love, and wisdom play in the application process? Why wait on God?
6. How can accountability partner and mentors assist you in applying your dream's understanding?

12

Practice on Your Own Dreams

"Perseverance is not a long race; it is many short races, one after another."
–Walter Elliot

My Waterfall Dream

I want you to know that I truly believe that you *can* master biblical dream interpretation, but you must work at it by consistently practicing until you know you've got it right. Let's begin with the dream I described in the first chapter. I call this dream my "waterfall dream" since it was the rain, the rushing waterfall and the underground rapids flowing through my house that captured my attention.

Aren't you just a little curious about what that wet and wild dream was all about? Please re-read it, but this time attempt to interpret it using the Get GUI steps that you studied. I'd like you to also think about how I should have applied God's wisdom regarding this dream. Then, after you have finished your analysis, permit me to share mine.

Using the Get GUI Steps, I hope you were able to ascertain the type of dream revelation, its purpose and the source of my dream relatively easy. Using the category approach, I also hope you visually recognized the house symbol and people symbols such as my friend, my husband, and my baby daughter. In addition, you should have noticed the clue of fresh water falling all over and the animal symbol of my yellow lab, who I affectionately named Gretchen.

I trust you realized that this dream was a complex one. It contained several messages regarding insight into my true self along with a preview of what God had planned next. And although it was *my dream* that you were trying to interpret, I hope you thought about testing it, for there are many falsities that are spoken in our dreams.[221] I wonder if you saw me accidentally trip due to those dream pitfalls.

When I first had this dream, I was so excited because I was sure that God was planning to pour His Spirit over my life, however, as I lived out the dream message and understood its meaning, I began to realize how clueless I was regarding my true self and the difficulties that would lie ahead.

This dream occurred when my daughter was a baby and I was having a big identity crisis as a stay-at-home mom. It was two weeks prior to an awful incident that I had experienced, which triggered powerful negative emotions from my past. Like that mighty waterfall flowing through my roof, I felt like I could not stand up under the pressure.

It all started at a ladies' retreat that I had attended. A women's ministry leader spoke some very personal words to me that were tremendously painful. I cried for days afterwards. This person's motives weren't evil, for I had honestly asked her what was wrong. However, she just blurted out the truth as she saw it, and I got more than I bargained for.

She spouted, "Your emotions are so out of control. You are always crying. It may look spiritual, but I don't believe it is. Also, I don't think you have more power because of the intonation of your voice either. That is not God."

In addition, this gal commented on my attire and intended it to be a compliment, but I wasn't able to receive it. Deeply hurt by her words, I was in shock. Although I was aware of my strong emotions, I felt that she was criticizing who I was.

While not everything she said was correct, I did have to get real and process it with God, yet He was the one who orchestrated this event.

Remember in my dream when my husband wanted to let that dirty dog (me!) in my clean house to be saved? In my initial interpretation I saw myself as good, as if I didn't need God. After all, I was getting food from my friend to give to others. I was acting in my usual performance mode, working my faith in my own strength.

I had never considered the notion that I, too, needed cleansing of my own carnal nature, my own righteousness. When I look back, I clearly see that God was shaking me up so that my desire to be perfect could be washed away, for God can't work with people that don't think they need Him.

Can you see how ironic it was to think my friend was so ill? I can't believe I actually shared this dream with her. While she recognized her own shortfall, I was totally unaware that I was the thin and sickly one that this dream was talking about.

Nevertheless, God still loved me and walked with me through my mess. This process is how dreams, and living your life, work. God Himself will teach you how to understand and apply your dreams step by step as you seek Him.

Please understand that God has many ways to speak and reveal truth to you, and that biblical dream interpretation is just one tool that He uses.

But if you want to learn it, you have to practice. I believe practice is how the great biblical dreamer Joseph learned. Practice is also how I acquired this gift, and I believe that's how you will learn, too.

Dream Discoveries Template

Now take the time to thoroughly examine the final conclusions for my "Waterfall Dream" using the *Dream Discoveries Template*. It should confirm what I've already mentioned above.

Part I: The Revelation
Here is my dream from the first chapter. I have purposely included it again so that you can view my dream and how I processed it.

Scene 1:
I am at a friend's house waiting for some food that she is preparing; however, I believe that this food is not for me. Noticing that my friend is extremely thin and weak, I wonder if she will be OK. I can see her china cabinet filled with many beautiful wedding gifts, but I take the food and leave.

Scene 2:
Next, I am at my house with my husband. My baby daughter is sleeping upstairs. We have a small steady stream of water running through our backyard. It begins to rain and the ceilings start to leak. The rain grows heavier, developing into torrential falls like Niagara. It breaks through the roof, sopping through the windows and walls. I think we cannot stand under this waterfall and remain alive.

Suddenly my house starts to shake. It appears that it is built on top of this stream which becomes a raging river flowing right through the foundation, rocking the house back and forth. I feel frightened.

Scene 3:
My husband wakes my daughter from her sleep and brings her downstairs due to the storm and raging river. For some reason, I wash my baby girl in the kitchen sink. Then, he brings our yellow Labrador retriever who is covered with mud inside our kitchen. I am so upset that I scream, "Why are you letting that dirty dog into our house?"

He answers, "So she can be saved." Ugh. I allow my husband to do this, but I let him know that he absolutely must wash that dog's feet before her grimy tracks tarnish our home interiors.

We were fearful of all the mighty waters, but we couldn't leave the house.

I woke up.

Dream title that I gave to this dream: My Waterfall Dream

Date/Time: Spring 2001 (Don't remember the exact date and time as I wasn't faithfully recording that info, but now I wish I had.)

Describe your location / situation / emotions when this dream occurred: This dream occurred about two weeks prior to my attending this ladies retreat. Although I didn't understand what God was about to do, I had a great sense of excitement.

Part II: The Interpretation

Get God's Understanding and Interpretation (Get GUI):

Step 1: Consider Your Dream and Its Source:
- **Type of Dream:** This dream was complex, symbolic, visual, supernatural and prophetic.
- **Purpose of Dream:** Normally complex dreams carry more than one purpose. This dream contained all three of the stated purposes for it:
  o   Revealed my true self (Heart and Soul Dream).
  o   Encouraged me (Encouragement Dream).
  o   Gave me a directional peek with where God was going to take me next (Directional Dream).
- **Dream Source:** God

Step 2: List and Decipher Your Dream Symbols
- **House** – my life
- **Food** – doing the spiritual will of my Heavenly Father[222]
- **Dining Room** – a place where I am serving God
- **China Cabinet and gifts** – storage unit with all the wedding gifts from my Heavenly Father
- **Rain** – God's Holy Spirit
- **River** – God's Holy Spirit
- **Husband** – my bridegroom and husband, Jesus Christ
- **Friend** – a reflection of my true self (sick)
- **Baby Daughter** – a reflection of my true self (innocent)
- **Dog** - another reflection of me (willing to beg for a treat and do whatever it takes to get people to love and accept me.)

Step 3: Write Your Dream Message(s)
- I was spiritually sick, thinking that I could serve others without God's help.[223]
- God is going to shower His Spirit over my life in a powerful way. But it's not about what I think. He was cleansing me of my performance based behaviors and compulsive desire to be perfect.
- You can stand under the pressure of those forthcoming events because God is in this process.

- Like my baby girl and dirty dog. God wanted to wash me and clean me up for His purposes, to grow and mature in Him.[224]
- I must open the door and let God deal with my sinful stuff.
- God has many beautiful gifts for me stored in my china cabinet.
- My identity was skewed. I thought I was good and clean because of what I did.[225]

Step 4: Test and Go
I tested my perfectionism with the perfect nature of God; and of course, I fell short.[226] I needed to go with God, recognize His truth, relinquish control and relax.

Part III: The Application

Apply God's Wisdom:
Lessons Learned:
- Using the Dream Discoveries Template, I can process my dream in a more systematic fashion such that I can learn biblical dream interpretation.
- This dream was about **me** as most my dreams are.
- God has the power to do amazing acts if I open my heart and cooperate with Him.[227]
- I can live my life processing my dreams and still rest in God's goodness.
- God gave me this dream and that event because He loves me. He disciplines those He loves.[228]
- I have a beautiful identity as God's child. It's not because of what I do, but because of what He has done.[229]

Prayer:

Dear Heavenly Father,
I can't tell You how thankful I am that You revealed my true self to me so that I could be set free. While I sure didn't like Your waterfall process when I was going through it, I do like the ultimate results. It's so good to know that I can completely trust You with my life and that I don't have to do anything to be unconditionally loved and accepted by You.

Your adoring daughter,
Barb

So what do you think? Isn't it amazing how you can glean so much from a dream? I feel so blessed that God revealed every detail. As He and I worked through this process, He gave me so much more than I asked.[230] As you work through all your dreams, I recommend that you use a template like this one to help you learn to master this skill. Don't forget that this is a process. Often answers won't come overnight, especially with complex dreams, so be patient.

I would also encourage you to write your dream messages, lessons learned, and even your prayers in your journal. In some cases, you might consider creating a comprehensive dream interpretation script. That's where you take the time to write down every element of your interpretation as you understand it thus far. You don't have to do this for every dream, just the significant dreams that are God-inspired.

When I first started learning how to uncover the mysteries in my dreams, I analyzed and prayed over every dream byte, even typed some of them up on my computer. I am aware of the arduous labor involved, however, I promise you will find these tasks worthwhile as God will divulge His secrets as you passionately pursue Him.

In fact, my journals have greatly assisted me in thinking through all those details. They provided a record of what I processed as I reinterpreted my understanding. Truly, your thoughts are better sorted and understood using the discipline of writing.

Finally, I suggest that you take this *Dream Discoveries Template* and make it your own. Write and pray as much or as little as you feel led. In the beginning days, I journaled everything because I wanted to learn from it all, but today, I usually journal only my dream revelations and my prayers. However, I must tell you. I still process all these details in my mind because I realize how each function can impact my overall interpretation and application. This is my process and it works for me, but you figure out what will work best for you.

I desire to discover God's understanding. I yearn for God to reveal my true self to me so that I may show His glory. As a matter of fact, God has a beautiful truth waiting just for you to discover—it's your true self, your identity in Him.

Your Beautiful Identity

Have you ever noticed various reflections of yourself in your dreams? While dreams can highlight your broken heart, battles within your soul, and your flaws and failures, they do not represent your identity.

Your identity is not based on your past or present either. It is never established through your education, talents, accomplishments, money or treasures, nor is it based on what people may say about you.

No. No. NO. You and your dreams do not reveal who you are.

You are defined by what God says about you.

You can't fathom it with your head as it requires experiencing it in your heart first. Once your heart receives it, you can begin to understand it with your mind. And when you live this truth of who God says you are, it will transform you from the inside out and change your life.

When I look back at my Waterfall Dream, I clearly see those pitfalls that tripped me as I interpreted and applied my dream. Regretfully, I had spiritual pride thinking I could do God's work in my own strength.[231] I misinterpreted several dream symbols making unholy connections, and definitely did not see my true self. I also believed the false truth that I was good because I was serving others.[232]

However, God desired to set me free of my works mentality. After all, God doesn't need me and my ministry. He can easily raise up another Barb anytime He wants. It's me that needs Him, for no mere human can do anything for a divine all-powerful God. All I had to do was cooperate with God, letting Him do this work. And I am so glad that I did.

This labor of God is what the Bible calls grace. It's a gift, a blessing you can't possibly work to obtain in your own efforts. It's the foundation of the true gospel of Jesus Christ.[233]

God loves you so much that He wants to call you His child.[234] He desires to put a seal on your life and make you an heir to all His heavenly riches.[235] Just trade-in your weaknesses for His strengths by identifying with what God's Son, Jesus, accomplished on the cross.[236]

This mystery of Christ, His dying for our sins and rising from the dead, is power for us who believe to become a son or daughter of God.[237] It's our beautiful identity because we accepted God's perfect love gift.[238]

Do you believe it though?

Mark 12:30 speaks of God's great commandment that you are to love the Lord your God with all your heart, with all your soul and mind, and with all your strength. Did you notice that this commandment starts with the heart? It's just the opposite of the way the world thinks.

Most people attempt to believe based on what their mind can understand, trying to figure out God with their intellect. They'll research, study and come to their own conclusions, however, they won't find Him.

The reason is because faith cannot be attained through the mind. Your mind naturally wants the scientific explanations that seem plausible, but that is not faith. Faith is the substance of things hoped for, believing when you don't understand.[239]

Most of us human beings hate not knowing, as we want to know how, but faith comes from hearing with your heart.[240] It's why you can't mouth faith by speaking positive words. It's why you can't intellectually explain faith using your head knowledge. For only with your heart can you understand that you are deeply loved.

Again this principle of a having a heart-felt experience first directly conflicts with the way the world does it. We are told that we must do to become. For example, if you want to be an athlete, play sports. If you desire to be a teacher, attend school, study, and become certified. If you hope to be a good person, do good things and be approved by others.

But God's plan works differently from the world. If we want to love like God, to be holy like God, to be good and perfect like Him, we can't do it in own strength.[241] We must first become His child, and then we can inherit His nature, through faith in Jesus Christ.[242]

I know this concept can be difficult for some of you to grasp, but have you tried opening you heart to God?[243] Even if you believe, try opening your heart with regards to something that you struggle with. It's hard to do this in your own ability.

But oh, how freeing it is when you grab hold of what He's done and what He wants to do for you.[244] I pray you will experience His love for yourself for it will change everything you know about who you really are.[245]

You can learn to hope and dream with purpose for you are His beloved, accepted in Christ, redeemed and forgiven.[246] He will never condemn you for He is for you all the time regardless of what hurts may happen in your life.[247] You are His masterpiece, the only one in the world who can accomplish His plans on earth with your life.[248] In fact, He calls you more than a conqueror; not because of what you do, but because of what He has done.[249]

God has dreams for you and your life, and I am confident that He will complete this good work that He has started.[250] So start practicing with your dreams for there are many things God wants to teach you. In fact, I believe that is exactly how the great biblical dreamer, Joseph, brilliantly mastered this marvelous gift.

And you know, when God sees that you are seriously paying attention to what He wants to say, He will give you even more dreams. So let's learn together using our dream stories.

Learning from Dream Stories

When I was a little girl I idealized the Bible character Joseph. Somehow in my feeble thinking I foolishly assumed that God snapped his fingers and this interpretation gift appeared. Well, that's a naïve view, isn't it?

I know that the Bible doesn't describe how exactly how Joseph learned biblical dream interpretation, but I have this sneaky suspicion that God taught him just like He taught me—through the school of hard knocks paired with the pursuit of God.

Deeply betrayed by his brothers, Joseph was sold into slavery, and then unjustly thrown into prison.[251] No longer having his natural daddy to call on for help, Joseph was forced to cry out God, for there was no one else to hear his cries. During that traumatic period, I bet that God continued to speak to Joseph in dreams, and that Joseph relentlessly pursued God for answers.

Certainly Joseph, like each of us, had some things to learn, but God showed mercy and favor on him while He was preparing Joseph for his destiny.[252]

Although I don't believe that I ever suffered like Joseph, I can attest that God has definitely positioned me to a place of trial where I had to solely rely on Him. I tried calling on friends and family, but God deliberately arranged my situation such that they were either unavailable or ill-equipped to help. How inconvenient, yet how necessary it was that I learned to depend on God and God alone.

Many times we think God would never send the bad stuff our way, and He is surely not the author of evil, but this process is exactly the stimulus that molds us into what He desires for our lives.[253]

Rather than run away, I pray that we all commit to learn from all our experiences using what I call the A-L-O-E instructions. It's a name I tagged because of an African aloe plant to keep on my window sill. When you squeeze the ends of this healing plant, a lovely juice is released which has a purifying medicinal quality that refreshes whenever it is placed on the skin. I often apply it to burns, cuts, dry skin, and even acne for healing.

Similar to this aloe plant and its juice, God has this A-L-O-E formula for you and me, but we need to apply it, especially with our dreams:

- **A - Ask** God to open your eyes and ears that you may see and understand.
- **L – Listen** carefully as God brings light into your situation.
- **O – Open** your heart and be **Obedient** to what He says.
- **E – Everything**. Do this with everything, practice and learn as you go.

Over the years God has spoken to me using many fascinating dreams regarding all kinds of situations in my life. As I have walked out these experiences with Him, I have been intentional about learning from each one. That's why I have so many dream stories to share that glorify His name and display His splendor.[254] Truly, He has taught me so many things about who He is and what He desires to do for me and you.

One night while I lay asleep, God spoke to me in a dream and said, "I want you to tell people how much I love them and how much I desire to heal them and to do miracles." I will never forget when God spoke that word to me in a dream. I had no idea how I would do this, but in my dumbfounded ignorance I said, "Yes Lord." Who would have thought that He could use biblical dream interpretation to communicate such a plan?

And so, beautiful dreamers, dream more beautiful dreams. Start practicing on your own dreams for God wants to give you a story where you will make your own dream discoveries with Him. Your story will be a testimony of what God has done in your life, describing how you learned to hope and dream with purpose with God.

Will you join me in this prayer request and see what God does next?

Dear God,
Please help me to practice with my dreams so that I can tell Your story of what You did in my life. I want to know who I am based on the beautiful identity that You have given me as Your child. Help me to learn all kinds of things from You and my dreams, including the gift of biblical dream interpretation. You did it for Joseph and I believe You can do it for me. Come, Lord God Almighty. I thank You and praise You for Your goodness. Amen.

Review

1. What did you see when you attempted to interpret and apply my "Waterfall Dream"?
2. How might you use the *Dream Discoveries Template* to process your own dreams?
3. What does a beautiful identity mean to you? How does this apply to the dream application process? How can it change your life?
4. Why do you need to experience faith with your heart first?
5. Describe God's A-L-O-E instruction and how you can learn using it.
6. Use the Dream Discoveries Template to practice on one of your own dreams. If possible, pick a God-inspired dream. How did this methodology work for you?

Dream Discoveries

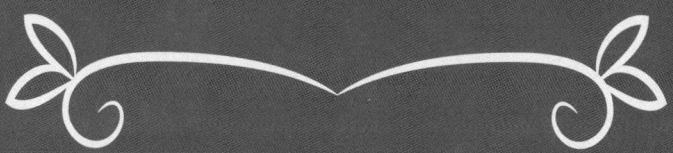

"And it shall come to pass in the last days, says God, That I will pour out of My Spirit on all flesh. Your sons and daughters shall prophesy, Your young men shall see visions. Your old men shall dream dreams."

–Acts 2:17

13

God Dream Stories

"And there are also many other things that Jesus did, which if they were written one by one, I suppose that even the world itself could not contain the books that would be written. Amen"
-John 21:25

Don't you just adore a great story? I sure enjoy being entertained and I certainly love a good laugh. I want action, drama, and inspirations that will last for days as I recollect the plot. It seems like God knew me, and He definitely filled my mind and my life with some spellbinding dreams, but that's why I also have many dream experiences with lots of stories and discoveries to share.

The next few chapters will describe a number of my personal dream stories that I hope will have you kneeling on the floor asking God about your own dreams. I have hand-picked these stories because they include a variety of dream types—God dreams, natural and occultic dreams, simple and complex dreams, symbolic and literal dreams, classic dreams and prophetic dreams, for every one of these dreams can be interpreted and processed with God.

I am optimistic that as you read my stories with my GUI summary info, for I am trusting God, that you will see similarities to your own dreams. It should reinforce the concepts that you already learned. It might even set off a spark or provide insight into some lessons that I learned along my dream journey. But for brevity's sake, I will only include the Get GUI Steps, and not the full dream parts, as that's the most crucial part of dream interpretation.

And so, the first three stories that I'd like to share are all God dreams that came directly from His throne room. The first dream, "Instructions about a Stolen Purse" is a directional dream that points to faith and answered prayer. The second dream, "A Phone Call from Heaven," is an encouragement dream that brought comfort in a time of sorrow, and the last dream, "Snow White at the Wishing Well" is one of my favorites that reveals my true self. As you read them, see if you can find what I discovered before you read the Get GUI summary.

Instructions about a Stolen Purse

You might instinctively think that I knew that God spoke in dreams, but that's categorically not the case. This story is one of my early experiences of hearing God speak, but before I share, I must provide a little background.

One Saturday afternoon my husband and I trekked out of the house to a gourmet ice cream parlor. As soon as we finished indulging in our delectable frozen treats, we headed home, but while on the return route, I suddenly remembered that I accidentally left my purse.

Big mistake. Naturally, we swung the car around and swiftly returned to the place where I left it, but sadly, it was gone.

Agonizing over the impending consequences, I began to realize that this thief had stolen more than my purse. He had my money, my credit cards, the keys to both cars, and the key to our house. He even knew where we lived since I had carefully marked my wallet with my name and address.

Although my husband rarely raises his voice, he did that day.

"Barb, how could you let this happen?"

In my defense, I shouted back in fake faith, "Don't worry. God will return it somehow."

I was attempting to believe, even cover up the gravity of my mistake, but on the inside, I was sweating.

The next day was Sunday, and I went to church as usual, enlisting others to pray for me and my stolen goods. For a day or two, I felt confident that God would answer those prayers, for it was a time in my life when I had decided that I was going to grow in my faith.

No need to notify the credit card companies of my blunder, I thought, however, after three days, I realized my sheer folly.

Along came shame and embarrassment, coupled with fear. Filled with anxiety, I knew my unwise actions contributed to an already terrible situation.

Still…no purse.

Finally, I embraced the steps to rebuild my identity. I purchased a new handbag, alerted the authorities and bank, obtained new keys for my car and house, and applied for a new driver's license. It was a painful process.

Scroll ahead two weeks.

I hear this little voice muttering in my mind, "You don't need the Lord to return your purse. You already recovered everything."

Ha! I knew those words were not from God, and it made me mad. Right then and there, I decided I would not give up on my original prayer, even if it appeared no longer probable.

"Lord, Your Word says that I can ask for anything in Your name and that You will do it.[255] Lord, this purse was mine, and some robber unlawfully pocketed it. Lord God, I am beseeching you to send it back, for I will to purposely believe You no matter how long it takes, no matter what."[256]

I know that prayer may sound strange and rather demanding, however, I also know that after I prayed it, something changed in my heart. My hope crossed over to faith, and I had the strangest dream that night:

I dreamt that my purse was returned.

Next I dreamt that I should put a small ad in the classified section of our local newspaper. I was to thank the person who returned my purse including my name and telephone number.

I woke up with this simple dream sealed in my heart.

Get GUI Summary

Normally, simple dreams don't need an explanation but here is how I processed it.

Step 1: Dream Consideration
- **Dream Type:** Simple, literal, visual, supernatural, and prophetic
- **Purpose:** Provide directions
- **Source:** God

Step 2: Dream Symbolism
No symbols exist with literal dreams.

Step 3: Dream Message
Have faith and believe God that He will return your purse.

Step 4: Dream Test & Go
Wait on God and do the next step. (Unfortunately, I didn't put the ad in the paper as instructed.)

Within three days, I received a peculiar brown manila envelope without a return address. Exactly nineteen days from the day, my purse had been returned with all its contents, including the cash.

Wow God! I can't explain it, but He sure proved to me that prayer in faith works.[257]

As the years have passed by though, I have often wondered what might have happened if I had put the ad in the paper as God had directed. Perhaps God would have done another miracle? Who knows, but looking back I definitely learned some lessons for next time.

One lesson that I learned is that I should pay more attention regarding such an important personal item. I have now trained myself to virtually affix my handbag to my personage in case my brain forgets again. The second thing that I learned is to always act wisely. Having faith does not contradict common sense. And the third thing is never to discount that God can speak in a dream. So begin building yourself a track record of personal experiences where God has proved Himself to you.

Conclusively, the last lesson was the best. Even if you make a mistake, God is able to turn it around. He is the master Mr. Fix-it who promises to work everything out for good to those who love Him.[258]

I know it's hard to continue to believe sometimes, but set your heart on hope amidst your trials that it may be your starting point to build faith.[259]

Phone Call from Heaven

Who wouldn't like to get a phone call from heaven?

I had a dear friend who was diagnosed with diabetes as a child and tragically suffered from complications of this awful disease. Her name was Shawne, and she was beautiful, optimistic and always hopeful of the healing promise she held in her heart in spite of her extreme health issues.

I met Shawne in her late twenties shortly after she lost her eyesight. During a short period of time, I saw her physical health decline as she was forced to avail herself to a home dialysis machine four times a day. This gal could make a pleasant picnic out of a bad situation.

How blessed I was that she called me friend, and just like girls naturally do, we spent hours chit-chatting on the phone about all sorts of things.

One time I asked her, "Shawne, how can you take algebra in college when you can't see the teacher's blackboard?" Being a former math teacher, I sure wondered how in the world she would be able to do such a thing.

Her response, "Oh, I use a felt-board and feel my way through those equations."

Truly, she was an amazing woman of faith with a strong spirit that could not be quenched, but sadly for me and her family, she went home to be with the Lord.[260]

Shortly after her passing, as I was strolling around my street's circle, I tearfully lamented to God.

"Father, I know Shawne is in a better place, but would you say, 'hello' for me? Please tell her how terribly I miss her."

That night I had the most extraordinary dream.

I dreamt the phone rang. When I answered it, I was in shock.

"Hi Barbara. This is Shawne. I am here in heaven sitting on my bed with my favorite dog, Freckles, watching cartoons. I am very happy up here."

Thrilled to hear from her, I tried talking, but every time I did, the line became full of static such that I couldn't hear what she was saying. Apparently, this call only worked one-way, and because I was trying to speak back, I couldn't hear everything she was telling me.

The call lasted just a few minutes, but I thoroughly enjoyed receiving this delightfully divine call from my friend.

I woke up permeating with encouragement.

Was this call really from my friend? I'd like to think so, but who can say?

In any case, this revelation was an encouragement dream personified. It gave comfort to my soul and a boost to my spirit, but the story gets better.

As I mourned my loss, I became friends with Shawne's mom. Since I knew that her mom didn't believe in all this supernatural stuff, I didn't dare approach her about my experience She was still grieving, and I wanted to walk in love and kindness allowing her time to heal. We often went places together for fun and enjoyed each other's company.

After a few years had passed, I felt led to share my experience one day at lunch as I hoped it might bring comfort.

> ### Get GUI Summary
> **Step 1: Dream Considerations**
> - ***Dream type:*** Simple, literal, visual and probably actual, supernatural, and prophetic
> - ***Purpose:*** Provide encouragement
> - ***Source:*** God
>
> **Step 2: Dream Symbols**
> No symbols exist.
>
> **Step 3: Dream Message**
> Your friend is happy in heaven.
>
> **Step 4: Dream Test & Go**
> Rest in God that all is well.

"Peggy," I timidly offered. "You might not believe this, but I received this unusual phone call from Shawne."

As I relayed my story, her eyes watered. Evidently she knew exactly what I was talking about because Shawne had called her, too. What a God surprise!

Dreams like this don't really need an interpretation because the message is simple, but again for the sake of working the interpretation process, take a look at the Get GUI summary.

Wasn't this experience remarkable? Today I remain awestruck.

Yet, I still don't understand so many things. Why did Shawne have to suffer so much? She was so joyfully full of life and touched so many. It was painful to watch her deteriorating body slip toward death. I don't understand why God would allow this blessing counter to leave earth unhealed.[261]

In many ways I think it's more challenging for those left behind, and so, I have many questions to ask God when I see Him, but this I do know. God used Shawne to touch the lives of many people and His glory shined all around her. I also know that dream was a God-send to encourage me.

Do you need comfort and encouragement today? You know, your heavenly Father God could use a dream to provide what you need.

Snow White at the Wishing Well

Very different from those other two dreams, here's a great example of a symbolic heart and soul dream which revealed my true self:

I dreamt that I was Snow White standing at the wishing well with all these beautiful little bluebirds chanting around me. Dressed in my scullery maid clothes, scrubbing the floors, I am singing, "Someday My Prince Will Come".

In the nearby trees, my Prince-Charming Jesus sees me, but I don't know He's looking. He is passionately in love with this ugly scullery maid—not the beautiful princess I hope to be.

When I discovered that He sees me, I get flustered and run away because I don't want Him to call on me looking so dirty and unkempt. It was quite an enchanting moment.

I woke up.

This dream was monumentally personal for as soon as I opened my eyes I had this profound sense that God sees me, that He knew me even as a little girl. I can't explain it, but I felt His overwhelming love overtake me in a powerful way that I wish everyone could experience.

Get GUI Summary
Step 1: Dream Considerations
- ***Dream type:*** Complex, supernatural, symbolic, visual, and prophetic
- ***Purpose:*** Reveal my heart and soul, provide encouragement
- ***Source:*** God

Step 2: Dream Symbols
- **Snow White** ~ reflection of me
- **Wishing well** ~ all my dreams
- **Bluebirds** ~ spirit of God
- **Prince Charming** ~ Jesus
- **Scullery maid clothes** ~ dirty, not good looking good, and definitely not good enough

Step 3: Dream Message
God sees me as beautiful and He loves me just the way I am.
Step 4: Dream Test & Go
Strengthen and encourage myself in God's words of love.

Funny thing is that my entire family would be cracking up with laughter if they heard about this dream for I was infamous for pretending to be the beautiful princess when I was a little girl. My parents had taken me to see the movie Snow White and subsequently bought me a record player and the soundtrack. Even though I knew I wasn't a daughter of an earthly king, I enjoyed play-acting that I was a beautiful princess just like Snow White at the wishing well. I often fantasized that my prince charming was on his way to the rescue.

Dressing up and dancing around the room singing "Someday My Prince Will Come," I am certain that I drove everyone around me crazy. In fact, my younger brother would constantly complain, "Please, *please* make her stop that music. I can't stand it anymore."

We were just kids, and of course, I didn't stop and he may be nuts today because of me. Well, maybe not because of moi? He had his own idiosyncrasies as everyone in my family is amusingly colorful, but seriously, have you the slightest clue what was that dream was all about. It took me about one year to figure out God's understanding and interpretation, for this dream was surely not a coincidence. It occurred about two weeks prior to that ladies retreat I attended. God knew what event was forthcoming in my future, for He was about to release a shaking and a waking to wash me off and clean me up.

This dream was His way of strengthening me prior to the storm by reminding me of His unconditional love. This visual reflects my beautiful identity for I was already beautiful to Him, and it was not because of how I looked or what I did.

Isn't it fascinating how God uses various dreams, even different dreams with similar messages, so that they may seep into your soul and seal His love into your innermost being? Can you see my examples of how God uses dreams to direct, encourage and reveal areas of your true self?

I'm dancing on the table, symbolically speaking of course, hoping and a praying you are thinking, *Oh, Yeah.*

And so, dear readers, let's decide to get God's understanding no matter what the cost, as His words are priceless.

Often people ask me, "How do you know which dreams are God dreams?"

Most of my God dreams ensue between the hours of 1:00am and 3:00am accompanied by a holy presence. It's just a sense I catch in the air accompanied by a memory that lingers. And although I don't have a specific formula, I believe you need to test your dreams and determine this for yourself.

Nevertheless, if you must choose a dream to Get GUI, pick a God dream as these dreams are the best. Don't miss even one of His love letters that are personally penned for you, for I promise that He will make it worth your while.

Review

1. What do you think of these God dream stories? What lessons, if any, can you learn from these experiences?
2. Do you believe that God hears our prayers and answers questions about our dream stories?
3. Have you had any of your own God dreams? If yes, what do you think God might be saying?
4. Explain the concept of an actual dream with an impartation. Have you ever had one? Can you be sure?

14

Natural and Occult Dream Stories

"Indeed, I am against those who prophesy false dreams," declares the Lord.
"They tell them and lead my people astray with their reckless
lies, yet I did not send or appoint them. They do not benefit
these people in the least," declares the Lord.
– Jeremiah 23:32

While natural and occult dreams are not always the nicest, you and I need to know about these dream types. We must know how to recognize them and how to properly deal with them; but first, let me start with some definitions.

A natural dream is conjured from your own will and emotions, revealing your innermost thoughts. They reflect what you truly have on your mind whether it is good or bad, fun or disturbing. These dreams can also contain incorrect information depending on your beliefs.

One of my happiest natural dreams was about the day I would marry. Like many young girls, I imagined myself dressed in the gorgeous white gown promenading down the aisle to "Here Comes the Bride" as my smiling Prince Charming would greet me with true love's kiss. No wonder my active imagination stimulated these dreams both before and after my wedding.

As a matter of fact, I distinctly remember whimpering to my new husband after our nuptial vows, that it was all over. Funny how these natural dreams reflect the real you on the inside, though not necessarily the truth.

Hugely stunned, my new man retorted, "Oh Honey, this is just the beginning." That was the initial start, not the end, of my marital bliss.

On the other hand, an occult dream has Satan as its source. If you are actively engaged in the occult, I suppose your chances of having a dream from Satan are likely. However, the sad news is that even if you are not actively practicing witchcraft, even if you are a committed Christian, you can have a dream which is inspired by the demonic.

"How?" you ask.

You can accidentally tap into the demonic spirit realm. Most of my occult dreams, which thank God are few, have resulted around a foul feast day such as Halloween, or being disturbed by a wicked presence from a foreign location such as a hotel room or other tainted space.

Incidentally, both natural dreams and occult dreams are often spoken of as false dreams. The reason is because their source and their messages are deceitful. Continue with caution because you cannot trust these dream types.

A good example of a false dream is a nightmare. Either a natural origin or a demonic root can fuel nightmares. In either case, you must find the foundational cause of the fear and cleanse the ground that provided the basis for that bad dream. Often I have learned to pray for protection beforehand whether it is for my child or for me sleeping in a strange space, however, if you forget, you can pray during that present moment in anticipation of the next time. For the point is to close all open doors so that the enemy can no longer terrorize.

Nonetheless, in this chapter, I have included four dream stories, two natural and two occult. While these false dreams are not as exciting as the God dream stories, I do hope that you will see some correlations to your own dreams. Again, see if you can guess the Get GUI Summary before you read them. And never forget, that no matter what the message of your dream is, even if it is false, that God has a good answer.

Off with Your Head

Not one of my most pleasing dreams, this one definitely revealed a battle brewing in my soul, for I was raised in an extremely strong-willed family. In fact, my parents, a few of my siblings, and I have all prided ourselves on our brawn and self-determination to keep pushing our way through life's situations so that we can deem ourselves significant.

"Dust yourself off" and "Never give up" were the combat mottos of mine and my family for we were determined to fight through life to victory. However, if your natural ability is fortified with your own resilient self, your personal power can hinder God's grace. God is such a gentle Father that He will let us have our own way. Actually, this attribute is not a strength, but a Spartan weakness, and it's especially true if you've never learned a healthy sense of community and interdependence.

Essentially, this dream revealed a recurring theme that reared its head in many of my dreams. Honestly, it's one of my silliest dreams, illuminating this one issue that I have often struggled with, and I wonder if you will perceive what I now see.

I dreamt I am standing in line, waiting for my turn at the guillotine. Naturally, I am afraid. Of course I am not happy with where I am, but this circumstance appears to be my lot in life.

Suddenly my turn comes.

I place my head between the blades in anticipation of being decapitated. Just as I have imagined, the blade falls and slices my neck, cutting off my head. As I gawp at the carnage seeing all the blood and flesh on the ground, I think "Oh no. I am finally dead. So now what?"

Yet, miraculously, I survived. Somehow, I find myself stitched back together in one piece.

And again, I stand in line waiting for my turn at the guillotine, waiting for my head to be cut off.

And again, I am sewn back together.

I attempt to speculate how many times I will have to die and then can come back to life. It's like I can't break away, because I am determined to crucify my carnal nature.

I woke up.

Get GUI Summary

Step 1: Dream Considerations

- ***Dream type:*** complex, symbolic, visual, natural and false
- ***Purpose:*** reveal my heart and soul, provide directions (albeit false directions)
- ***Source:*** Natural (me)

Step 2: Dream Symbols

- **me** ~ reflection of me, afraid, worrying, continually willing to die to myself
- **guillotine** ~ cutting off
- **neck** ~ will, stiff-necked, stubborn spirit of God
- **head** ~ authority

Step 3: Dream Message

I am willing to die again and again to crucify my flesh. It's got to be done and repeated over, and over again (and that's the lie).

Step 4: Dream Test & Go

Receive God's free gift of grace. Rest in His completed work on the cross. He died for me so I can freely live.

This dream definitely caught my curiosity for I had fallen in love with France a few years back when my husband, my two-year-old daughter, and I had lived there for five months. I fancied experiencing all the gourmet culinary delights that satisfied my carnal pleasures, but never could I have conjured up a trip to the guillotine.

What in the world was this dream all about?

At first, I thought this dream divulged my true self as I dealt with crucifying my flesh and my desire to die for Christ. I knew I must detach from my prideful self and was working hard to overcome, however, why did I have to repeat this negative experience? You would think that if I had my head cut off just once it would have killed me for good.

But this false dream, like all false dreams, was portraying a lie. It was a very subtle lie, so you have to look closely because in some warped way, my continual dying appeared to me as a noble act.

Most of the times we won't recognize the lie for our faulty belief system has covered it up. Do you see it?

The lie was found in my need to continually repeat that vicious guillotine cycle. God does not require me to purposely repeat the death process. I shouldn't have to worry or continually be afraid. Jesus Christ suffered on the cross for my sins. He was chastised for my iniquities, not His wrongdoings. He was punished so that I would not have to be punished. I should not have to condemn myself.

Also, I am in Christ and my life is in Him. Death should no longer sting.[262] Since He conquered all sin and suffering on the cross, I have only to surrender my life to Him once, believe that what He did is enough, and rest in His finished work.

This dream was a complex one with a simple solution. Hallelujah.

It's All Your Fault

No one should ever have to endure a nightmare that unsettles one's slumber for the Lord desires to give us peaceful sleep.[263] While the source of a nightmare could involve the demonic, it does not have to be. Here is a recurring nightmare retold to me by one of my friends.

I dreamt that I am working at my job with all my coworkers. Everyone keeps coming to my office and criticizing me.

"It is all your fault. You were responsible and you are the reason why this task has failed." I try to explain myself, but it is to no avail. They keep blaming me over and over again.

I wake up in a panic.

The situation at my friend's job was, indeed, very difficult. For certain, her coworkers lacked basic organization and administration skills, and they were constantly blaming her whenever their projects performed at a subpar level. While my friend was to provide advice and support, these failures were a result of their irresponsibility, not hers.

Reliving this situation in her dreams must have been awful, but as she further inspected the root cause, it pointed to something that occurred in her younger years, not the current situation.

Her mom was an insecure person. Whenever anything negative happened in my friend's childhood, her mom always assumed it was her fault saying, "What did you do to cause this problem?"

Whenever you have a false dream, always attempt to look beyond the shallow interpretation so that the lie will be uncovered in the light. In this gal's case, the problem wasn't the blaming by her peers. It was her deep-seated insecurity stimulated by a critical mother.

This nightmare revealed a need for inner healing of the emotions that she felt as a child. Once she received prayer and resolved those feelings of self-doubt with faith in what the Lord did for her, she could confidently set aside her co-worker's comments and not allow their guilt to infiltrate her mind.

When she did this, the nightmares miraculously disappeared, for God wants to heal us. Sadly, the root problems in our dreams often remain unhealed until we decide to go before the Lord and walk out our own healing.

On one occasion, a gal conveyed a recurring nightmare to me regarding her playing the flute. In her dream, no matter how hard she tried, this awful sound would resonate into the atmosphere.

"I know I can play the flute," she coached herself, "I know I can."

However, the off-key vibrations kept echoing in her dreams such that she would wake up in a cold sweat.

Essentially, the flute was a

> ## Get GUI Summary
> **Step 1: Dream Considerations**
> - *Dream type:* Simple, literal, visual, natural, and false
> - *Purpose:* Reveal my heart and soul
> - *Source:* Natural (My friend)
>
> **Step 2: Dream Symbols**
> Literal dreams do not have symbols.
>
> **Step 3: Dream Message**
> You are to blame. However, that was the lie. For the project managers were the ones responsible for their assignments.
>
> **Step 4: Dream Test & Go**
> Receive healing and shake off the blame.

dream symbol of this young gal, as she did play the flute, however, this dream revealed a personal inner struggle that she felt she could never perform well enough with her life's activities. Similar to my friend's dream, she needed inner healing of her heart.

Our wonderful God is always the one who will cheer us on. He does not condemn us. Our accomplishments are not important to Him, for it is not about what we do, but about what He did. Dreamer friends, make the decision and choose to walk out your freedom because He wants it for you more than you do.

Hubby or Old Boyfriend?

As I mentioned in the "Off With Your Head" dream story, I adored my time in France. It couldn't have happened at a better time in my life. After a few years of grueling infertility treatments, my husband and I finally had our beautiful baby girl.

So when Jim received a temporary work assignment in the Rhone-Alps region of southeastern France, in the city of Lyon, Anika and I bundled our belongings, and stowed away in his hotel room at the luxurious *La Reine Astrid.*

My baby bird and I had so many delightful days exploring the city together, yet at night, I'd have these dreadful dreams. In particular, there was this one recurring dream about an old flame from high school.

I dreamt that my old high school boyfriend, John, suddenly emerges to court me. I feel the excitement of a possible affair that could be fermenting, but I continually find myself asking these questions...

"Who will I choose? John or Jim?"

After much deliberation, I finally stand up and take charge, "I made the decision years ago. I pick Jim."

And I wake up.

If this dream happened only once, I might have ignored it, however, it persistently appeared. Indisputably, I knew that my heart no longer carried romantic feelings for another. I was confident that my choice was always for Jim, but why did I continue to have this strange dream?

And so, I inquired of the Lord, and He revealed that this dream was the result of a territorial adulterous spirit that hovered over that part of the city. Its mission was to tempt people to seek love in the wrong places.

Thank God I knew to take authority over it in

Get GUI Summary

Step 1: Dream Considerations
- ***Dream type:*** Simple, literal, visual, supernatural, and false
- ***Purpose:*** Provides directions on where not to go
- ***Source:*** Satan

Step 2: Dream Symbols
No symbols in this literal dream.

Step 3: Dream Message
You can still choose your old boyfriend instead of your husband, and it's OK. (That's the deception.)

Step 4: Dream Test & Go
Bind the enemy's scheme and pray for protection from evil spirits entering my hotel room.

the name of Jesus. I declared that our nouvelle nest was a safe place, that it was guarded by angels and that no evil dreams could enter. Once I protected our petite place with prayer, I never had the problem again.

I can only imagine what can happen to innocent people who are caught off guard by such spirits, as the enemy loves to weasel his way into a hurting heart to destroy a person's life, for this is how demonic dreams work.[264]

Satan will deliberately vex your emotions, whispering wicked temptations, obscenities, or fears to cart you off to the wrong course. That's why it is imperative to recognize an occultic dream and bind the devil with the authority God has given you in Christ.

It's not by accident that this demonic dream occurred in a different place from my ordinary routine. Over the years I've discovered that hotel rooms are often havens for the demonic to torment an unsuspecting victim. I can only imagine what can happen to an innocent person who is unaware of their goings-on. Don't be afraid to take charge over the atmosphere before you lay your head to rest.

This next dream is an excellent example of a demonic deception, a net purposely cast to entrap me using my own natural desire to have another child. Oh how Satan doesn't play fair, so be aware.

Deformed Baby Blessing

One weekend our family decided to visit one of our senior friends at their new retirement home at the beach. During that time in my life, I yearned to have another child, but given our circumstances, it was not to be.

As I lay asleep in their house, I had this bizarre dream that spoke directly to my heart. Unbeknownst to me, I was tricked by its seemingly good pretense.

I dreamt this older woman came to visit with some news from God. She tells that God was going to give me and my husband a baby. Immediately, I felt excitement and leaped for joy.

Then, she tells me the other news…

"This baby will be born severely deformed with many abnormalities so that God can teach you human compassion."

As my heart sank, I thought, "God, I don't want that, but if this is You, I will joyfully receive your plan."

I woke up with mixed emotions.

I am so grateful to God that when I told this dream to my husband, he looked directly into my eyes and firmly stated, "That is *not* from God."

You would have thought that I would have recognized the deception, but I was too caught up in my emotions. Needless to say, I wasn't onboard with his response, at least not at first, but like all my dreams, I quietly asked the Lord. It was better than arguing my point.

Within the hour, God confirmed that my husband was correct. God's will is always to give life abundantly, healthy life, too. While sickness does occur here on earth, it was never part of God's original plan. I suspect a few of you might have difficulty understanding this concept, but I beseech you to genuinely seek Him for yourself on this topic.

As I thought more about this dream, I also realized that God does not teach "human" compassion. He is the source of enduring mercy and abundant grace that will confound intellectual, political and religious views. In plain man's terms, I don't get it, but I do believe that He is perfect love. I know that He is good all the time.

Most likely that woman in my dream symbolized a demonic spirit who wanted to torture me about my future by deceiving my mind with a false truth. Once I realized it, I shook off that message from my heart and declared God's goodness over me and my family.

Now that you have processed seven of my dream types, I'd like to summarize a few things in hopes that you saw what I saw in the last two chapters. The three prophetic dreams all had their source as God, and each one spoke truth, even about bad situations, because God doesn't lie. Conversely, the four false dreams had a natural source or a demonic root, and each one contained some type of lie or deception.

I also hope you noticed that five of the dreams were supernatural; three had God as a source, and two were demonic. You should have also detected that complex dreams have more than one purpose, and that not all dreams are symbolic. In addition, some supernatural dreams could actually be real, although I can't say for sure.

Get GUI Summary

Step 1: Dream Considerations

- **Dream type:** Simple, literal, visual, supernatural and false
- **Purpose:** Revealed my heart & soul
- **Source:** Satan

Step 2: Dream Symbols

This dream was probably literal, but I suspect that woman was a demonic spirit speaking to me in my dreams.

Step 3: Dream Message

God was going to give me another baby, with abnormalities to teach me. (That was the deception; God does not create deformities.)

Step 4: Dream Test & Go

Shake off that message and its lie. Believe God for good things because He is good.

As I look back and see how God has taught me through my dream journey, I continue to find all my dream stories fascinating. Have you enjoyed reading my dream stories? Maybe you are thinking about your dreams in a different light? Can your caramel apple get any sweeter?

Maybe not, but we can have another gooey chewy apple if we want, or we could dip the one we have in chocolate.

Review

1. What do you think of these natural and occult dream stories? What lessons, if any, can you glean from these experiences?
2. How can you discern between a natural dream and a supernatural one?
3. Explain the concept of a false dream versus a prophetic dream. Are you able to discern the differences?
4. Out of all the dream stories told so far, which one was your favorite?
5. Could any of these dream lessons be applied to your own dreams?

15

More Dream Stories

"We may not pay Satan reverence, for that would be indiscreet,
but we can at least respect his talents."
–Mark Twain

Years ago I expressed to some employees that worked for me that I am always looking for my next job. They smiled with disbelief as they thought I was happy at that company, but really, I was only saying that I wanted to stay alert and look for that next big wave of opportunity.

Do you remain alert as you gaze upon your dreams? God has some super exciting revelations for you to perceive, like surfing waves of His Holy Spirit, but you have to get wet and be ready to ride.

Even if you are new to surfing in His Spirit, God would love to give you a dream where you must deeply seek Him for understanding. If you couple your dream revelations by asking for God's wisdom, the Lord will use them to help you with your life.

Here in this chapter, I describe three interesting dream stories and some big lessons that I learned from God. A "Great Deal on a New Car" is one of my journey dreams where I learned more about forgiveness and God's grace. "Flush Three Times" is, you guessed it, a bathroom dream that revealed my desire to wash up and a call to obey. And last, "My Stolen Purse" is a very common identity dream.

Beautiful dreamers, even though the enemy will attempt to derail you, God wants to encourage you to ride those spiritual waves of His goodness, to allow Him to teach you on your dream journey, for He some brilliant lessons just for you. So have fun riding those waves, this one and the next.

A Great Deal on a New Car

While the possibility of driving off the lot in a brand new car sounds fun, this dream reflects a hard spot in my heart with some divine advice when I was struggling with some family relationships.

Have you ever had a skirmish that has not been amicably settled? Oh mercy me, the Lord is not in that.

Scene 1:

I see my parents shopping for a car. They find a really cool van with all the newest features and gadgets, but the only catch is that they must purchase it in Canada.

The vehicle's list price was $19,000, but, they were not willing to pay that amount. However, as luck would have it, they were able to purchase this fine-looking new vehicle for only $15,000. It was a great deal.

You'd think that I would have rejoiced over their good fortune, but instead I howled, "You know, you may have purchased that car at a good price, but the price of gas required to drive it is going to be outrageous. It will cost you."

They bought the car anyway and were as happy as can be.

Ironically, after a little more thought on the matter, I decided to buy that same car as this deal was too amazing to pass up.

Scene 2:

I see myself with my husband driving a car in my childhood neighborhood. We travel down a very steep slippery road that is covered with snow and ice. Jim pumps the brakes exactly as needed, and we miraculously stop at the next intersection without having an accident.

Funny how all the houses in the neighborhood have recently rebuilt their foundations including newly constructed front porches. It is lovely.

I woke up.

This dream clearly spoke about my life's journey with my parents. I was angry about some things, from my past and in my present, and I would not let it go.[265] Of course, this dream never divulged what it was that I was so irritated about, but I knew in my heart.

My inner struggles stemmed from the revelation that I wrote about in my shopping dream, that I felt unloved and unimportant while growing up, and this complicated our relationship.

God was very familiar with my problem, which is why He was undeniably giving me some very helpful instructions to rebuild the foundation of my future.[266] If I would choose His ways, trading my sin, my sorrows, and my prideful path, He would remove the garbage flooding His amazing grace on my path.

Do you have an unresolved issue with a family member or friend? Don't let Satan have his way, for God would love to speak to you about it in your dream. It will cost you something, but not as much as you think, for in reality His grace is the greatest deal ever.[267]

GET GUI SUMMARY

Step 1: Dream Consideration
- *Dream type:* complex, symbolic, visual, supernatural, and prophetic
- *Purpose*: reveal my heart and soul, provide encouragement
- *Source:* God

Step 2: Dream Symbols
- **Shopping** ~ buying a truth or lie
- **New Car** ~ new journey
- **$15,000** ~ cost of freedom
- **$19,000** ~ cost of shame, barrenness, self-righteousness
- **Gas** ~ cost of journey without grace
- **Canada** ~ north of where I live, i.e. look up to heaven.
- **Slippery Road** ~ difficult path
- **Intersection** ~ stop at the Cross
- **Front Porch** ~ future revealed with a new foundation

Step 3: Dream Message
- God's grace is for everyone, even when you don't deserve it.
- Brake when the road is slippery; be cautious and wise, and all will be well.
- Stop at the cross, God's intersection.
- God desires to rebuild your life and give a beautiful future, and He will do this for others, too.

Step 4: Dream Test & Go
Forgive. Stop trying to make others pay for their mistakes, when Jesus paid for it all. Soften your heart and receive His amazing grace; it's for everyone. It won't cost you, except for your pride.

Flush Three Times

God tells us that it is impossible for offenses *not* to come. Because we live in a broken world, this dilemma, my dear friends, is the absolute wretched truth. It's just a matter of time, but you and I will get hurt by someone or something. In fact, Jesus told us that offenses *will* come, but woe to the man who brings the offense.[268]

Furthermore, we are told not to hold onto those offenses, not because they don't deserve justice, but because it will hurt you the most. Despite how we feel, we must leave every offense at the cross, for if we don't, Satan's snare will hold you captive.

Here is a profound dream that occurred several years after a trip that I made to visit my mom and dad with my sixteen month old baby. Attacked by their ill-mannered rottweiler named Brutus, I lost my sense of safety in their home.

As I look back, this situation wasn't normal in so many ways. Why did it bother me so much? Why couldn't I control those tears? Why wouldn't my parents comfort me in my time of distress?

As they walked away ignoring my cries, I felt so deeply rejected. Sobbing for three straight days, I then developed a severe migraine that incapacitated me, leaving me unable to function and care for my child. Finally, when I was able to compose myself, I wept in my heart for years afterwards carrying that hurt and anger. Without doubt, the enemy had lodged a deep offense in my heart.

Unable to shake off my raw emotions, I suffered a form of betrayal. I no longer felt secure as their cherished daughter who they cared about. Due to trauma that I had experienced as a little girl, my tears resurfaced, and along with it, a bitterroot that I wasn't valued.

As fate would have it, both my parents refused to kennel their dog for next time.

I suppose people didn't talk about their problems back in the olden days, as you were expected to bury your feelings and move on, but miserably I was unable to do so.

Although I tried to talk to my parents, my words fell on deaf ears.

"But the dog didn't hurt you," Mom exclaimed, "You are fine. And I won't have you demand what I do in my house."

I didn't think I was demanding, but maybe to her, I was. Yet, I believed I suffered a deep breach of trust one too many times. No matter how hard I tried, I couldn't stop sniveling over this dreadful event.

And so, because they refused to honor my feelings, I refused to visit them in their house. Naturally, I justified my actions. After all, I live over five hundred miles away and it cost me time and money to travel that far.

Consequently, and most sorrowfully, an offense was born.

Of course, we saw and spoke to each other, even loved one another as we politely worked through our disagreement, but I snubbed the idea of ever stepping foot in that dog's house again until one day when I awoke with this unusual dream.

It was a house dream and a bathroom dream with a complex story line.
I am in my childhood home on Cherry Blossom Drive.

My heavenly Father comes and asks me if I will accompany Him on a visit to my earthly father who is now residing in Long Island, NY. Although I want to go, I am unable to commit.

"I can't. I can't face this situation." I yelp in trepidation.

My heavenly Father is very sad, but He says He understands.

Next thing I know, I decide to venture out with a girlfriend to have some fun, however, in order to get ready, I need to wash off and clean up.

"Heavenly Father," I inquire, "is it okay if I take a shower in your master bathroom?"

"Of course," He graciously responds allowing me that privilege. That is huge especially since all of the kids in our house were forbidden to ever shower in my parent's bathroom.

Proceeding into the bathroom, I attempt to turn on the water, but for some reason, I cannot get the faucet to work.

Suddenly, I see why. Someone has stuffed a plastic bag and an empty orange juice carton in the commode creating a big clog.

I run back to my Heavenly Father and ask. "How can I get the water to flow?"

He replies, "Flush three times."

I declare, "Daddy God, that clog is way too big for that to work, I don't think that will work. But because You said to do it…I will."

As instructed, I flush three times and the clog miraculously disappears. The water starts flowing again, and I take my shower. Woohoo!

I woke up.

Oh how amazing is the kindness and patience our heavenly Father has toward us.[269] Almighty God could have forced His instructions on me, even for my own good, but instead He flooded me with His love and goodness.[270] And because He did, I learned so much from my situation and this dream.

I had been wronged and wanted justice. I wanted things to be made right with my idea of what it should look like, but alas, that was never going to happen. For sure, I needed to forgive, as that is a huge condition for freedom, however, this dream revealed the source of my struggle.[271]

Take another look and see if you can discover why I had such difficulty removing this offense? Why wouldn't the water flow? What was causing the clog?

Have you reexamined my dream? Know the answer?

My problem uncovered by the dream stemmed from a deep root of rejection and I simply did not have the strength to fight it off. However, the truth is that I was not rejected by Jesus.[272]

In some warped way, I was looking to my parents to care about my cries, but that's looking to a person. Whenever we look to people, money, resources, or anything other than God, we will be disappointed.[273]

<u>Get GUI Summary</u>

Step 1: Dream Consideration
- *Dream type:* complex, symbolic, visual, supernatural, and prophetic
- *Purpose:* reveal my heart and soul, provide directions and encouragement
- *Source:* God

Step 2: Dream Symbols
- **Childhood Home** ~ my life as a child
- **Heavenly Father** ~ God
- **Natural Father** ~ my dad, my parents, or possibly a reflection of me and my future alone on an island if I don't change
- **Girlfriend** ~ a reflection of me, wanting to go out but desiring to wash off first
- **Shower** ~ need to wash off
- **Bathroom** ~ place of cleansing
- **Commode** ~ need to eliminate sin
- **Trash Bag** ~ spirit of rejection
- **Empty OJ Container** ~ no energy left
- **Water** ~ God's word / Holy Spirit
- **Flush** ~ remove sin / offense
- **Three Times** ~ obedience to Christ

Step 3: Dream Message
- I can't visit in my own strength; my emotions are too raw.
- I need to let go of the offense to be free.
- I am having trouble eliminating the offense because of deep feelings of rejection and my lack of energy to fight it.
- Obey God, and the clog will miraculously be removed, and the water will start flowing again.

Step 4: Dream Test & Go
Don't let the enemy win. Go visit your parents in spite of how you feel. Very hard to do, but very freeing.

I was waiting for a person to make it right, but God was waiting for me to shake off that victim mentality. I had to surrender my right to be right for God had already done His work through Christ's shed blood on the cross.[274]

Can you consider this truth regarding your own offenses?

Remember in my dream, I actually told God that I didn't believe what He said would work, but I did tell Him that I would give it a try only because it was Him who said so. Should there have been any doubt that He was right? During this time my husband had been suggesting a trip to New York to visit some historical places like Washington Irving's Sunnyside homestead and President Roosevelt's estate, and of course, we would stop in to visit my parents for a short period.[275]

For so many years and so many past problems, I was apprehensive to travel there, however, as soon as I had agreed, a mysterious event occurred around that same hour. The basement walls of my parent's house had caved in, jeopardizing the foundational structure of their home. Fortunately, no one was hurt and it was able to be fixed better than before, but I did receive a phone call from mom asking for prayer.

Do you think a physical sign such as that was a mere coincidence? Could it have symbolized a breakthrough in the spirit?

All I can say is that God's words of wisdom worked better than I could have ever imagined. The moment I stepped through the door of my parent's house, I was set free from that offense. My only regret is that it took me so long to take that step.

Do you know that God has a breakthrough for you? You may never openly do evil to another, but maybe you, like me, hold on to a grudge. Perhaps you were truly wronged and are looking for your situation to be made right. Perhaps you are relying on someone or something to make that change. Remorsefully I say, these thoughts are wicked.

The lesson that I learned is that God desires for us to come up higher. If we allow God, He will use every situation, every God-awful thing you wish never happened, and even the bad things that you actually did of your own accord, to work for His good purposes.[276]

I can't explain how He does it except to say that it was God who used that attack dog to reveal my need for deliverance. He wanted me to know and deeply experience that He did not reject me. He loves me and you. He loves my mom and my dad, and all my family, and He loves everyone, for He has a divine purpose, a beautiful identity for each one of us.

The Stolen Purse Dream

This last dream and its many variations is a very popular one with many people, yet most don't understand what it means. In fact, I have consistently received comments and questions on my blog from all over the world.

To aid in your understanding, I have summarized this complex dream. So take a look and see if you can discover its meaning.

Traveling down the mountain along a treacherous path, I am on my way to Las Vegas. Although I arrived safely, I found myself among some thieves who mysteriously stole my purse and all its content. I was so upset. I felt so helpless, too, for I didn't know where to begin to find my stolen goods. Ugh!

Next thing I know, I meet a gal named 'Singular Ruth'. What a very lonely and frightened girl she is, but we quickly become friends. Surprisingly, she takes me right to the place where I am able to repossess everything that was stolen.

Once again, I see those thieves and I hear them say, "Oh, we thought you were worth more than that! You only had $6."

Thank God for Singular Ruth, for she assisted me to recover all my stolen goods! Suddenly, I see that there is not just one Singular Ruth – but many Singular Ruths."

I woke up.

When I had this dream, I knew it was from God. Yet, I had no clue as to its meaning for the longest time. However, I did exactly as I have told you in this book. I journaled and prayed to God for the interpretation.

Today you have the benefit of me having lived through this dream. Read through the Get GUI summary and see if this interpretation makes sense. This complex dream was about my stolen identity, which I believe happened when I was a little girl. It provided directions, encouragement and revealed elements of my true self. Although it took two years to figure it out, the interpretation clearly stares me in the face today.

As I've described so many times throughout my dream journey, I thought my identity was based on what I did. I considered myself valuable because of my accomplishments and the approval of others, however, I only need to care about what He thought of me.

He calls me His precious daughter with a beautiful identity in Him for His good pleasure. This revelation continues to be huge for me and I am so thankful He is teaching me this lesson.

Because people are so unique, I have seen many deviations of this dream type because our identity could be based on various things like how much money we have, where we live, our careers and talents, and so on. If you believe your identity has been stolen, you will have to ask God.

Nevertheless, this I know for sure: You don't have to work to figure this out. You can rest in this God who calls you His child, the One who saves and heals through His grace. Isn't that great news?

Now look at the last part of this dream for it's the best. Here, I saw that there were many Singular Ruths. This symbol represents a woman who is both compassionate and courageous. She is not single, nor a lone survivor of any disaster, but a singular, a one-of-a-kind woman who obeys God and tenaciously works through every one of her problems with faith in God. This woman will birth God's blessings into existence, not just for herself, but for others.

Are you one of those Singular Ruths? You have more worth than you can ever know simply because you are His and He is yours.

Now let's look at prophetic signs and other loose ends to ride some more waves, for God always has more.

Get GUI Summary

Step 1: Dream Considerations

- **Dream type:** complex, symbolic, visual, supernatural, and prophetic
- **Purpose:** reveal my heart and soul, provide encouragement and directions
- **Source:** God

Step 2: Dream Symbols

- **Las Vegas** ~ sinful place
- **Treacherous Path** ~ journey of betrayal
- **thieves** ~ enemy stealing
- **purse** ~ my identity, who I am
- **$6** ~ my value to man
- **Singular Ruth** ~ a representation of lonely, fearful me, who braves it out to recover my stolen identity
- **Singular Ruths** ~ other women like me who are courageous and compassionate, who desire to birth the blessings of God.

Step 3: Dream Message

You are a singular woman of compassion and faith, similar to biblical Ruth, who has worth in Christ.

Step 4: Dream Test & Go

I opened my heart to God, and continued on my healing journey dancing with Jesus.

Review

1. What unique messages and lessons have you discovered in your dreams?
2. Explain the cost of God's grace for our lives. Why is it the best deal ever?
3. Have your dreams ever revealed offenses or hurts? Did you want justice? What does the Lord want you to do about it?
4. Have you had encountered a stolen purse or stolen wallet dream?

Or another type of identity dream? What did it reveal about you?

5. Share some of your personal spiritual breakthroughs. Did you encounter a physical breakthrough as well?

16

Prophetic Loose Ends

"Never be afraid to trust an unknown future to a known God."
-Corrie ten Boom

Beautiful dreamers, I want to affirm you. You *can* be prophetic in the biblical sense, for all that means is "God speaking to you." If you are one of God's sheep, *you can hear from Him.*[277] The enemy would delight in deceiving you to believe otherwise, but God wants to personally speak to you for the purposes of encouraging and strengthening you.[278]

God will employ any number of methods including prophetic symbols and prophetic words and prophetic dreams accompanied by glorious wonders that will draw you closer to Him, for He always desires to do a new thing. In this chapter, I will describe some more information about seeing and hearing through prophetic symbols, signs and dreams.

Prophetic Symbols

Did you know that God can use dream symbols to speak in your everyday life? I absolutely love hearing God speak in this way because it feels like I am experiencing His words in a more powerful way. Let me give a few examples.

While driving on the interstate one day at rush hour, my husband and I saw a triple rainbow. Normally, we would have smiled at a single rainbow, but a triple one caused some big rejoicing. While this appearance seemed insignificant to the other cars whizzing past us, we knew it was a God-moment confirming His promises during a difficult time.[279]

Another time my young girl came running into the house with her friend screaming about a snake in our driveway. Oh Lord, I don't like snakes. I've even experienced tormenting dreams with snakes, however, as I ventured out to view the situation, I discovered this snake was a dead one.

Apparently, I had accidentally driven over it with my car. I think it died shrieking in pain as it tried to escape my house. When I inquired of the Lord, I felt Him say, "The enemy is so terrified of you that He has to flee."

Well then…he should be scared.[280]

When I first started teaching dream workshops, I noticed that others seem to hear God speak using this method, too. One lady told me she accidentally broke a bowl in her kitchen sink. A few hours later, her husband broke a similar bowl in that same sink.

"Barb," she candidly remarked, "normally, we would have ignored the incident, calling it bad luck, but because you told us to ask the Lord, we did. We felt Him declare, 'I am breaking you out of your comfort zone.'"

Since then, I've heard all kinds of stories. Another lady told me that while she was walking around her neighborhood, she kept finding loose change on the street. It appeared that much of her neighborhood was under construction, it also seemed to be a very special moment with the Lord.

First she saw a penny, and another, and another, and then a dime. After prayer, she felt that the Lord was speaking to her about some upcoming changes, that God was starting some reconstruction on her spiritual house. Over time that word materialized into a great work of God in her life.

Who would ever imagine seeing a red bird could have significance? Yet, my blog post entitled, "The Sign of the Red Cardinal" is one of my most popular.[281] One of my girlfriends shared about always encountering a red cardinal while walking in the woods, and she allowed me to write her story. At the time, she was heartbroken along with her kids because their young golden retriever was unexpectedly diagnosed with cancer, however, all of them chose to believe God for a miracle.

Every time she'd take her stroll, she would stumble upon a scarlet-feathered friend and feel the presence of Lord, it was like He was saying, "I am here for you. Trust me."

As it turned out, God did heal their beloved pet. Now if God would use an encouraging bird symbol and heal their dog, think what He would do for you.

For certain, God loves to use physical symbols and signs to confirm His word. Actually, this phenomena occurs throughout the Bible and here are a few great examples.

When Jesus died on the cross, there was darkness over the whole land for three hours.[282] The veil of the temple was torn in two from top to bottom and the earth quaked.[283] After His resurrection, graves were opened and many bodies of saints who had fallen asleep were raised.[284] Truly, these signs of darkness, of the veil tearing, of holy people waking from the dead were God speaking, but many missed them.

Will you see the signs when they appear?

Prophetic Signs

God loves to use prophetic signs to wake us up.[285] He can even use angels.

I had been on a business trip and was reading a book about angelic beings; it taught me that they are ministering spirits created by God to answer our beckoning calls.[286] That one day I needed directions to where I was going, and I decided to ask for God's help using an angel.

As I was standing in line waiting, this Irish-looking, young man dressed in a blue suit with a Beatle haircut from the 60s caught my attention. He strutted right in front of me to the counter, turned the pages of this book, and then walked away. I wondered what he was doing, but when my turn came I discovered that book. It was open to the exact page that contained the information that I needed.

I thought, *that's strange.*

A night later, I had this dream where that same gentleman appeared to me with great excitement. He waved hello and confirmed my suspicions, "Hi there. I am your angel here to assist you."

Nice. I fell back to sleep with a smile knowing that He sees me.

Beloved child of God, I pray that you will begin to believe that God really wants to help you with your life. In fact, sometimes God will even give you a little peek at the future. Like your dreams, this glimpse could be either good or bad. It's just a sign of what *could* happen.

Given my role as an intercessor, I am often forewarned by the Lord of various prayer needs, and it often happens in the middle of the night. Happily it doesn't bother me as I am such a good sleeper. I rise from my bed, pray, write down what the Lord said, and fall right back to sleep.

When I was very young in the Lord, I remember the first time I experienced a prayer alert in my dreams. I saw that my grandfather unexpectedly died. Very upset by this news, I prayed continuously asking God to save his life. Several weeks later, I received this very interesting phone call.

"Hi there, Barb. It's your Grandpop. I was just thinking about you and wanted to tell you how much I love you. Did you know that I was in a car accident about six weeks ago? I was seeing double, but I am fine now."

Even back then, God was teaching me so much. My grandfather never called me in his entire life except for that one time. I expect God moved on his heart to let me know my prayers were working.

Another time I heard my friend Shawne calling me in the middle of the night.

"Help me, Barbara. Help me," she desperately cried. I knew Shawne had serious health problems, so when I heard her voice I knew God was ringing the prayer bell. And so, I rose up and prayed for her until I felt a release even though I didn't know what was going on. When I saw her later that week, I asked her if anything unusual had happened earlier that week.

"Honestly," she replied, "I was having a terrible attack and almost called 911, but suddenly the pain subsided."

Truly, the Lord is so good to alert us to pray so that situations can be averted or at least lessened through the power of prayer.

And of course, future signs can be given through a prophetic dream. I've already mentioned several examples where God gave prophetic dreams to people like Joseph, Pharaoh, and Nebuchadnezzar, and even me, but do you think that this could actually happen to you?

I guess you know my answer.

The truth is that I have heard of others who have had prophetic dreams, too. I want you to know that there is a God in heaven who *sees you*. As you read through my next two dream stories, I pray God activates your faith to reveal His hope and future for your life.

An Old House Remade

Dreams like the one I am about to share are the best. You wake up in wonderment reflecting on all the riches that have just captivated your attention. Even the date when this dream occurred, 1/12/08, was significant.[287]

I didn't need to attend a conference or receive a word from a prophet of God, and neither do you. God will give you your own glorious prophetic word through a personal dream. At first, I didn't understand everything He was saying to me, but as I practiced interpreting dreams, I obviously improved. I wonder if you'll get the understanding before reading my Get GUI summary.

I dreamt that my husband and I had moved back to our old home located at 111 Coatbridge Circle. A French couple lived there now with their two children.

They had renovated my home with a cool new contemporary look using stunning colors. Included in their décor were all these scenic pictures, lovely vases, and all kinds of neat knick-knacks and interesting collectibles.

I always loved that house when I lived there, and was so glad that they loved it, too. This house was, obviously, lovingly cared for. While it always had a charm to it, it was even more so. Now it had a view of the ocean and you could walk right up to the water.

In the backyard there was a beautiful fountain and swimming area.

Amazed at the old master bathroom, I noticed its high ceilings with new window treatments that perfectly covered the old style. The long curtains were made of the prettiest material embossed with a reddish-orange and yellow-gold pattern. It was heavy, durable and exquisite. Ironically, you could still see the decorations that I had previously done, yet it was somehow covered up.

When I looked out the bathroom window, I saw many more houses - not just the ones across the street. Everything was so much more built up. I absolutely loved all the updates that this French couple had made to my old house! I also wondered how they did this. It seems that they had a live-in houseguest.

Out of the blue, I discovered a sliding door on the second floor to the attic. I slipped open the white and purple polka-dotted door and found the most amazing thing. This houseguest was a kind, older gentlemen, who served as both a worker and an artist.

I couldn't figure out how he could live in the attic when there was no space there, but somehow he painstakingly finished this entire attic, and it was fantastic. There was a well-designed table and chairs for the kitchen, as well as other belongings that he needed to live. I thought how wonderfully delightful.

This gentleman even built the wooden flooring in the attic that gently sloped upwards towards the roof. If you wanted, you could go to the inside of the top of the house and look out the window. From there, you could see the ocean, the swimming area and the fountain in the backyard. In the front, you could see all the houses.

This house became such a cool house! I loved it when I was young, and I still love it, however, it is so much more than when we first lived there.

I woke up.

Just take a look at all those fantastic dream symbols. The imagery in a dream like this is priceless. God said so much more with a picture than I would have understood with words. It was an outstanding experience and He gave it directly to me. Even today, this prophetic dream continues to encourage me.

But what do you do with a prophetic dream like this one? Always remember that it is God who is doing this work. He will perform His word. You don't have to work at it. You only need to be willing to cooperate with Him and rest in faithfully knowing that He's got you.

Do you know that God loves to remake old houses? He is a master artist and decorator for your life. Your house won't look like mine, but I do believe it will be great. He will make it perfectly fit your personality and calling.

Make sure you record your dream when it happens, for you don't want to miss your moment of visitation. For you definitely will want to gaze upon your God dream because He is always making beautiful new things.

Get GUI Summary

Step 1: Dream Considerations

- **Dream type:** complex, symbolic, visual, supernatural, and prophetic
- **Purpose:** reveal my heart and soul, provide encouragement and directions
- **Source:** God

Step 2: Dream Symbols

- **The French couple, new owners** ~ me and my Lord, my new beginnings
- **Old home** ~ my old life
- **Décor** ~ loving things in my life
- **View of ocean** ~ I see the sea of humanity, including my own human condition.
- **Backyard** ~ my past made beautiful
- **Fountain** ~ God's Spirit & Word
- **Swimming Area** ~ place to allow God's Spirit to transform my past
- **Master bathroom** ~ place of cleansing
- **High ceilings** ~ deep and high
- **Window treatments** ~ seeing with His eyes
- **Reddish-orange** ~ fiery love
- **Yellow-gold** ~ glorious marriage with God
- **House-guest** ~ my heavenly Father, God's Holy Spirit dwelling with me
- **Artist-worker** ~ God creatively working
- **Sliding door** ~ gateway
- **Second floor** ~ intimacy
- **White purple polka dots** ~ pure, royal, fun
- **Attic** ~ renewing my mind
- **Kitchen table and chairs** ~ communion and rest preparing to do Father's will
- **Wooden flooring** ~ grounded on the cross
- **Roof** ~ covering, anointing for your life
- **Renovated house** ~ my old life remade new
- **Front** ~ future

Step 3: Dream Message

- God is doing a great remodeling of my life
- My past is being beautifully transformed.
- The Holy Spirit dwells in me. He is renewing my mind through intimacy with Him.
- Commune and rest, and cooperate with God to allow Him to do His creative work.
- As I come up higher with God, my anointing will allow me to see so much more than before.
- I have a blessed life and great future in God.

> **Step 4: Dream Test & Go**
> This personal word was from God for me.
> Contiue walking with Him.

Surgery and a Pool

While most of my dreams are symbolic, every so often I have a literal dream. I had this amazingly prophetic dream in the middle of the night while I was fasting and praying. It was an open vision. That's when your eyes are open, and you see both the physical realm and the spiritual realm.

As you read through the dream, there isn't much of an interpretation because the dream is literal; however, there is a great story that surrounds this prophetic word for my life.

Scene 1:

I am in the hospital having surgery. The doctors are poking me with lots of needles, and it hurts. (I sense this surgery was related to having children, but I was afraid to ask the Lord.)

Scene 2:

I look out my kitchen window and am stunned at the beautiful in-ground pool in my backyard. Ever since I was a little girl, this was one of my heart's dreams.

I am already awake.

If I am totally truthful with you, I didn't know what to think about this dream except to say that I liked the idea of having a pool in my backyard. This dream was rather scary to me.

Somehow in my heart, I knew the surgery was related to having children, but at the time I was so afraid of becoming a mother, that I wouldn't even ask the Lord. However, God knew the deep desires of my heart. I knew that I wanted a pool, but He also knew that I wanted a child.

So when you have a prophetic dream such as this one and don't know what to do, tuck it away in your heart and wait for God. He will reveal its meaning at the proper time.

The reality of this dream only came to light later. For years, I always thought that I would get pregnant, but that's not how it worked for me. Finally, in my mid-thirties I thought I'd go to the doctor just to ask what's going on. Before you knew it, I was having all kinds of tests and discovered that I had a severe infertility problem. Then, came the surgeries and more tests ending with infertility treatments at the Duke Clinic.

I went through four IUI procedures, three IVF procedures and one miscarriage before I got pregnant with my daughter.[288] It was a very uncomfortable time.

If it wasn't for this dream, and a word from the Lord about having a baby, I don't think I would have endured all these treatments, but this dream came true exactly as I saw it, including the many needles.

In a way, God used the infertility treatments to change my fear of motherhood to faith to become a mother. I'd love to tell you how I was this great woman of faith throughout this entire ordeal, but that was certainly not the case. I cried every day, and begged God to give me a child.

Get GUI Summary

Step 1: Dream Considerations
- **Dream type:** simple, literal, visual and actual, supernatural, and prophetic
- **Purpose:** reveal my heart and soul, provide encouragement and directions
- **Source:** God

Step 2: Dream Symbols
Literal dreams do not have symbols.

Step 3: Dream Message
There is a surgery in your future with lots of needles. An in-ground pool is also there waiting for you.

Step 4: Dream Test & Go
Tuck this message in your heart and wait on God to see what this is all about.

I also experienced a magnification of the enemy's lies. Of course, I was devastated when I had a miscarriage, but I thought we could try again.

Sadly, after so many unsuccessful tries, the clinic thought that I was wasting their time and my money. They said they were only trying to be a reputable facility by telling me the truth.

"Mrs. Koob," they sternly stated their professional medical opinion, "you are not going to have a baby. You need to come up with another alternative."

With tears flooding my watery eyes, I stood my ground, "But the Lord has told me that I would have a child." He hadn't told me in this dream, but I remember the day. It was the day after Hurricane Fran tore through our area, September 7, 1996. The Lord had also divulged to my husband that we would have a child many years prior.

They thought I was delusional, one of these crazy Christians.

So they continued with their best medical naysaying voice, "Mrs. Koob, we are so sorry that you will never have a child. It is impossible."

I definitely didn't feel like a person of faith, but wasn't willing to heed their advice and would not leave their office until they agreed to allow me one more IVF procedure. Their only stipulation was that this would be my last IVF procedure.

Miraculously, I obtained a positive pregnancy test!

You would think they would have been happy for me, but they wanted to be right with their medical opinion. The head nurse actually left a negative message on my answering machine with a positive report.

"Barbara," she informed me, "you probably already know you are pregnant, but don't tell anyone because we don't believe it will stick."

Well, they were wrong. I had a very normal pregnancy with no complications, and it resulted in the birth of a beautiful baby daughter. I even took her back to the clinic to show her off to everyone, but only one nurse came out to congratulate me.

I am telling you to say this. The enemy doesn't like when we win a victory for the Lord. Even when we get a positive report, he will attempt to put a negative spin on it. Even when you have your triumph, he will snub you. Don't let what the enemy says affect you. God wants you to be more than a conqueror in your life.[289] While you shouldn't fight a war unless God leads you into that battle, be relentless in your battles. Don't ever give up unless God says to let it go.

No matter what is going on in your life, no matter what trial or adversity, God can make your dream, the one God placed in your heart, come to pass, for nothing is impossible for Him.[290] He is good; He delights in giving you the desire of your heart, even when you don't know that's your desire.[291]

And you know what else? Not only did I get the baby, but He gave me the pool, too. Yeah God!

Your Dream Story

Do you know that God desires to give you a dream story?

All of my dream stories represent only a handful of what God has done in my life, but I hope you can see repetitive information that revealed my heart and soul and common themes. I believe that because I took the time to journal and seek God, He answered my heart's cries. I also believe that God loves to use biblical dream interpretation to point people to Himself... so that we can tell our story through His story. Don't you think everyone should have at least one really good story to tell? Don't let the enemy talk you out of it.

Let's pray that we open our eyes, ears and hearts to see and hear God's messages to us.

Dear God,

Please help me to see all Your signs and wonders. I ask you to give me prophetic dreams about my future that would bring encouragement to my heart and strength to my soul so that I can hope again. I ask for my personal dream story so that I can dream with purpose. You did it for Joseph, and you did it for others, and I believe You will do this for me. I want to tell my story through His story for Your glory. Thanks, God. I praise You. Amen.

Review

1. Has God ever used physical symbols to speak to you? If yes, please describe.
2. Have you ever seen an angel? Describe the experience.
3. Has God ever given you a prayer alert in a dream? Describe what happened.
4. What prophetic dreams concerning your future has God give you?
5. Do you have a dream story yet? How can you tell His story with your story?

17

Your Dream Discoveries

Now there was a young Hebrew man with us there, a servant of the
captain of the guard. And we told him, and he interpreted our dreams for us;
to each man he interpreted according to his own dream.
– Genesis 41:12

Dream Breakthroughs

Thank God that I am no longer lost in my dreams. As you read through my stories, I hope you truly saw how it was God who gave me breakthrough after breakthrough. Instead of discarding those dream messages, He opened my spiritual eyes. Rather than wondering what in heaven's name was happening, God showered His understanding such that I was able to successfully walk out my dream journey, and He will do the same for you.

What dream discoveries have you and God made thus far?

At this point I hope you feel confident enough to say that you have conquered the basics. You should unequivocally know that God does, indeed, speak in dreams. You should be able to recognize and distinguish the different types of dream revelations and how to obtain God's understanding for yourself. You ought to have a general sense of biblical symbolism, and how to correctly apply your dreams. I am guessing that God might have walked a few of you through a little healing, too.

Yet, there's always more with God. It might have started with a dream, but God always desires to give breakthroughs such that your life will give Him glory. He wants to raise up dream interpreters to help others with their life's journey, so they can give Him glory, too. Yes, God desires modern day master dreamers like Daniel and Joseph to come forth for people are hungry and searching.

In this new age, the world abounds with false revelatory gifts to fill this black hole just like in the days of Daniel and Joseph. So many people live in darkness today; they do not know that God exists, let alone that He is a good and loving heavenly Father who desires to shed His light on their situation. People's lives can be changed if God's light is allowed to reveal truth, to encourage, to comfort and to direct them for His good purposes.

However, someone must stand up strong in the knowledge of who God is so that others may find Him. Interpreting a dream should never be the goal. We must learn how to understand and apply God's wisdom, not just for ourselves, but for others…so that His hope can break forth and redeem.

Could you be that someone?

A Message of Hope

Joseph thought that he was someone. He even had two amazing dreams that revealed of his future greatness.[292]

Can you imagine Joseph's **great** anguish when things did not go the way he planned? In one day, he was demoted from being the favorite son and heir to the family fortune to a forgotten slave in a foreign country.[293] **Then**, while faithfully serving his master Potiphar, he was thrown into prison for a crime he didn't commit.[294]

I wonder how many times Joseph retraced his steps and thought *how in the world did I end up here?* Nevertheless, there was nothing he could do about it except cry out to God. This life experience is what God calls our refining process, and I have to say, it's not my favorite pastime.

However, if we choose to cooperate with God, it can be an amazing time of spiritual growth. As a matter of fact, the Bible says that if you want to be great, you should be a servant first.[295] It also says if you want to be first, then you need to be a slave.[296]

A slave? Really? I would have thought that, at least a little self-promotion might be in order. Not true, for God is the one who will promote you and me.

No matter what our challenges, you and I need to follow Joseph's example once he arrived in Egypt. He pressed on with God and God showered His amazing favor over everything Joseph did in spite of his bleak circumstances.[297] He allowed God to mold him into a humble man of strong integrity, and God matured him through this purifying process in preparation for his destiny. And if we let Him, God will grow us in wisdom and stature, too.[298]

It was during those difficult days that Joseph learned many things including the gift of biblical dream interpretation. Actually, slavery in prison was Joseph's divine appointment. For it was there, while serving time, that Joseph met Pharaoh's cupbearer and Pharaoh's baker. Although Joseph didn't realize it, interpreting their dreams was a God connection for his future.

The cupbearer dreamt of a vine with three branches blossoming into clusters of grapes, followed by seeing Pharaoh's cup in his hand.[299] The baker dreamt of three baskets sitting on his head with all kinds of baked goods for Pharaoh, but his dream concluded with birds coming to eat out of the basket.[300]

Because Joseph knew that interpretations belong to God and Him alone, he was able to reveal what each dream meant, and they came true exactly as predicted.[301] Within three days the cupbearer was restored to his position, and alas, the baker was beheaded, impaled, and the birds ate his flesh.

What a great word of encouragement for the cupbearer to receive. When Joseph gave this word to him, He pleaded, "Please remember me to Pharaoh for I have done nothing wrong to be thrown into prison."[302]

Still, such a tormenting one for the baker. I don't know how you feel, but whenever I read about the baker's terrible ending, I am very sad. Of course, the Bible doesn't tell us what this poor soul did and why he wasn't forgiven, but why would Joseph deliver such a message of despair? Shouldn't biblical dream interpretation always confer hope?

Absolutely yes!

For example, couldn't there have been something that the baker could have done in three days such that his life might have been saved? Maybe he could have pleaded for mercy and made good on his mistake? Or he could have called out to God Almighty to deliver him?

But Joseph hadn't been rescued yet, nor had he received God's revelation of hope for his life. He was powerless to save the baker's life, as he was not the Pharaoh, supreme ruler of Egypt. However, I suspect that if he had the opportunity to speak to that baker today, I bet he'd be telling him about Jesus, King of all Kings, and his life-giving power.[303] For Joseph's entire story is one of God's salvation and hope.

Not only did God rescue Joseph and redeem him (albeit it wasn't in Joseph's timeframe), God also used Joseph to save many others, including his own brothers that betrayed him. In fact, the paradox is that God used the very sin of his brothers to save them all from an impending famine. For sending Joseph to Egypt, ahead of his family, was actually all part of God's amazing plan to save them.

Then, at just the perfect time, God supplied Pharaoh with two double dreams that no one could interpret.[304] And interestingly, that cupbearer who had forgotten Joseph conveniently remembered him and his ability to interpret dreams.[305]

And so, when Joseph stood before Pharaoh to interpret those dreams, something in him was different. His interpretation and application process had been matured such that it provided God's wisdom; it provided hope.[306]

Not only did Joseph interpret Pharaoh's double dreams, but Joseph also provided a way of escape. Those dreams foretold of seven years of abundance followed by seven years of famine, but Joseph also spoke to Pharaoh about finding a discerning and wise man to store one-fifth of all the grain from the plentiful years in preparation for the lean years.[307]

Suddenly, Joseph was ready for promotion. Pharaoh had seen the Spirit of God within him and raised him up to be second-in-command.[308] Do you know that you can have God's Spirit within you, too?

As believers in God's forgiveness through Christ's shed blood on the cross, we have the power to change any situation through prayer.[309] We can bring God's kingdom which is already being done in heaven down to earth so that others can be saved.[310] We can be like this transformed Joseph bringing a message of hope wherever we go.

For indeed, hope must be one of the keys when interpreting someone else's dream.

Interpreting Another's Dreams

At first, I was afraid to interpret another's dream. What if I was wrong in my interpretation? What if they based their life on what I said? Fortunately, their decisions are not up to me but I have learned more than I bargained for when I stepped out. God even protected me as He taught me to discern the motives of an individual first.

Some people ask me only because they want to test me. They really don't care to know; they just want to see how I will react. Some have hard hearts, and while they may say that they are seeking God's will, they are not. I no longer waste my time on such people and their endeavors to trip me up. If they want to know, they can go to God for themselves just like me.

Still others want to understand, but are not able to see clearly as their spiritual eyes are blinded because of wounds, offenses and other sins. If someone sincerely asked me and I am released by the Lord to assist, I will walk alongside them and pray for a breakthrough.

One time my missionary friend asked me regarding a dream concerning one of her supporters. This lady dreamt that she had pieces of broken glass in her mouth. I had no idea what this meant, but agreed to pray. The next day I found myself cut and bleeding because of broken glass that I was sweeping up at an apartment rental.

All of a sudden I knew. The broken glass represented the women's transparent words. She spoke things as she saw them, even if her words were sharp, hurting herself and others. When I shared this insight to my friend, she grievously gasped, "Ah yes, this does make sense coming from this individual."

That was a simple dream, however, often God gives complex dreams which reveal our true self, but we have to know how to process them. And of course, we have to want to know and be willing to seek truth.

Every October one of my good friends hosts a harvest party. One year there was this woman, a professional photographer, who had heard about my dream interpretation skills, and she was looking to speak with me.

"I am sorry." I responded, "I do not interpret people's dreams as I cannot be someone's Lord and hear His voice for them."

In the sweetest demeanor she replied, "I know that, but could we just talk about one of my dreams?"

For this reason, I agreed to walk with her through a very complex God dream. Looking back, I quickly noticed many self-revealing clues, but I never could have uncovered those symbols without her, as they were uniquely personal. This dream was confirming her value, both as an individual and as a business owner, so that she would be confident in her calling as a bona-fide professional worthy of the prices she charged. At the end of our little chat, we both were amazed at what God did, for He had clearly laid out His understanding and next steps for her.

Another time I met a young woman while ministering one weekend at a Loved Retreat, and we quickly became friends, for we had much in common.[311] Our husbands both spoke German, her mom's name was Barbara, and we were both God lovers and God dreamers.

One day she sent me a Facebook message regarding a complex dream. As usual, I prayed and then we spoke about what it could mean, as I never know until God shows me. While her dream divulged problems in her present life, some of the bitterroots that we discussed in the healing section of this book were also exposed.

Remember though, God never sheds His light to condemn us. Growing up in several foster homes, this gal had been severely neglected as a kid, and became incapable of receiving correction from anyone, including those trying to help her.[312] The reason wasn't because she didn't want to change; it was because she lived through much trauma and very little authentic love.[313]

And so, with tender care, I validated her beautiful identity in Christ for I knew that God desired to heal her, to strengthen her in her innermost being with His unconditional love. Then, I approached the subject of her dream offering some possible interpretations regarding the negative clues that I saw. I was astonished as she was able to listen and process this information without feeling condemned. Offering the truth in love rather than pushing your interpretation is always more effective.

At the end of our discussion, she exclaimed, "That was the first time I was ever able to receive constructive criticism."

Dear readers, always remember that God does not disapprove of us. Rather He desires to help us in our time of need. Use the same principles I outlined in the application process—pray first, walk in love, and wait on God for His instructions. But when we do interpret another's dreams, it must always be with the intent to shed hope and bring breakthrough.

Now here is one of my favorite experiences as a dream interpreter that was totally God. I didn't stand before a King like Joseph, but the true King Jesus definitely healed and delivered, and I didn't' have to work at it. I've affectionately named this story *The Scarlet Letter 'R'*

The Scarlet Letter 'R'

While speaking at a women's conference regarding our identity in Christ a few years ago, I mentioned my website and blog posts about biblical dream interpretation. Well, several people seemed captivated. One sweet lady was so interested that she searched through my entire entourage of dream posts and felt led to write me about a dream that she had.

When I read her extremely complex dream, I immediate thought *"Oh no. I can't do this."* Seeing many symbolic clues, I had an inkling of what might be going on, but couldn't be sure. And so, I prayed and asked God for wisdom. Then, after a few days, we talked on the phone.

We walked through each dream scene, and I pointed out that her dream was not about ministering to someone else; it was probably about her. I can't tell you how many times I see this mistake, and still, I myself can fall into this trap if I am not careful.

Anyway, as I spoke with this lovely lady, I could tell a tear or two was welling up over the phone. I learned that she had been adopted at birth, but had a wonderful mother. I didn't want to upset her but I shared what I thought her dream could mean.

I reiterated my convictions, "Dear one, you don't have to believe me. This dream is between you and God. Just ask Jesus. He will show you what you need to know."

We prayed together and hung up.

Here's the note I received from her about an hour later:

Barbara - Wow. I have been on a quick journey of healing since you called. As you were speaking into my dream, I felt the Holy Spirit tugging on me in certain areas. When I hung up, I became very teary. I prayed and felt the Lord was revealing some things. I called my hubby and shared, and the Lord brought a deliverance and new peace. The Lord used you mightily this morning.

It is amazing how the Lord works. Even while I was typing out my dream to you, I thought, "Why am I doing this?" But I felt led to send it to you.

It seems that there was this anger. The Lord revealed rage, and it would well up inside me at times. It wasn't often, but it was there. This rage seems connected to the adoption and rejection as well as other rejection that had happened in my life.

After talking with my husband, the Lord gave me a vision where I saw myself with an "R" on me, like the Scarlet Letter. Then I saw the "R" disappear for I belong to Him. The peace of God just came. The Lord said that deliverance has come to this house today. Praise God! I know that God has brought much healing to me in this area before now, but obviously there was an even deeper work that needed to be done.

I know that there may be more that the Lord desires to show me, but I wanted you to know and to thank you for sharing with me. God bless you!

In His Great Love,

C.A.

Beautiful dreamers, it was God who healed that day—not me. I am as amazed as you for He did what He does best—save, heal and deliver.[314] This story exemplifies God's ultimate purpose for dreams—to point us to God and help us to cooperate with what He wants to do in our lives. For God, our great Redeemer always desires to receive, renew, and restore us.

This testimony is just one fantastic dream story, but I believe that God is going to give many more stories that tell of His love. You won't have to read my stories or someone else's stories. You can have your own dream stories, and that would be so much better.

Want to know how?

There's an enchanting place where you can go and I take pleasure in sharing about it.

Review

1. Have you conquered the basics of biblical dream interpretation? If not, what areas of your expertise still require clarification or most practice?

2. Why did Joseph have to endure such hardships as being sold into slavery and thrown into prison? Was this necessary for his promotion? How has God used adversities in your life?

3. Explain how hope is key to God's use of biblical dream interpretation.

4. Do you feel you can interpret another's dream? When should you and how?

5. Describe God's ultimate purpose for biblical dream interpretation for you and for others.

18

The Greatest Discovery

May He grant you according to your heart's desire,
And fulfill all your purpose.
–Psalm 20:4

Dream University

For sure, God has a really special place where you can learn what His plan is for your life. I call it Dream University, and it's where you can make your greatest discovery as you learn to grow in your faith.

Dream University is not a physical location. Rather, it is a habitation in your heart, where God's Spirit can dwell inside you and do things that you cannot do on your own. It is a spiritual school with God where you can intimately know who He is and who you were created to be.

Here, in Dream University, people experience God and learn how His truth can set them free. Of course, they learn about biblical dream interpretation, but they also learn about the wonderful destiny God has planned for their life's dream. The teacher is God's Holy Spirit and the enrollment is absolutely free.[315]

Sound like a hoax? I agree it sounds too good to be true.

One day when I was sixteen years old, I stood by the kitchen sink peeling potatoes with my mother as we were making dinner. She announced to me, "Someday you will know Jesus. He is the most important person in the whole world."

I thought she was out of her mind.

She continued, "You don't believe me, do you?"

"Honestly, no. I don't."

At that time in my life I had my own plans. I was certainly not going to give my life over to this Jesus so that He could destroy all the grandiose plans I had for my future. But as life moved ahead, I quickly discovered that even my best laid plans had problems. What I thought was going to work didn't. The things that did happen according to my plans never gave me the happiness and satisfaction I sought.

Have you reached this point yet?

Here's the bottom line. God wants to walk and talk with you forever, even help you with all your discoveries regarding your life's plan, but He can't until you open the door to your heart, for God can't mix with sin.

Sadly, we human beings, the imperfect ones, cannot touch a perfect God. Or, to put it another way, we are sinners.[316] No matter how hard we try, we can never be like God, never reach perfection. Unless there's a miracle, we can't be with God.[317]

Even if we make improvements or mend one area of our lives, often another thing will go amiss. Just look at the earth today, and see how we are utterly incapable of solving its problems—wars, sickness, suffering, and so on.

On the other hand, God, who is a perfect being, can't mix with our mess. So how can the two of us meet?

It is simply impossible for us to defeat our shortcomings in our own strength. That's why we need a Savior to wash us clean of all sin so that we can commune with God. It's why God sent His Son, Jesus Christ, the Perfect One to come into this world to show His love.[318] Because of God's great mercy, Jesus suffered and died on the cross shedding His blood for your sins and mine.[319] Then, on the third day, He rose from the dead making a way for us to access God.[320] Without Jesus, there is no way to get to God.

Are you still having trouble with this concept? Perhaps you are thinking that you live a fairly righteous life, so what's the big deal? After all, would a kind and loving God pass judgment on someone who was trying to be good? Please allow me to share some more.

If someone committed a crime against you, wouldn't you want justice?

Perfect justice demands that a suitable payment is made for the crime. By letting a criminal walk free without consequences, the judge is ignoring the crime, and he wouldn't be a perfect judge. And if you were the one who was lied to, mistreated, beaten, robbed, raped, or some other crime, would it be fair that your assailant walked? Even if the criminal act was small, should it not be made right?

Of course it should. But where does the plumb line fall?

Our judicial systems attempt to bring justice but often with flaws. Who then should decide the case? You? Me? Someone bigger? I believe the definitive answer points to God.

God is not just perfect love; He is a perfect judge.[321] Someone must pay for the crime of sin or we will receive just punishment—hell after death. That's where the miracle of Jesus comes in. His sacrifice on the cross totally pays for all sin. Jesus is our ransom from hell and the grave regardless of whatever sins we have committed. If you accept Him into your life, believe that He died for your sins and rose again, and confess your belief to another, you are saved.[322] It's that easy, but you have to do it.

In some ways, it's like paying a bill collector. Even if you have the money to pay, it doesn't count until you actually pay your bill. Nevertheless, we are incapable of paying our bill of sin. It is like saying we are perfect, and we've already established the fact that you and I can never be that.

Even though Jesus completely paid your bill of sin, you must authorize the payment. If you don't, the bill is left unpaid and with consequences.[323] However, when you make that authorization, it's done once and forever. You have crossed over from the death of sin to the life of God's love.

This step is the first one to starting a new life in Christ Jesus. Officially, He now calls you His child with all the benefits of being an heir to His kingdom.[324] If you believe this—that God is your heavenly Father—then you are filled with hope.[325]

Plus, you are now able to enroll at God's Dream University.[326] God is knocking on your door, but you cannot hear the sound with your natural ears. You must listen closely with your heart to hear.

So will you open the door?

A Knock on the Door

My memory recalls that my mom told me about God when I was about three years old. Somehow in my childlike mind, I thought I could really talk to Him. And so, I remember going outside to our front porch, sitting on this rocking chair, looking up at the sky, and having this simple chat.

"God, I know you are up there, but maybe someday you and I could talk?"

Little did I know that was the cry of His heart as well.[327] I never heard Him speak that day, but I sure do recall that moment. It was as if He already knew and was preparing me.

One day at school when I was in first grade, I heard this knock on our classroom door. It was a nun who I had never seen in our Catholic school before.

"Miss Whooley," she kindly commanded, "I must speak to the children."

Of course, our teacher would have never said no to a Sister. That would have been unthinkable, especially back in those days.

Without faltering, Sister spoke, "Children, I have something very important to tell you today, so listen carefully."

Even though I was a severely distracted kid who couldn't sit still in her seat, that nun caught my attention. There was something different about her. She didn't just know of Jesus. She *knew* Jesus, and she explained the entire story about Jesus dying on the cross for our sins so that we could go to heaven. I hung on her every word for that day was the first time I heard the salvation message.[328]

I have no idea who that nun was, and I never saw her again, but I definitely remember this incident because the following Sunday at church, I had a God encounter at six years old. During Mass, my eyes caught a glimpse of a Catholic cross depicting Jesus' suffering on the main altar, and I *knew* it was true.

In childlike faith I called upon His name, "Jesus, thank you so much for dying on the cross for me so that I could go to heaven."[329]

Suddenly I felt this lovely sensation all over me and tears streamed down my face. For weeks afterwards, I prayed that same prayer, but never had quite the same experience that I did that first time. It was the tangible presence of Jesus coming into my life; I just didn't know what it was.

That morning Jesus came and dwelt with me, and He has remained ever since I invited Him into my heart.[330] Have you ever felt such a feeling? Did you perceive His presence during your dream journey? He delights to join you on your life's adventures.

Unfortunately, I never attended Dream University at the start of my early Christian years. It wasn't because I didn't want to. I simply didn't realize that I wasn't in a place where I could learn and grow in my faith.

However, all that changed when my husband and I married and moved to North Carolina. It had been about two months after we settled into our new home and new jobs, and once again, it started with a knock on the door.

School Days

A lovely couple was strolling by my house on their evening walk after dinner. Both kind-hearted souls, they were grandparents to most everyone on our street. That evening, the Holy Spirit clearly told them to knock on my door.

"Hi there. We're your neighbors, Gene and Betty. We live down the street and wanted to welcome you to the neighborhood. Do you know Jesus?"

"Yes...I do." I answered a little indignantly, for who asks such a question.

Then I responded, "I attend Saint Michael's Catholic church." Erroneously, I equated going to church with knowing Him.

What an interesting reception as the Lord guided our conversation.

They had a story to tell about their rebellious son and the power of the Holy Spirit. God had delivered their son and changed them in the process. We only talked for a few moments, but I will never forget how they shared God's love.

Still, there was more for God was answering one of my prayers.

Shortly before we moved to NC, I began seriously thinking about God again. I had this thought… *I should at least know what the Bible says before I reject it*. However, as I tried to read that big thick book, I found it too complicated. I never shared with anyone, but I had been praying that God would help me to understand His word.

And wouldn't you know it, my new heaven-sent friends, Gene and Betty, started a Bible Study every Wednesday night. All I had to do was walk three houses down from where I lived. There, I could ask all my questions and learn how to read my Bible.

In addition, Gene and Betty shared their experiences with the Holy Spirit, including the spiritual gifts that are described in 1 Corinthians 12.[331] As I saw what they had in Christ, I became hungry for more. I wondered if God would give such gifts to me and I started asking Him for them.[332]

And wow! God opened the floodgates of heaven and poured out His Spirit. While I can't explain all this spiritual stuff here in this book, and a book about biblical dream interpretation is probably not the place, I can say this—seek God and ask Him for yourself.[333]

I don't know how God will do it for you, but I am positive that He desires to bless you with spiritual gifts that are beyond anything that you can imagine.[334] Hey, I've even heard of folks that have had dreams and received spiritual gifts, for nothing is impossible for Him.

This season of my life was the beginning of my school days at Dream University. It was an exciting time as I walked with my friends, Gene and Betty, in our small group. I read God's word, and I learned from the Holy Spirit; I even experienced God working through me to heal when I didn't know how to pray.

At Dream University, I studied and trained like I did when I was in school, but this time I was walking with God on His exciting adventures. I wish I could tell you that it was easy, and that everything always went perfectly, but then you'd know I was lying.[335]

For going to school can be challenging. You have to attend class, listen to your teacher, complete your assignments and take tests as you practically apply the information you learned. Fortunately, God is gracious and will lead your every step. You can even take a test over again if you don't pass it the first time.

It is also important that you keep fit and exercise as you attend Dream

University. So, if you haven't done this already, I suggest you buy a study Bible and start reading it, along with journaling with God. Joining a small group to connect with other Christians, breaking bread and celebrating Christ is also a must for spiritual growth.

Nevertheless, the good news is that the Holy Spirit is the most awesome teacher on the planet. Imagine Jesus right beside you leading you everywhere you go. Talk with Him just like you would speak with someone sitting next to you. Then be quiet and listen for many times you'll find God in that quiet voice within. Of course, you'll also find He speaks in dreams and visions, and now you have a basis for interpreting them.

Remember when I started this book saying that I was lost in my dreams? Well, if you attend God's Dream University and faithfully walk with Him on a daily basis, you won't be lost. Before you know it, you'll be ready to graduate and fulfill the marvelous dream He has for your life.[336]

Your Life's Dream

So what do you think is your greatest discovery?

For me, it was learning who I am and knowing what my life's purpose is. Like I described earlier regarding your beautiful identity, you first need a heart experience followed by a head understanding.

Sadly, I started out by doing the reverse. When I was trying to decide on a life occupation, I thought about what I would do with my life and how I would earn money to support myself. Sorrowfully, I never considered the passions that lay inside of me.

But God knew.

As a child I was always enthusiastic about going to school and often pretended to be a teacher. As I grew, I realized that I liked mathematics and music, which eventually led me to a mathematics education degree.

Yet, somehow I veered off into a career in software engineering. At first, I liked the job and the better pay, but within a few years, my spirit dried up as I hated working behind a desk. I needed to get out of the office and converse with people.

In spite of all these things, God had a plan and was using all these things for good. As I joyfully stepped into motherhood, He connected the dots, little by little, and one day I began to see the big picture.

I would have never believed that I would one day write a book since English was never my favorite subject. While I had the thought of teaching, I had no clue that God would use my natural math abilities to develop a biblical dream methodology to teach about hope and healing.

I also suspect that He wants to use my gifts of mercy and compassion to minister to the sick because I am drawn to hurting people. You know, both my mother and my paternal grandfather grew up fatherless. I am quite familiar with the long-term generational devastation it causes in families due to abandonment. It's why the Lord has given me a heart for missions especially for orphans. And maybe, if I am lucky, I might get to explore the world on some mission trips as I love to travel.

Isn't it amazing how God is connecting all these dots? I am blown away at how God opened my eyes to see who I am and what He has called me to do.

For I believe that my greatest discovery includes seeing myself as He sees me. I am His beautiful one, called to write, speak and teach people how to learn to hope and to dream with purpose. He has revealed to me that I am a biblical dreamer with a passion for healing and prayer. I am desperate to see God splash His blessings on people so that they can welcome God into their lives, receive His healing touch and walk in their God-given destiny. This God revelation is my greatest discovery, my life's dream.

Please realize that my plans did not happen overnight, but by taking one step at a time.[337] Often I had immense difficulty believing that God would use one such as me. I once had my manager's manager, confide in me how I happen to obtain this prestigious job at this big blue corporation.

"Barbara," he kindly shared his secret, "We only gave you this job because we didn't have the money to hire someone more qualified. There was no one else available. We thought you'd fail."

Yet, I didn't tumble on my "tushie" as he had predicted. While I suffered in self-doubts, I knew to call on the God of the universe to move those mountains. With His help, I became a successful software engineer and product manager, even though that job wasn't my ultimate destination.

Although I didn't believe in myself, I learned that what actually qualifies a person to blossom and thrive in any environment is them not relying on their own adequacies. If we walk in our own strengths, we will not be walking in His power.[338]

Therefore, I hold dear to all my weaknesses so that I am able to run with God more perfectly.[339]

And when you run with God, don't think the devil is going to roll over dead while you walk out your God-sized dream.[340] During the final course of writing this book, my husband and I have experienced the most challenging moments of our lives with our teenage girl. Some of these episodes were even life-threatening to our family as the devil stopped at nothing to thwart the plans of God for us.

But my God is bigger. He has promised me that everything will be OK, and I trust Him at His word. I know that He is always with us in the storms of life. I know that He will use everything for good because I love Him.[341] He is connecting the dots so that I can share the gospel through my testimony.

And you know what?

God will connect the dots for your beautiful life's dream, too. Your greatest discovery probably won't look like mine, but I promise you, it will be great when God gets His hand on it![342]

Now let's look back to the beginning of your dream excursion. If you remember, I invited you on a dream journey back in the first chapter. Did you find God? Hear Him speak? Receive His understanding? Experience any miracles? I hope you heard Him speak in your dreams along with receiving His understanding and that you are well on your way with biblical dreaming. I pray that you know without a doubt that He desires to do something beautiful with your life, and that you will join me in this one last prayer, which I call the sweet dreams prayer.

But as I told you from the start, it is your choice as to what you believe and act on. No matter when you decide, I wish you the sweetest dreams in both your sleep and your waking hours, and always remember—God yearns to dream with you.[343]

Sweet Dreams Prayer

Dear God,

Thank You for sending Your Son Jesus Christ to pay the price for all my sin with His shed blood on the cross. Because of Your amazing grace, I receive Your gift of salvation and eternal life by faith today.

I am so grateful that You are my Heavenly Father and that I am Your beloved child. I am thrilled to be accepted into Your Dream University so that we can walk together connecting the dots regarding every part of my life.

Please send Your Holy Spirit to be my teacher and fill me with Your hope so that my life may give You glory.

Thanks, Father God, for continuing to speak to me

in my dreams, so that we can dream with purpose together, for You are an awesome, mighty God and worthy of my praise.

All in Jesus' name. Amen and Amen!

May the Lord Jesus bless you and always keep you near. May you know yourself as dear to Him, your loving heavenly Father who delights in lovely you.

Sweet dreams, my beautiful dreamer friend. I hope to see you in heaven someday. And I'll be looking forward to hearing about all the beautiful things He did for you while you walked the earth.

Review

1. What does God's Dream University mean to you? Are you planning to attend?
2. Has God ever knocked on the door or your heart? When? How did you answer?
3. Describe your school days with God. Did it include reading your Bible, following the Holy Spirit and participating in a Christian community or small group study?
4. Explain the concept of the greatest discovery for your life. Have you been able to connect the dots yet?
5. What are your hopes and dreams for your future? Have you asked God to reveal them? How are you and God dreaming together?

Appendices

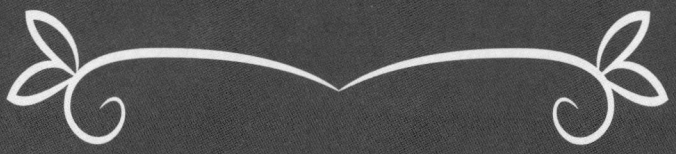

House Symbols

The *house symbols* define all kinds of information pertaining to your life. They depict characteristics of the "real" you, your true self within.

House: Life, either yours or another person's (2 Cor 5:1)
> **House – Childhood Home:** Your life when you were a child
> **House – Moving:** A change in your life
> **House – New House:** New life
> **House – Old House:** Old life apart from Christ, past life (2 Cor 5:17)
> **House – Renting a House:** Not owning your life, a non-freehold estate
> **House – Selling Your House:** Trying to sell your life, move / change something in your life

Apartment: Non-freehold estate, your life in captivity

Attic: The thoughts in your life, your mind, attitude (Phil 3:13)

Basement/Cellar: Substandard living space, storage place for old things you are not ready to get rid of (Jeremiah 38:6)

Bathroom: Desire or need to eliminate or wash off sins (Psalm 51:2)

Bedroom: Place of rest, intimacy, meditation (Psalm 63:6, Psalm 4:4)

Camper: Temporary housing for your life. Not settled and grounded in a particular area of your life

Dining Room: Being served the will of your Father; i.e. Jesus' food was doing His Father's will. (John 4:34)

Door: Entrance or way of escape (John 10:7)

Kitchen: Preparing for the will of your Father; i.e. Jesus' food was doing His Father's will. (John 4:34)

Living Room: Your everyday life revealed

Porch: Open and exposed part of your life

Roof: Covering over your life

Walls of a Room: The thoughts you carry regarding a specific part of your life. (Check the wallpaper & paint color.)

Window: Revealed opening (Joel 2:9)

Yard: Grounds surrounding your house, your life

Vehicle Symbols

Vehicle symbols define your life's journey. Unlike house symbols which represent you, vehicles depict where you are going, how and with whom.

Airplane: What you do, either work or ministry (Rev 14:6)

> **Airplane – Jet:** Powerful work/ministry, moves with great speed
>
> **Airplane – Rocket**: Powerful ministry, swift progress; could be an unexpected attack

Automobile – Car: A personal journey in one's life (Gen 41:43)

Automobile – Convertible: Journey that is uncovered and exposed

Automobile – Motorcycle: Individual journey, traveling alone

Automobile – Wreck: Journey of calamity, strife, contention (Nahum 2:4)

Bicycle: Journey of the flesh, human peddle power (Gal 5:19)

Boat: Support for your life's journey, floating on the waters, usually a spiritual voyage (Luke 8:22)

> **Boat – Battleship:** Prayer or intercession support.
>
> **Boat – Cruise Ship:** Support for missions - team, resources, and locations
>
> **Boat – Raft:** Support adrift, floating aimlessly
>
> **Boat – Rowboat:** Personal support through an individual, human paddle power
>
> **Boat – Speedboat:** Fast, powerful support for your spiritual journey
>
> **Boat – Submarine:** Submersible support in the spirit

Bus: Journey traveling with others

Bus – School Bus: Journey to learn or teach, usually with a team.

Elevator: Changing position

Roller Coaster: Unstable, wavering with twists and turns, doesn't go anywhere but round and round (James 1:6-8)

Roller Skates: Fast, Skillful

Tractor (for farming): Slow but powerful work ministry of the gospel (James 5:7, Mark 4:1-9)

Train: Continuous, unceasing fast journey, some stops allowed (Acts 2:42)

Truck: A personal journey, either natural work or ministry

Walking: Your personal journey on foot, powered by you (Ephesians 5:2)

People Symbols

People symbols reveal a part of your true self. They symbolize characterizations of that person or person type. Most often they are a reflection of you.

Baby: A reflection of your true self, your innocent self, or reveals new birth, new idea, new work, beginning (1 Cor 3:1; 1 Peter 2:2; 2 Cor 5:17)

Boy: A reflection of your true younger self, could refer to being spiritually young

Bride: The Church, the Bride of Christ (Isaiah 65:2)

Brother: A reflection of your true self

Clown: Foolish

Doctor: Healer

Driver: One who is in control

Family: Relatives, Spiritual family

Father: Father God, Natural Father, Satan as Father, Authority, Source (Matthew 6:32; Ephesians 6:2; John 8:44)

Father-in-Law: Father based on the Law, Authority, Legalism (Exodus 18:17)

Friend: A reflection of your true self, Look to the character or circumstance regarding this friend.

Girl: A reflection of your true younger self, could refer to being spiritually young

Grandchild: Heir

Grandparent: Inheritance (Proverbs 13:22)

Husband: Christ, husband of the bride (Ephesians 5:23)

Judge: Authority (Psalm 75:5)

Lawyer: Advocate, Christ is our advocate (1 John 2:1)

Man – New Man: Spiritual man in Christ (2 Cor 5:17)

Man – Old Man: Carnal man not in Christ (Romans 6:6)

Mother: Source, Church (Genesis 3:20)

Mother-in-Law: Legalistic Church

Police: Authority, protector, enforcer of a curse

Preacher: Messenger, God's representative (Matthew 11:10)

Prostitute: Harlot, seductress (Rev 17:5)

Sister: A reflection of your true self

Soldier: Spiritual warrior (2 Timothy 2:3-4)
Thief: Hidden One who deceives, steals, destroys (John 10:10)
Wife: Covenant of agreement, joined (Ephesian 5:31)
Woman – Strange Woman: Seducing spirit, temptation (Proverbs 2:16; Proverbs 23:27)

Place Symbols

Place symbols represent a particular building type like a hospital or school. In addition, place symbols can represent characteristics of a physical location.

Buildings

Airport: Waiting, preparing for work or ministry
Bank: Secure, safe, place where money/treasures are stored (Matthew 25:27)
Barn: Storehouse, provision, may relate to ministry depot Deuteronomy 28:8
Church: Church, congregation (Matthew 16:18)
City / Country: Use characteristics of that city or country
Courthouse: Judgment, trial, justice (Exodus 18:26)
Factory: Production, accomplishing tasks
Farm: Sowing and reaping for Kingdom of God, Ministering Word of God (Matthew 13:3)
Hospital: Healing, Caring for the sick
Hotel: Public location for rest or business (Luke 10:34)
Library: Knowledge, research
Movie Theatre: Watching your life story, not participatory
Prison: Captivity, confinement (Genesis 39:20)
School: Education, either learning or teaching
Shopping Mall: Pleased to make a purchase, selection of stores to buy truth or lies
Zoo: Strange, confusion, chaos, pertaining to animal "carnal" characteristics

Locations

Africa: Missions (as I'm called to missions in Africa)

Long Island, N.Y.: Lonely, alone for a long time (as in no man is an island)

New York: Empire state

Poughkeepsie, NY: Where my true love and I live

Russia: Communist nation with no freedom

San Diego: Missions (Basilica San Diego de Alcala)

Victoria, Canada: Victory (play on the word Victoria)

Wisconsin: Land of milk and cheese

Animals Symbols

Animal symbols describe your carnal nature as reflected in the characteristics of that creature or they can also refer to a spirit. Ecclesiastes 3:18 says, "I also said to myself, 'As for humans, God tests them so that they may see that they are like the animals.'"

Alligator: Ancient as alligators are old world animals, danger

Bat: Spirit of Witchcraft (Isaiah 2:20)

Bear: Destroyer, economic loss (bear market), danger, opposition, Russia (Proverbs 28:15; Daniel 7:5)

Beaver: Busy, industrious

Bird: Spirit, can be Holy Spirit or evil spirit (John 1:32; Revelation 18:2)

> **Bird – Chicken:** Spirit of ear, coward
>
> **Bird – Dove:** Holy Spirit (John 1:32)
>
> **Bird – Eagle:** Holy Spirit, Super Eyesight, Swift in flight (Ezekiel 1:10; Hosea 8:1; Isaiah 40:31)
>
> **Bird – Hawk:** Predator, evil spirit, sorcerer (Deuteronomy 14:14-16)
>
> **Bird – Owl:** Spirit of the night, could be wise as in wise old owl (Isaiah 34:14)
>
> **Bird – Parrot:** Copy, mimic, mock, repeat
>
> **Bird – Red Cardinal:** Red spirit, could symbolize the Spirit of Christ
>
> **Bird – Rooster:** Spirit of pride, boasting, bragging,

Bird – Raven: Confusion, chaos, causes envy or strife (Isaiah 34:11)

Bird – Turkey: Large spirit, foolish, clumsy, dumb, could refer to Thanksgiving

Bird – Vulture: Scavenger, impure (Proverbs 30:17)

Bug: Unclean

    Bug – Ant: Industrious (Proverbs 6:6; Proverbs 30:25)

    Bug – Bee: Chastisement, offense, stinging words or wounds (Judges 14:8; Isaiah 7:18)

    Bug – Flea: Irritating nuisance, Insignificant (1 Samuel 24:14; I Samuel 26:20)

    Bug – Fly: Unclean, nuisance, curse (Exodus 8:21; Ecclesiastes 10:1)

    Bug – Hornet: Affliction, chastisement, stinging (Deuteronomy 7:10)

    Bug – Lice: Conviction, shame, condemnation, guilt (Jeremiah 43:12)

    Bug – Maggot: Corruption, filth, evil (Job 25:6; Isaiah 14:11)

    Bug – Moth: Deterioration, loss through deceit (Matthew 6:19-21)

    Bug – Roaches: Infestation, unclean, hidden sin

    Bug – Spider: Evil, deceptive web, snare, temptation, false doctrine (Job 8:14; Isaiah 59:4-6)

    Bug – Spider-Black Widow: Deadly, great danger, slander

    Bug – Termites: Corruption, hidden destruction, secret sin

    Bug – Tick: Hidden, unaware of true-self, parasite, pest

    Bug – Wasp: Affliction, chastisement, stinging

Bull: Persecution, spiritual warfare, opposition, bull market, economic increase (Exodus 21:29)

Butterfly: Freedom, transformation, metamorphosis

Camel: Endurance, long journey (Genesis 31:16-18; Genesis 37:25)

Cat: Untrainable, self-willed, could represent your pet

Cow: Idolatrous, false worship (calf), prosperity, increase (Exodus 32:4; Genesis 41:3; Deuteronomy 15:19)

Deer: Graceful, swift, timid, could mean "dear" (2 Samuel 22:34)

Dog: Devour, ruled by stomach, will do anything for a treat, contentious, strife (1 Kings 21:23)

    Dog – Barking: Warning, danger

    Dog – Bulldog: Stubborn, unyielding, dangerous

    Dog – Personal Pet: Man's best friend

    Dog – Rabid: Extreme danger, overzealous, foaming at the mouth

    Dog – Wagging Tail: Friendly, accepting

Dolphin: Spiritual guide, mentor

Donkey: Stubborn, self-willed, unyielding, obnoxious (Genesis 16:12)

Elephant: Large, invincible or thick-skinner, not easily offended

    Elephant – Baby: Potential for greatness

    Elephant – Ears: Extra-sensitive hearing

    Elephant – White: Not wanted, Reusable

Fish: Spirit or soul of a person, can be good or bad (Matthew 13:47; Matthew 4:19)

Fox: Deception, cunning (Luke 13:32; Song of Solomon 2:15)

Fly: Unclean, nuisance, uncle (Exodus 8:21)

Frog: Unclean spirit, demonic, curse (Exodus 8:2; Exodus 8:7; Revelation 16:13)

Goat: Sinner, unbelief, unyielding (Matthew 25:33)

    Goat – Scapegoat: Blamed for another's wrong doing (Leviticus 16:10)

Horse: Work, Strength; works of the Spirit or works of the flesh (Joshua 11:4; Revelation 19:14; Revelation 9:19)

Kangaroo: To jump, to jump to a conclusion, prejudiced

Lamb: Jesus, Passover, blood of lamb takes away sin (Exodus 12:21; John 1:29)

Leopard: Powerful, predator, unchanging evil person (Daniel 7:6; Revelation 13:2)

Lion: Dominion, Christ, King, or Satan, bold, powerful (1 Peter 5:8; Revelation 5:5)

Monkey: Foolishness, clinging, mischievous, dishonest, "monkey business," "monkey on your back"

Mouse: Curse, devourer, timid (1 Samuel 6:4)

Penguin: Black and white, legalistic, southpaw

Pig: Swine, carnal, unclean (Matthew 7:6)

Rabbit: Increase, multiplication, unclean (Leviticus 11:6)

Raccoon: Night raider, mischief, rascal, thief

Rat: Unclean, wicked person, jerk, plaque (1 Samuel 6:4)

Sheep: Innocent, saint, unsaved (Matthew 10:6; Matthew 18:12)

Seal: Dogs of the sea, or "seal of approval," endorsement (Nehemiah 9:38)

Sloth: Lazy, lethargic, slow (Proverbs 19:15)

Snake: Sin, craftiness of Satan, curse, demonic, threat, danger (Genesis 3:1; Numbers 21:9)

Stork: Expectant, new birth, new experience

Weasel: Wicked, renege on a promise, betrayer (Leviticus 11:29)

Wolf: Predator, devourer, evil person (John 10:12)

Worm: Corruption, filth, evil, devourer (Isaiah 51:8; Jonah 4:7; Acts 23:12)

Body Parts and Face Symbols

Body part symbols figuratively describe a characteristic or function of the body using a biblical reference.

Body Parts
Ankle: Faith (Psalm 18:36; Ezekiel 47:3)
Arm: Healing (Psalm 136:12)
Back: Support, carrying burdens; or, going back, returning (Isaiah 30:6; Luke 15:18)
Bones: Spirit, condition of the heart (Matthew 23:27; Proverbs 17:22)
Face: Reflection of your heart, who you are (Proverbs 27:19)
Feet: Your walk (Job 18:8; Psalm 56:13; Acts 14:10)
Finger: Writing, words, or works; can also indicate pointing a finger at someone. (Exodus 31:18; Proverbs 6:13; Exodus 8:19)
Hand: Work(s) (Nehemiah 4:17; Genesis 5:29)
Head: Authority (1 Cor 11:10; Revelation 13:3-4)
Hips: Out of joint or not; loins of your mind (Genesis 23:25; 1 Peter 1:13)
Legs: Support to stand or walk (Psalm 147:10)
Neck: Your will; can be stiffed-necked or strong-willed (Exodus 33:3; Jeremiah 17:23)
Thigh: Strength, either natural or supernatural (Revelation 19:16; Genesis 24:9)

Face
Beard: Covering, relating to the heart
Ears: Hearing and attentiveness (Matthew 13:9)
Eyes: Reveals knowledge and understanding, desire, thoughts, window to the soul (Genesis 3:5; 2 Peter 2:14)
Hair: Covering, either old sinful nature or glorified one (1 Cor 11:14-15)
Lips: Words, either good or bad (Revelation 19:15)
Nose: Discerning; can also mean busybody, sticking your nose in someone's business (1 Peter 4:15)
Teeth: Wisdom, experience; or animal's teeth for devouring, danger (Song of Solomon 4:2; Proverbs 30:14)

Teeth − Brushing: Cleansing one's thoughts

Teeth − Wisdom: Wisdom, working out your salvation, growing in experience

Teeth − Animal: Danger of being clawed or devoured

Teeth − Baby: Immaturity, without experience, wisdom or knowledge, innocent

Teeth − False: False wisdom or knowledge

Teeth − Toothache: Trial, trouble

Teeth − Broken: Bad experience, gaining wisdom through suffering

Clothing Symbols

Clothing symbols refer to a covering over a body part, either righteous or wickedness.

Coat: Tunic, cloak, mantle; could represent destiny, anointing, power (Genesis 37:32; 2 Kings 2:13; 1 Samuel 28:14)

Gloves: A covering for the work of your hands

Hat: A covering/protection for your head (authority) (1 Cor 11:1-12)

Shoes: Protection/support for your life's walk (Ephesians 6:15)

Night and Day Symbols

Day: Revealed in the light; works/evil/sin exposed; truth/knowledge discovered, true-self exposed (Genesis 1:5; 1 Cor 3:13; 2 Timothy 1:10)

Night: Hidden in the darkness: works/evil/sin concealed; ignorance, unknown, unable to see your true self (Genesis 1:5; Psalm 139:11-12)

Darkness: Outside God's Kingdom; weeping and gnashing, pestilence (Matthew 8:12; Psalm 107:10-11)

Light: Jesus, the light of the world, God's Kingdom revealed (John 8:12; John 1:4-9)

Covenants of Agreement Symbols

Covenants of agreement symbols indicate that you are joined, contractually obliged by a particular thing in your life. Usually these symbols work in conjunction with the *people symbols*.

Adultery: Sin idolatry (Ezekiel 23:27)
Dating: Courting of contractual agreement. (Exodus 23:32)
Kissing: Touch of contractual agreement (Psalm 85:10; Proverbs 27:6)
Marriage: Joined together, intimacy, oneness (Ephesians 5:31-32; 1 Cor 7:1-7; Hebrew 13:4)
Sex: Agreement, joined (1 Cor 6:15-16; Hebrews 12:16)

Direction Symbols

East: Enter in (as in the Lord enters through the East gate), beginning (sun rises in the east to begin a new day) (Ezekiel 4:34)
North: Look up to the heavens, to God (on your left when facing east) (Deuteronomy 2:3; Psalm 75:5-7)
South: Natural (on your right when facing east) (Luke 12:54-56)
West: End (sun sets in the west) (Psalm 103:12)
Left: Spiritual, weakness of man; God's strength (Matthew 25:33; 2 Cor 12:9)
Right: Natural, strength of man, power of God reveal through flesh (Matthew 5:29-30)
Back: Past (as in back door, back yard) (Philippians 3:13)
Front: Future or now (as in front porch, front yard) (Zachariah 3:9)

Travel Way Symbols

Air: Spirit, Breath of life; atmosphere; presence of God; appearance, countenance, aura (Psalm 18:10; 1 Thessalonians 4:17; 1 Cor 9:25-27)

Air – Crash: Failure, disaster

Air – Flying Near Electrical Power Lines: Danger, caution, need prayer

Air – Flying Too Low: Insufficient power, preparation or training, (not being led by the Spirit)

Air – Flying or Soaring: Moved by the Spirit (ministering in the gifts of the Spirit)

Bridge Support: crossing way, as in trial or faith (Isaiah 43:2; Genesis 32:22)

Elevator: Changing position: up – elevated; down – demotion or trial

Ladder: Ascend or Descend, a way of escape (Genesis 28:12-13)

Railway: Unchanging, traditions

Road: Travel way (Isaiah 55:8; Genesis 6:12)

Road – Dead End: Stop, change directions (Haggai 1:5-7)

Road – Dirt/Muddy: Man's carnal way, flesh, weak (Psalm 69:2)

Road – Highway: God's way of life in the fast lane (Isaiah 35:8)

Road – Stones, Pebbles, Gravel: God's way, using His word and His Spirit (Jeremiah 6:16)

Road – Under Construction: Preparation of God's way (Matthew 7:13-14)

Stairs: Ascending or descending

Water: Spirit, either the Spirit of God, man or of the enemy; can also refer to the Word, cleansing with God's Word (John 1:33; John 3:5)

Water – Lake: God's Spirit; catch fish (Matthew 13:47)

Water – Ocean /Sea (Salt): Sea of Humanity, nations of the world (Isaiah 57:20; Isaiah 60:5)

Water – River, Rapids (Fresh): Living Holy Spirit flowing, peace like a river (John 7:38; Isaiah 66:12)

Water – Rushing Stream (Fresh): Fountain of wisdom, purifying (Proverbs 18:4)

Spiritual Element Symbols

Earth: Lord's creation, originally dark and void, but now called to be blessing (Psalm 24:1)

Earth – Dry: Dark and void (Genesis 1:2)

Earth – Fertile: Fruitful and able to multiply seed (Genesis 1:28)

Fire: God's spirit, holy purifying presence (Hebrews 12:29)

Fire – Smoke: Manifest presence because there is a fire, glory of God, prayer ; or offense, temporary cover-up as in smoke screen, (Isaiah 6:3-4; Revelation 8:4; Proverbs 10:26)

Water Spirit: Words (of God, of man or the enemy); to make holy, to cleanse (Proverbs 18:4; Ephesians 5:26)

Water – Flood: Overwhelm, either good or bad (Job 27:20; Psalm 29:9-11)

Water – Fountain: Spirit of man; Holy Spirit (James 3:11-12)

Water – Fresh: Spirit of God, God's word (James 3:10-12)

Water – Hail: Spirit of Destruction, judgment (Psalm 18:12-13; Exodus 9:23-25)

Water – Ice: Hard saying, harsh words, slippery, dangerous (Job 37:10; Job 6:15-16; Job 38:28-30)

Water – Muddy: Polluted Spirit of God, Corrupted or contaminated of God's Word (Psalm 69:2; Isaiah 57:20)

Water – Rain: Life, God's Holy Spirit, God's Word; depression, trial Zachariah 10:1; Matthew 7:27)

Water – Salt: Spirit of the world, unclean, undrinkable, doubts in God (Psalm 68:22; James 1:6)

Water – Snow: Covering, pure, grace (Isaiah 55:10-11)

Water – Well: Source of the Spirit, either man or God; can be deep, dry (John 4:10-14; Jeremiah 6:7)

Wind: Spirit or doctrine; holy or demonic (John 3:8; Acts 2:2-4)

Wind – Storm/Hurricane: Disturbance, change spiritual warfare, sudden calamity; or God' powerful revival (Isaiah 25:4; 2 Peter 2:17)

Wind – Tornado: Spirit of the Lord; or terrible destruction (2 Kings 2:11; Nahum 1:3)

Related Element Symbols:

Clouds: Covering, canopy, can be good or bad (Exodus 16:10; Exodus 19:9; Zephaniah 1:15)

Cloud – Dark: Covering, canopy (Psalm 18:11)

Earthquake: Upheaval, Crisis, Disaster (Isaiah 29:6; Matthew 28:2)

Moon: False Worship, works of darkness (2 Kings 23:5)

Rainbow: Promise, covenant (Genesis 9:13)

Storm: Disturbance, spiritual warfare, sudden calamity or destruction, trial, persecution; or white storm being God's power, revival (Isaiah 29:6; Nahum 1:3)

Sun: Heat, God, light, goodness; or affliction, persecution, trial (Psalm 84:11; Malachi 4:2)

Thunder: Change, a warning of impending judgment or trouble, The Lord speaking (1 Samuel 2:10; Psalm 18:13; John 12:28-29)

Volcano: Eruption, sudden violent reaction to pressure (Psalm 11:6; Deuteronomy 32:22)

The Four Seasons

Spring: Beginning, revival, fresh start (Isaiah 43:19; Song of Solomon 2:11-12)

Summer: Harvest, opportunity, or trial, heat of affliction (Psalm 32:4; Proverbs 10:5)

Autumn: End, Completion, change, repentance(Jeremiah 8:20)

Winter: Barren, death, dormant, waiting, cold (Matthew 24:20; Acts 27:12)

Numbers Symbols

One: Beginning, first, new, united (Genesis 1:1,5; Mark 12:29)

Two: Divide, separate, judge (1 Kings 3:25; Genesis 1:6-8)

Three: Obedience to Christ, likeness of Jesus, conform (Genesis 1:11-13; Matthew 28:19)

Four: Reign, rule, govern (Matthew 24:31; Revelation 11:15; Genesis 1:16-19)

Five: Grace, fruitful, multiply, blessing (Matthew 16:9; Genesis 1:20-23)

Six: Image of man, carnal, flesh (Genesis 1:26-31; Revelation 13:18)

Seven: Complete, finished, rest (Genesis 2:3)

Eight: Put off the old man, new beginnings (Acts 7:8; Colossians 2:11)

Nine: Harvest, fruitfulness; or judgment (Galatians 5:22; Matthew 13:29-30)

Ten: Measured, period of trial or temptation for the purposes of either accepting or rejecting; accepted through God's Son (Matthew 25:1-3; Romans 5:10)

Eleven: End, last, finish (Jeremiah 1:3; Jeremiah 39:2; Matthew 20:9-12)

Twelve: United, government, apostolic number (Luke 9:1-2; Luke 22:30)

Thirteen: Rebel, revolution, rejections, occult (Genesis 14:4)

Fourteen: Double completion; recreated, reproduced <7+7>; or bond slave, employee (Genesis 31:41; Numbers 28:16)

Fifteen: Grace with boundaries, finite fruitfulness, sin covered (not removed) (2 Kings 20:6; Hosea 3:2)

Sixteen: Free spirit without boundaries, salvation <8+8> (Acts 27:34-38)

Seventeen: Incomplete, unfinished, immature, a babe in Christ (Genesis 37:1-3)

Eighteen: Put on, either judgment, destruction, captivity or the Spirit of Christ <9+9> (2 Samuel 8:12-14; Luke 13:11-16)

Nineteen: Barren, ashamed, repentant, selflessness (2 Samuel 2:30)

Twenty: Holy, tried and accepted <2 X 10> (Revelation 4:4)

Thirty: Time to begin ministry; value, price paid for Jesus <3 X 10> (Luke 3:23; Matthew 27:9)

Forty: Freedom, rule, reign after period of captivity or testing <4 X 10> (Genesis 7:16-18; Matthew 4:2)

Fifty: Jubilee, free from all debts, abundant grace <5 X 10> (Leviticus 25:8-15)

Hundred: Fullness, full measure, full completion, full reward <10 X 10> (Genesis 26:12; John 21:11; Mark 10:30)

Thousand: Maturity, mature service, mature judgment <10 X 100> (Deuteronomy 1:15; Romans 11:4; Galatians 4:4)

Color Symbols

Black: Absence of color, lack, sin, evil grief and mourning (Revelation 6:5-6; Isaiah 59:8-10; Jeremiah 4:28)

Blue: Spiritual gift, divine revelation, heavenly, as in the sky; Holy Spirit, God's Word as blue is the color of water; or depressed as in singing the blues; or innocent little baby boys (Numbers 4:6-12; Number 15:38; Exodus 39:1)

Brown: Dead as in brown grass, no life, without spirit (Genesis 3:19; 1 Peter 1:24; Psalm 102:10-11)

Gray: Not defined, gray areas between right and wrong, vague, not specific, hazy, deceived; or if gray hair if can mean wisdom, age, or weakness (Proverbs 20:29; 1 Kings 2:8-10)

Green: Life, moral or eternal life; or not ripe, not mature, inexperienced, carnal, flesh; or green with envy; or fresh as in from the garden (Genesis 1:30; Psalm 23:1-3; Luke 23:31)

Orange: Danger, great jeopardy; or bright orange can mean power, force, energy, danger, even fire (Exodus 24:17)

Pink: Flesh, sensual, immoral; or a female baby that is innocent, moral and chaste.

Purple: Royal, rule, majestic, noble; can be good or evil (John 19:5; Esther 8:15)

Red: Passion, love, enthusiasm, zeal, or emotion, anger, hatred, lust, sin (Isaiah 1:18; Revelation 1:5; Revelation 6:4; Revelation 12:3)

White: Pure, unblemished, spotless, righteous, blameless, innocence (Revelation 7:14; Psalm 51:7)

Yellow: Gift of God or from God, glory of God; or marriage, family honor; or caution as a yield sign; or welcome home as in a yellow ribbon (Psalm 68:12-13)

Metal Symbols

Brass: Words, sounds, resounding gong or clanging cymbal (1 Cor 13:1)

Gold: Glory of God, wisdom, truth (Proverbs 8:10)

Iron: Strength, power usually with a stubborn stronghold (Isaiah 48:4)
Lead: Weight of the world, heavy burden of win (Zechariah 5:8)
Silver: Knowledge of God, revelatory knowledge (Matthew 27:9; Proverbs 2:3-4)

Miscellaneous Symbols

Arrows: A person, or words; either accusation, gossip, or prayer and deliverance (Psalm 64:3; Proverbs 25:18; Psalm 64:7)

Ashes: Ruin, destruction; memories (2 Peter 2:6; Job 13:12)

Axe: Word; either gospel, preaching, or rebuke and repentance (Proverbs 27:17; Matthew 3:10)

Bells: Sign indicating a change, or presence of the Holy Spirit; or vanity, pride (Exodus 39:25; 1 Corinthians 13:1)

Bikini: Uncovered, carnal, flesh revealed (Isaiah 47:3)

Birth: New life, new beginning for either sin or blessing (James 1:15)

Blind: Ignorant, unseeing, without understanding (1 John 2:11; Matthew 23:26)

Blood: Life of the flesh, covenant; unclean or Christ's cleansing blood (Leviticus 17:11; Leviticus 15:19; John 6:53)

Bomb: Power either Holy Spirit outpouring; or sudden destruction (Acts 1:8; Acts 2:17)

Book: Record, remembrance (good or evil), witness written on our hearts (Malachi 3:16; Revelation 20:12; 2 Corinthians 3:2)

Bread: Life, word of God, Jesus, provision (John 6:36; Matthew 4:4)
    Bread – Stale: Unfit old life, stale (Joshua 9:5; Malachi 1:7)

Bullets: Words, accusations, slander, gossip (Psalm 64:3)

Christmas: Gift, season of rejoicing, good will to men (Luke 11:13)

Coffee: Wake-up call, stimulant; can be bitter memories (Ephesians 5:14; James 3:14)

Darts: Words, either accusation, gossip; or prayer and deliverance (Psalm 64:3; Proverbs 25:18; Psalm 64:7)

Death: Termination, end, loss, sorrow (John 12:24; Hebrews 2:14)

Desert: Place of barrenness/testing (Deuteronomy 32:10)

Ditch: Habit or snare to causes one to fall (Psalm 7:15; Matthew 15:14)

Dynamite: Powerful miracle; severe danger (Luke 10:19)

Egg: New Promise, new thoughts, new plans, fragile; or rotten egg as in bad person (Isaiah 34:15; Isaiah 59:5)

Electricity: Power (1 Cor 4:20; Acts 1:8)

Explosion: Sudden change, either expansion or destruction (Isaiah 48:3)

Falling: Unsupported (Proverbs 11:28; Proverbs 16:18)

Fence: Boundaries, barrier, obstacles (Job 19:8; Psalm 62:3)

Flowers: Glory, as in glory of man is as the flower of grass (Proverbs 25:11; Song Of Solomon 2:12)

Food: Doing the spiritual will of your Father (John 4:34)

Furniture: Tools for your life (Exodus 31:6-8)

> **Furniture – Bed:** Rest for your life, place for sleep
>
> **Furniture – Chair:** A position of rest for your life; can also mean position of authority, i.e. like a chair on an executive board

Garbage: Rejection (2 Kings 10:27; Mark 9:47)

Gun: Weapon, powerful, can be words (2 Cor 10:4)

Honey: Sweet, strength, Holy Spirit anointing, pleasant experience (Psalm 19:10; Numbers 14:8; 1 Samuel 14:26-30)

Horns: Revelation 17:12

Intersection: The Cross pictured like two streets intersecting (Hebrews 12:2)

Jewel: Treasure, God-made (Song of Solomon 7:1; Isaiah 61:10)

Jewelry: Idolatry, adorning yourself, man-made (Ezekiel 16:17)

Lightening: Power, instant miracle or judgment (Luke 10:17-18)

Mirror: Looking at oneself, could be vanity, seeing only in part (James 1:23; 2 Cor 3:18; 1 Cor 13:12)

Miscarriage: Failure, unjust loss (Exodus 23:26)

Money: Value or worth, can mean self-worth; power to attain wealth (1 Timothy 6:10; Deuteronomy 8:18)

Mountain: Stronghold of God; obstacle, challenge, a stronghold of sin (Exodus 24:12-14; Psalm 48:1; Mark 11:23-24)

Music: Worship (from the heart), prophesying (Daniel 3:5; 1 Chronicles 13:8; 2 Kings 14-16)

Name: Your identity, who you are, true self (Proverbs 22:1; Genesis 16:13; Revelation 3:12)

Nudity: Uncovered flesh, sins exposed (Genesis 3:7)

Oil: Holy Spirit Anointing, Healing (1 Samuel 16:13; Mark 6:13)

Painting: Covering (Jeremiah 22:14; 2 Kings 9:30)

Perfume: Influence, sweet or seduction (Isaiah 3:19-21; Ecclesiastes 10:1; Song of Solomon 4:10)

Photo: Memories, past experiences (Mark 4:10; Numbers 33:52)

Pot/Pan/Bowl: Vessel to be filled (Exodus 25:29; Genesis 43:11)

Pregnancy: Expectant, in process either sin or righteousness (Isaiah 66:9)

Purse: Identity, treasure, self-worth (Proverbs 1:13-15; Matthew 6:21)

Refrigerator: A storage place for food/doing the will of your father (John 4:34)

Rose – Red: Romance, passion, courtship (Song of Solomon 2:1)

Rose – Yellow: Romance, Marriage (Song of Solomon 2:1)

Salt: Seasoning or preservative (Mark 9:50; Matthew 5:13)

Sand: Flesh, improper foundation, weakness; numerous, prosperous (Matthew 7:26-27; 1 Kings 4:20; 1 Kings 4:29)

Sign: External action or event that signifies something important; directions (Genesis 9:13; Acts 4:30; Hosea 12:10)

Sleep: Unconscious, unaware (Isaiah 29:10; Romans 13:11)

Smile: Friendly, kind (Job 9:27; 1 Samuel 2:1)

Star: Person, shining star, saint (Genesis 22:17; Daniel 12:3)

Suitcase: Personal storage for traveling, temporary (Luke 23:35)

Table: Communion (Luke 14:1)

Tears: Grief, sorrow; prayer, repentance and crying out to God (Mark 9:24; Psalm 34:6)

Telephone/Cell Phone: Communications (Acts 2:21)

Title/Deed: Ownership, possession (Genesis 23:20)

Tree: Person or Covering (Psalm 37:35; Psalm 52:8)

Veil: Hidden or concealed (2 Cor 3:13-16)

Wallet: Identity, treasure, self-worth (Matthew 6:21; Psalm 22:16-18)

Wine: Intoxicant, either filled with the Holy Spirit or other spirit (Ephesians 5:18)

Healing Clues and Symbols

The following list contains various clues which could reveal a need for inner healing. Please note that the sickness could possibly symbolize a spiritual one.

Baggage: Lies that you believe and carry around in your life (Matthew 23:4)

Bathroom: Place for cleansing (Psalm 51:2-3)

    Bathroom – Bath/Washbasin: Washing/cleaning (John 13:6-10)

    Bathroom – Flush: Remove offenses, sin, sickness (Luke 17:1)

    Bathroom – Shower: Washing/showering clean (Ezekiel 34:25-27)

    Bathroom – Toilet: Eliminating sin, sickness, offenses (2 Kings 10:26-27)

Urinating: Need to relieve oneself of pressure (2 Kings 18:27)

Burglars/Thieves: Person/evil spirit stealing from you (John 10:10)

Doctor: Healer (Jeremiah 8:22; Luke 5:31-32)

Hospital: Place for healing

House Issues – Back Door Break-In: Issues in your life—violation from your past (2 Cor 5:1; Job 24:14)

House Issues – Setting Occurs in a Past House: Issues in your life —refers to your past, your childhood (Exodus 22:2)

Intruders: Person/evil spirit breaking into your life (John 10:1)

Prison: Place of captivity (Isaiah 61:1; Acts 16:25-26)

Rape: Symbolic act of violation against your will (Deuteronomy 22:23-24)

Rope/Cord: Bondage (Proverbs 5:22)

Sickness: Physical or spiritual sickness (Matthew 9:12)

Stolen Goods: Items stolen from your life such as peace and joy stolen from your abundant life (Obadiah 1:5; John 10:10; 1 Peter 5:8)

Weeds: Works of the flesh, sin, neglect (Proverbs 24:30-31)

Dream Discovery Template

Part I: The Revelation

Journal your dream revelation exactly as you saw it.

Give your dream a title:_____

Write the date and time of your dream:_____

Describe your life situation / emotions / location when this dream occurred:

Part II: The Interpretation

Get God's Understanding and Interpretation (Get GUI):

Step 1: Consider Your Dream and Its Source:

Type of Dream (circle one or more that apply):

Simple or Complex
(With simple dreams you know the meaning. Complex ones require more thought, and sometimes the help of a skilled dream interpreter.)

Symbolic or Literal
(Symbolic dreams use various characters to represent a specific meaning. Literal dreams happen as you see them. If your dream contains anything which you know can't be true, then assume your entire dream is symbolic.)

Visual and maybe Actual
(All dreams are visual but not all are actual. An actual dream contains some type of impartation, like a gift of faith, word of knowledge, healing, etc.)

Supernatural or Natural
(Supernatural dreams are from either God or Satan. Natural dreams are from you.)

Prophetic or False
(Prophetic dreams refer to God speaking in your dreams, and sometimes they can refer to the future. False dreams are not from God, and they always contain some type of lie or deception. They come from either your own natural mind or Satan.)

Purpose of Dream
(circle one or more that apply; note that complex dreams can have more than one purpose):

-To reveal your true self (Heart & Soul Dream)

-To encourage you (Encouragement Dream)

-To direct your next steps including where to go or not to go (Directional Dream)

Dream Source (circle one): God, Natural, Satan

Step 2: List and Decipher Your Dream Symbols

☐ _____

☐ _____

☐ _____

☐ _____

☐ _____

☐ _____

Step 3: Write Your Dream Message(s)

Step 4: Test and Go

Part III: The Application

Apply God's Wisdom

- Use God's word, God's will, and God's way.
- Watch out for the dream pitfalls: Pride, unholy connections and false truths.
 - Start with yourself, pray, walk in love and have faith in God.

Lessons Learned:

Write Your Prayer to God:

Further Resources

For more information, visit Barb's *Learn to Hope and Dream with Purpose* website at BarbaraKoob.com.

- Want to understand more about who God says you are? You can obtain a free bookmark entitled, **"You are Beautifully Made"** to learn about your true identity in Christ.
- Do you desire to know the "heart" truth about inner healing? God longs for you to be free to dream again. Read Barb's article, **"Will You Take THIS Dance? An Introduction to Inner Healing"** and take the next steps.
- Are you interested in assessing your knowledge about biblical dream interpretation? Test your skills with Barb's *Dream Quizzes.*
- Obtain a free softcopy of Barb's *Dream Discoveries Template* for personal journaling of your dreams.

Check out Barb's calendar for upcoming happenings, or contact Barb to speak at your next event.

Here are other suggestions for related ministries, books and resources:
- *The Dunamis Institute* at dunamisinstitute.org
- *Presbyterian Reformed Ministries International* at prmi.org
- *The Connecting Point Ministry and their Loved Retreats* at connectingpointloved.com
- *Hope Chapel Apex Women's Ministry* at hopechapelapex-women.com
- *A Beautiful Life Women's Ministry* at abeautifullifeministry.org
- *Let Jesus Heal Your Hidden Wounds* (book) by Brad Long and Cindy Strickler

And if you'd like to share *your dream story* for possible inclusion in an upcoming *Stories of Dream Discoveries* book, please use the *Dream Discoveries Template* found on the website and send it to Barb. She'd love to hear what discoveries you and the Lord have made, along with the lessons you've learned.

1. Rick Joyner, "The History and Future of the Present Revival – Part 5," Morningstar Ministries, 5/30/08, https://www.morningstarministries.org/resources/special-bulletins/2008/history-and-future-present-revival-part-5#.VrwRbbdvPow

2. Philippians 2:12-13 "12 Therefore, my beloved, as you have always obeyed, not as in my presence only, but now much more in my absence, work out your own salvation with fear and trembling; 13 for it is God who works in you both to will and to do for His good pleasure."

3. Jeremiah 29:15 "And you will seek Me and find Me, when you search for Me with all your heart."

4. Matthew 5:8 "Blessed are the pure in heart, For they shall see God." (NKJV)

5. Genesis 20:3 "3 But God came to Abimelek in a dream one night and said to him, 'You are as good as dead because of the woman you have taken; she is a married woman.'" (NIV)

6. Genesis 28:12 "12 Then he dreamed, and behold, a ladder was set up on the earth, and its top reached to heaven; and there the angels of God were ascending and descending on it." (NKJV), Genesis 31:10 "10And it happened, at the time when the flocks conceived, that I lifted my eyes and saw in a dream, and behold, the rams which leaped upon the flocks were streaked, speckled, and gray-spotted." (NKJV)

7. Genesis 31:23-24 "23Then he took his brethren with him and pursued him for seven days' journey, and he overtook him in the mountains of Gilead. 24 But God had come to Laban the Syrian in a dream by night, and said to him, "Be careful that you speak to Jacob neither good nor bad." (NKJV)

8. Genesis 37:5-11

9. Genesis 40:5-6 "5Then the butler and the baker of the king of Egypt, who were confined in the prison, had a dream, both of them, each man's dream in one night and each man's dream with its own interpretation. 6 And Joseph came in to them in the morning and looked at them, and saw that they were sad." (NKJV)

10. Genesis 41

11. Judges 7:12-14

12. I Kings 3:5 "5At Gibeon the LORD appeared to Solomon in a dream by night; and God said, 'Ask! What shall I give you?'" (NKJV), 1 Kings 3:6-15

13. Daniel 2

14. Daniel 4

15. Daniel 1:17 "17As for these four young men, God gave them knowledge and skill in all literature and wisdom; and Daniel had understanding in all visions and dreams." (NKJV)

16. Matthew 1:20 "20But while he thought about these things, behold, an angel of the Lord appeared to him in a dream, saying, 'Joseph, son of David, do not be afraid to take to you Mary your wife, for that which is conceived in her is of the Holy Spirit.'" (NKJV)

17. Matthew 2:18 "A voice is heard in Ramah, weeping and great mourning, Rachel weeping for her children and refusing to be comforted, because they are no more." (NKJV)

18. Matthew 2:19-23

19. Matthew 2:12 "Then, being divinely warned in a dream that they should not return to Herod, they departed for their own country another way." (NKJV)

20. Matthew 27:18-20

21. Acts 2:17 "And it shall come to pass in the last days, says God, that I will pour out of My Spirit on all flesh; Your sons and your daughters shall prophesy; Your young men shall see visions, Your old men shall dream dreams."

22. Zechariah 10:2 For the idols speak delusion; The diviners envision lies, And tell false dreams; They comfort in vain. Therefore, the people wend their way like sheep; They are in trouble because there is no shepherd. (NKJV)

23. Jeremiah 23:32 Behold, I am against those who prophesy false dreams," says the LORD, "and tell them, and cause My people to err by their lies and by their recklessness. Yet I did not send them or command them; therefore, they shall not profit this people at all," says the LORD. (NKJV)

24. Hebrews 11:6 "But without faith it is impossible to please Him, for he who comes to God must believe that He is, and that He is a rewarder of those who diligently seek Him."

25. Proverbs 25:2 "It is the glory of God to conceal a matter, but the glory of kings to search

out a matter.'"

26. Stephen C. Foster, Beautiful Dreamer, song, Wm. A. Pond & Co., 1864; Foster is the Father of American Music. and this song is one of his most popular melodies.

27. Genesis 1:26 "Then God said, 'Let us make man in our image, according to our likeness; let them have dominion over the fish of the sea, over the birds of the air, and over the cattle, over all the earth and over every creeping thing that creeps on the earth.'"

28. John 15:14-15 "14You are My friends if you do whatever I command you. 15No longer do I call you servants, for a servant does not know what his master is doing; but I have called you friends, for all things that I heard from My Father I have made known to you."

29. Numbers 12:6 "He said, 'Listen to my words: Where there is a prophet among you, I, the LORD, reveal myself to them in visions, I speak to them in dreams'".

30. Psalm 139:23-24 "Search me, O God, and know my heart; Try me and know my anxieties. And see if there is any wicked way in me, and lead me in the way everlasting."

31. Jane Hamon, Dreams and Visions: Understanding Your Dreams and How God Can Use Them to Speak to You Today (Christian International Ministries Network, 1997), 68-81.

32. Sigmund Freud, The Interpretation of Dreams.

33. 1 Samuel 3:2-10

34. Like 18:16 "But Jesus called them to Him and said, 'Let the little children come to Me, and do not forbid them; for of such is the kingdom of God.'"

35. James 4:2 "We do not have simply because we don't ask."

36. John 14:14 "If you ask anything in My name, I will do it."

37. Luke 17:5-6 "And the apostles said to the Lord, 'Increase our faith.' So the Lord said, 'If you have faith as a mustard seed, you can say to this mulberry tree, be pulled up by the roots and be planted in the sea, and it would obey you.'"

38. Deuteronomy 4:29, Matthew 7:8, Luke 11:10.

39. James 1:27 "Religion that God our Father accepts as pure and faultless is this: to look after orphans and widows in their distress and to keep oneself from being polluted by the world."

40. Gonxha means rosebud or little flower. (https://en.wikipedia.org/wiki/Mother_Teresa#Early_life)

41. Rapid eye movement sleep (REM sleep) is a normal stage of sleep characterized by the rapid and random movement of the eyes.

42. James W. Goll and Michal Ann Goll, Dream Language: The Prophetic Power of Dreams, Revelations, and the Spirit of Wisdom (Shippensburg, PA:Destiny Images Publishers, Inc, 2006), 65-78.

43. Ibid.

44. Mother Teresa and Brian Kolodiejchuk, Mother Teresa: Come Be My Light (The Mother Teresa Center, 2007).

45. Malcolm Muggeridge, Something Beautiful by God, (The Mother Teresa Committee, 1971).

46. "Do It Anyway" is a poem credited to Mother Teresa, similar to the "The Paradoxical Commandments" poem by Dr. Kent M. Keith.

47. Proverbs 4:1 "Hear, my children, the instruction of a father, And give attention to know understanding."

48. Goll, Dream Language, 141.

49. Job 33:15-16 "In a dream, in a vision of the night, When deep sleep falls upon men, While slumbering on their beds, Then He opens the ears of men, And seals their instruction." (NKJV)

50. Hamon, Dreams and Visions, 31.

51. 1 Cor 14: 3 "For he who prophesies speaks edification and exhortation and comfort to men."(NKJV)

52. Hoagy Carmichael, Heart and Soul, song, 1938.The tune features just four repeated chords (I-vi-ii-V) and is very easy to play on the piano, commonly played by two people.

53. Job 33:15-16 "In a dream, in a vision of the night, When deep sleep falls upon men, While slumbering on their beds, Then He opens the ears of men, and seals their instructions."

54. Proverbs 4:1 "Hear, my children, the instruction of a father, And give attention to know understanding."

55. 1 Cor 14:13 "Therefore let him who speaks in a tongue pray that he may interpret." (NKJV)

56. Job 33:14 "For God does speak – now one way, now another--- thought no one perceives it.", Ecclesiastes 3:11 "He has made everything beautiful in its time. He has also set eternity in the human heart; yet no one can fathom what God has done from beginning to end."

57. Isaiah 61:3 "To console those who mourn in Zion, To give them beauty for ashes, The oil of joy for mourning, The garment of praise for the spirit of heaviness; That they may be called trees of righteousness, The planting of the LORD, that He may be glorified."

58. Daniel 2:27-28 "27Daniel answered in the presence of the king, and said, 'The secret which the king has demanded, the wise men, the astrologers, the magicians, and the soothsayers cannot declare to the king. 28 But there is a God in heaven who reveals secrets, and He has made known to King Nebuchadnezzar what will be in the latter days.'"

59. Jeremiah 29:11 "11For I know the thoughts that I think toward you, says the LORD, thoughts of peace and not of evil, to give you a future and a hope."

60. John 10:10 "10 The thief does not come except to steal, and to kill, and to destroy. I have come that they may have life, and that they may have it more abundantly."

61. Acts 10: 9-16

62. Ira Milligan, Understanding the Dreams You Dream, Volume II: Every Dreamer's Handbook (Shippensburg, PA: Destiny Images Publishers, Inc, 2000), 1-3.

63. 2 Cor 5:1 "For we know that if our earthly house, this tent, is destroyed, we have a building from God, a house not made with hands, eternal in the heavens." NKJ

64. John 4:34 "Jesus said to them, 'My food is to do the will of Him who sent Me, and to finish His work.'" (NKJV)

65. Genesis 37:5-7 "5 Now Joseph had a dream, and he told it to his brothers; and they hated him even more. 6 So he said to them, 'Please hear this dream which I have dreamed: 7 There we were, binding sheaves in the field. Then behold, my sheaf arose and also stood upright; and indeed your sheaves stood all around and bowed down to my sheaf.'" (NKJV)

66. Genesis 37:9 "9Then he dreamed still another dream and told it to his brothers, and said, 'Look, I have dreamed another dream. And this time, the sun, the moon, and the eleven stars bowed down to me.'" (NKJV)

67. Genesis 37:8 "8And his brothers said to him, 'Shall you indeed reign over us? Or shall you indeed have dominion over us?' So they hated him even more for his dreams and for his words." (NKJV)

68. Genesis 39:10 So it was, as she spoke to Joseph day by day, that he did not heed her, to lie with her or to be with her.; Genesis 39:19-20 19 So it was, when his master heard the words which his wife spoke to him, saying, "Your servant did to me after this manner," that his anger was aroused. 20 Then Joseph's master took him and put him into the prison, a place where the king's prisoners were confined. And he was there in the prison. (NKJV)

69. Genesis 41:1-4

70. Genesis 41:5-8

71. Genesis 41:14-15

72. Genesis 41:16 1"6 So Joseph answered Pharaoh, saying, 'It is not in me; God will give Pharaoh an answer of peace.'"

73. Romans 8:28 "And we know that all things work together for good to those who love God, to those who are the called according to His purpose."

74. John 10:10 "The thief does not come except to steal, and to kill, and to destroy. I have come that they may have life, and that they may have it more abundantly."

75. 2 Corinthians 5:1 "For we know that if our earthly house, this tent, is destroyed, we have a building from God, a house not made with hands, eternal in the heavens." (NKJV)

76. Luke 4:34 "Jesus said to them, 'My food is to do the will of Him who sent Me, and to finish His work.'" (NKJV)

77. Genesis 37:28 "Then Midianite traders passed by; so the brothers pulled Joseph up and lifted him out of the pit, and sold him to the Ishmaelites for twenty shekels of silver. And they took Joseph to Egypt." (NKJV), Genesis 41:43 "And he had him ride in the second chariot which he had; and they cried out before him, 'Bow the knee!' So he set him over all the land of Egypt." (NKJV)

78. John 3:29 "He who has the bride is the bridegroom; but the friend of the bridegroom, who stands and hears him, rejoices greatly because of the bridegroom's voice. Therefore, this joy

of mine is fulfilled." (NKJV)

79. Isaiah 9:6 "For to us a child is born, to us a son is given, and the government will be on his shoulders. And he will be called Wonderful Counselor, Mighty God, Everlasting Father, Prince of Peace." (NIV)

80. Gal 1:10 "Am I now trying to win the approval of human beings, or of God? Or am I trying to please people? If I were still trying to please people, I would not be a servant of Christ." (NIV)

81. Matthew 4:19 "Then He said to them, 'Follow Me, and I will make you fishers of men.'" (NKJV)

82. Revelation 18:2 "And he cried mightily[a] with a loud voice, saying, 'Babylon the great is fallen, is fallen, and has become a dwelling place of demons, a prison for every foul spirit, and a cage for every unclean and hated bird!'" (NKJV)

83. Matthew 3:16 "When He had been baptized, Jesus came up immediately from the water; and behold, the heavens were opened to Him, and He[a] saw the Spirit of God descending like a dove and alighting upon Him." (NKJV)

84. Exodus 8:2 "But if you refuse to let them go, behold, I will smite all your territory with frogs." (NKJV)

85. Ecclesiastes 3:18 "8I also said to myself, 'As for humans, God tests them so that they may see that they are like the animals.'" (NKJV)

86. 2 Kings 2:8 "Now Elijah took his mantle, rolled it up, and struck the water; and it was divided this way and that, so that the two of them crossed over on dry ground." (NKJV)

87. Isaiah 64:6a "But we are all like an unclean thing, And all our righteousnesses are like filthy rags." (NKJV)

88. Tim Allen is an American comedian, actor, voice-over artist and entertainer. He is known for his role in the successful sitcom Home Improvement. (https://en.wikipedia.org/wiki/Tim_Allen)

89. Luke 8:17 "For nothing is secret that will not be revealed, nor anything hidden that will not be known and come to light." (NKJV)

90. John 15:5 "I am the vine, you are the branches. He who abides in Me, and I in him, bears much fruit; for without Me you can do nothing." (NKJV)

91. Proverbs 3:6 "In all your ways acknowledge Him, And He shall direct[a] your paths." (NKJV)

92. Ezekiel 43:4 "4And the glory of the LORD came into the temple by way of the gate which faces toward the east."

93. Matthew 24:27 "For as the lightning comes from the east and flashes to the west, so also will the coming of the Son of Man be."

94. Matthew 5:29-30 "If your right eye causes you to sin, pluck it out and cast it from you; for it is more profitable for you that one of your members perish, than for your whole body to be cast into hell. 30 And if your right hand causes you to sin, cut it off and cast it from you; for it is more profitable for you that one of your members perish, than for your whole body to be cast into hell." (NKJV)

95. 2 Corinthians 12:9 "And He said to me, 'My grace is sufficient for you, for My strength is made perfect in weakness.' Therefore, most gladly I will rather boast in my infirmities, that the power of Christ may rest upon me." (NKJV)

96. Romans 5:21 "So that as sin reigned in death, even so grace might reign through righteousness to eternal life through Jesus Christ our Lord". (NKJV)

97. Genesis 48:14 "Then Israel stretched out his right hand and laid it on Ephraim's head, who was the younger, and his left hand on Manasseh's head, guiding his hands knowingly, for Manasseh was the firstborn." (NKJV)

98. Philippians 3:13 "Brethren, I do not count myself to have apprehended; but one thing I do, forgetting those things which are behind and reaching forward to those things which are ahead." (NKJV)

99. Genesis 1:2 "The earth was without form, and void; and darkness was on the face of the deep. And the Spirit of God was hovering over the face of the waters." (NKJV)

100. John 4:14 "But whoever drinks of the water that I shall give him will never thirst. But the water that I shall give him will become in him a fountain of water springing up into ever-

lasting life." (NKJV)

101. James 1:6 "But let him ask in faith, with no doubting, for he who doubts is like a wave of the sea driven and tossed by the wind.";John 7:38 "He who believes in Me, as the Scripture has said, out of his heart will flow rivers of living water." (NKJV)

102. John 3:8 "The wind blows where it wishes, and you hear the sound of it, but cannot tell where it comes from and where it goes. So is everyone who is born of the Spirit." (NKJV)

103. Psalms 24:1 "The earth is the LORD's, and all its fullness, The world and those who dwell therein." (NKJV)

104. Genesis 1:2a "The earth was without form, and void; and darkness was[a] on the face of the deep.";Genesis 1:28 "Then God blessed them, and God said to them, 'Be fruitful and multiply; fill the earth and subdue it; have dominion over the fish of the sea, over the birds of the air, and over every living thing that moves on the earth.'" (NKJV)

105. Genesis 1:10 "And God called the dry land Earth, and the gathering together of the waters He called Seas. And God saw that it was good.";Matthew 13:24 "Another parable He put forth to them, saying: 'The kingdom of heaven is like a man who sowed good seed in his field.'" (NKJV)

106. Genesis 1:2b "And the Spirit of God was hovering over the face of the waters.";Deuteronomy 6:3 "Therefore hear, O Israel, and be careful to observe it, that it may be well with you, and that you may multiply greatly as the LORD God of your fathers has promised you—a land flowing with milk and honey.'" (NKJV)

107. John 3:8 "The wind blows where it wishes, and you hear the sound of it, but cannot tell where it comes from and where it goes. So is everyone who is born of the Spirit." (NKJV)

108. James 1:6 "But let him ask in faith, with no doubting, for he who doubts is like a wave of the sea driven and tossed by the wind." (NKJV)

109. Hebrews 12:29 "For our God is a consuming fire." (NKJV)

110. Genesis 2:2 "And on the seventh day God ended His work which He had done, and He rested on the seventh day from all His work which He had done."(NKJV)

111. Acts 7:8 "Then He gave him the covenant of circumcision; and so Abraham begot Isaac and circumcised him on the eighth day; and Isaac begot Jacob, and Jacob begot the twelve patriarchs." (NKJV)

112. Matthew 25:1 "Then the kingdom of heaven shall be likened to ten virgins who took their lamps and went out to meet the bridegroom." (NKJV)

113. Genesis 7:12 "And the rain was on the earth forty days and forty nights." (NKJV)

114. Mark 12:29 "Jesus answered him, 'The first of all the commandments is: "Hear, O Israel, the LORD our God, the LORD is one."'" (NKJV)

115. 1 Kings 3:25 "And the king said, 'Divide the living child in two, and give half to one, and half to the other.'" (NKJV)

116. Matthew 28:19 "Go therefore[a] and make disciples of all the nations, baptizing them in the name of the Father and of the Son and of the Holy Spirit." (NKJV)

117. Matthew 24:31 "And He will send His angels with a great sound of a trumpet, and they will gather together His elect from the four winds, from one end of heaven to the other." (NKJV)

118. Rev 11:15 "Then the seventh angel sounded: And there were loud voices in heaven, saying, 'The kingdoms[a] of this world have become the kingdoms of our Lord and of His Christ, and He shall reign forever and ever!'" (NKJV)

119. Matt 16:9 "Do you not yet understand, or remember the five loaves of the five thousand and how many baskets you took up?" (NKJV)

120. Genesis 1:26, 31 "26 Then God said, 'Let Us make man in Our image, according to Our likeness; let them have dominion over the fish of the sea, over the birds of the air, and over the cattle, over all[a] the earth and over every creeping thing that creeps on the earth.' 31 Then God saw everything that He had made, and indeed it was very good. So the evening and the morning were the sixth day." (NKJV)

121. Rev 13:18 "Here is wisdom. Let him who has understanding calculate the number of the beast, for it is the number of a man: His number is 666."(NKJV)

122. Genesis 2:3 "Then God blessed the seventh day and sanctified it, because in it He rested from all His work which God had created and made." (NKJV)

123. Acts 7:8 "Then He gave him the covenant of circumcision; and so Abraham begot Isaac

and circumcised him on the eighth day; and Isaac begot Jacob, and Jacob begot the twelve patriarchs." (NKJV)

124. Col 2:11 "In Him you were also circumcised with the circumcision made without hands, by putting off the body of the sins[a] of the flesh, by the circumcision of Christ." (NKJV)

125. Gal 5:22 "But the fruit of the Spirit is love, joy, peace, longsuffering, kindness, goodness, faithfulness…"

126. Matthew 13:29-30 "29But he said, 'No, lest while you gather up the tares you also uproot the wheat with them. 30 Let both grow together until the harvest, and at the time of harvest I will say to the reapers, "First gather together the tares and bind them in bundles to burn them, but gather the wheat into my barn."'"

127. Matthew 25:1-3 "Then the kingdom of heaven shall be likened to ten virgins who took their lamps and went out to meet the bridegroom. 2 Now five of them were wise, and five were foolish. 3 Those who were foolish took their lamps and took no oil with them."

128. Romans 5:10 "For if when we were enemies we were reconciled to God through the death of His Son, much more, having been reconciled, we shall be saved by His life." (NKJV)

129. Exodus 18

130. Psalm 89:11 "The heavens are Yours, the earth also is Yours; The world and all its fullness, You have founded them." (NKJV)

131. Ephesians 1:6 "To the praise of the glory of His grace, by which He made us accepted in the Beloved." (NKJV)

132. Acts 2:1-4 Scripture references to the Day of Pentecost and the coming of the Holy Spirit

133. Romans 6:6 "Knowing this, that our old man was crucified with Him, that the body of sin might be done away with, that we should no longer be slaves of sin."; 2 Corinthians 5:17 "Therefore, if anyone is in Christ, he is a new creation; old things have passed away; behold, all things have become new." (NKJV)

134. Luke 12:7 "But the very hairs of your head are all numbered. Do not fear therefore; you are of more value than many sparrows." (NKJV)

135. Exodus 39:1 "Of the blue, purple, and scarlet thread they made garments of ministry, for ministering in the holy place, and made the holy garments for Aaron, as the LORD had commanded Moses." (NKJV)

136. Genesis 1:30 "'Also, to every beast of the earth, to every bird of the air, and to everything that creeps on the earth, in which there is life, I have given every green herb for food'; and it was so." (NKJV)

137. Exodus 24:17 "The sight of the glory of the LORD was like a consuming fire on the top of the mountain in the eyes of the children of Israel." (NKJV)

138. Isaiah 1:18 "'Come now, and let us reason together,' Says the LORD, 'Though your sins are like scarlet, They shall be as white as snow; Though they are red like crimson, They shall be as wool.'" (NKJV)

139. John 19:5 "Then Jesus came out, wearing the crown of thorns and the purple robe. And Pilate said to them, '"Behold the Man!"'" (NKJV)

140. Psalm 68:12-13 "Kings of armies flee, they flee, And she who remains at home divides spoil. Though you lie down among the sheepfolds, You will be like wings of a dove covered with silver, And her feathers with yellow gold." (NKJV)

141. Revelation 7:14 "And I said to him, 'Sir, you know.' So he said to me, 'These are the ones who come out of the great tribulation, and washed their robes and made them white in the blood of the Lamb.'" (NKJV)

142. Genesis 3:19 "In the sweat of your face you shall eat bread till you return to the ground, For out of it you were taken; For dust you are, And to dust you shall return." (NKJV)

143. 1 Peter 1:24 "For, 'All people are like grass, and all their glory is like the flowers of the field; the grass withers and the flowers fall.'" (NKJV)

144. Jeremiah 8:21 "For the hurt of the daughter of my people am I hurt; I am black; astonishment hath taken hold on me." (NKJV)

145. James W. Goll, Exploring the Nature and Gift of Dreams: How to Understand Your Dream Language (Shippensburg, PA: Destiny Images Publishers, Inc, 2006), 72.

146. Job 28:1 "There is a mine for silver and a place where gold is refined." (NKJV)

147. Ezekiel 28:4 "By your wisdom and understanding you have gained wealth for yourself and

Endnotes

massed gold and silver n your treasuries." (NKJV)

148. Exodus 25:10-12 "10 Have them make an ark[a] of acacia wood—two and a half cubits long, a cubit and a half wide, and a cubit and a half high.[b] 11 Overlay it with pure gold, both inside and out, and make a gold molding around it. 12 Cast four gold rings for it and fasten them to its four feet, with two rings on one side and two rings on the other." (NKJV)

149. Proverbs 8:10 "Choose my instruction instead of silver, knowledge rather than choice gold." (NKJV)

150. Matthew 28:9 "Then what was spoken by Jeremiah the prophet was fulfilled: "They took the thirty pieces of silver, the price set on him by the people of Israel." (NKJV)

151. Proverbs 2:3-4 "Indeed, if you call out for insight and cry aloud for understanding, and if you look for it as for silver and search for it as for hidden treasure." (NKJV)

152. Isaiah 48:4 "For I knew how stubborn you were; your neck muscles were iron, your forehead was bronze." (NKJV)

153. Zechariah 5:8 "He said, 'This is wickedness,' and he pushed her back into the basket and pushed its lead cover down on it." (NKJV)

154. 1 Corinthians 13:1 "If I speak in the tongues[a] of men or of angels, but do not have love, I am only a resounding gong or a clanging cymbal." (NKJV)

155. Hebrews 12:5-6 "And have you completely forgotten this word of encouragement that addresses you as a father addresses his son? It says, 'My son, do not make light of the Lord's discipline, and do not lose heart when he rebukes you, because the Lord disciplines the one he loves, and he chastens everyone he accepts as his son.'" (NKJV)

156. Romans 8:1 "Therefore, there is now no condemnation for those who are in Christ Jesus." (NKJV)

157. John 10:10a "The thief does not come except to steal, and to kill, and to destroy." (NKJV)

158. James 1:6-7 "But let him ask in faith with no doubting, for he who doubts is like a wave of the sea driven and tossed by the wind. For let not that man suppose that he will receive anything from the Lord." (NKJV)

159. 2 Corinthians 10:5 "We demolish arguments and every pretension that sets itself up against the knowledge of God, and we take captive every thought to make it obedient to Christ." (NKJV)

160. John 10:10a "The thief does not come except to steal, and to kill, and to destroy."

161. Frederick Loewe and Alan Jan Lerner, I Could Have Danced All Night, song, 1956. "I Could Have Danced All Night" is a song from the musical My Fair Lady. The song is sung by the musical's heroine, Eliza Doolittle, expressing her joy after an impromptu dance with her tutor, Henry Higgins..

162. Acts 28:26-27 "Go to this people and say, 'You will be ever hearing but never understanding, you will be ever seeing but never perceiving.' For this people's heart has become calloused, they hardly hear with their ears, and they have closed their eyes. Otherwise they might see with their eyes, hear with their ears, understand with their hearts and turn, and I would heal them." (NIV)

163. Acts 9:18 "Immediately there fell from his eyes something like scales, and he received his sight at once; and he arose and was baptized."

164. 1 Kings 19:11-12 "'Go out, and stand on the mountain before the LORD.' And behold, the LORD passed by, and a great and strong wind tore into the mountains and broke the rocks in pieces before the LORD, but the LORD was not in the wind; and after the wind an earthquake, but the LORD was not in the earthquake; and after the earthquake a fire, but the LORD was not in the fire; and after the fire a still small voice."

165. John 4:5-26 The Samaritan Woman Who Met Her Messiah

166. Romans 6:18 "And having been set free from sin, you became slaves of righteousness." (NKJV)

167. Romans 8:2 "For the law of the Spirit of life in Christ Jesus has made me free from the law of sin and death." (NKJV)

168. Deuteronomy 5:9 "You shall not bow down to them nor serve them. For I, the LORD your God, am a jealous God, visiting the iniquity of the fathers upon the children to the third and fourth generations of those who hate Me." (NKJV)

169. Deuteronomy 7:9 "Therefore know that the Lord your God, He is God, the faithful God

who keeps covenant and mercy for a thousand generations with those who love Him and keep His commandments." (NKJV)

170. Romans 8:28 "And we know that all things work together for good to those who love God, to those who are called to His purpose." (NKJV)

171. Isaiah 61:1 "The Spirit of the Lord GOD is upon me, Because the LORD has anointed me to preach good tidings to the poor; He has sent me to heal the brokenhearted, to proclaim liberty to the captives, and the opening of the prison to those who are bound." (NKJV)

172. Genesis 1:27 "So God created man in His own image; in the image of God He created him; male and female He created them." (NKJV); "The human heart, made in the image of God, is designed to flourish in the context of loving relationships like those of the pre-Fall Garden of Eden"; Brad Long and Cindy Strickler, Let Jesus Heal Your Hidden Wounds:Cooperating with the Holy Spirit in Healing Ministry (Grand Rapids, MI:Chosen Books, 2001), 110.

173. "Defense Mechanism Table," Long and Strickler, Let Jesus Heal Your Hidden Wounds, 110-111.

174. Band-Aid is a brand name of American pharmaceutical and medical devices giant Johnson & Johnson's line of adhesive bandages and related products. Despite common misconception, Band-Aid is a generalized trademark in the Unites States. The term "band-aid" has entered usage as both a noun and verb describing a temporary fix. (E.g."Band-aid solutions were used to fix the leak.")

175. Demons can cause violently trembling within an individual. Mark 1:25 says, "'Be quiet!' said Jesus sternly. 'Come out of him!' 26 The impure spirit shook the man violently and came out of him with a shriek." (NIV)

176. Mark 4:22 "For there is nothing hidden which will not be revealed, nor has anything been kept secret but that it should come to light." (NKJV)

177. Presbyterian Reformed Ministries International, prmi.org; Introduction to the Community of the Cross, prmi.org/coc-introduction

178. Dunamis Institute, dunamisinstitute.org

179. The Community of the Cross is a ministry of the Presbyterian Reformed Ministries International (PRMI) and the location of the PRMI office. It is located on 24 acres of land in the mountains of western NC and it provides the spiritual support base for PRMI's involvement in the worldwide advancement of the gospel of Jesus Christ.

180. "Inner healing, then, is evangelism to the unbelieving hearts of believers." John and Mark Sandford, A Comprehensive Guide to Deliverance and Inner Healing (Grand Rapids, MI:Chosen Books, 1999), 19.

181. Ephesians 3:16 "I pray that out of his glorious riches he may strengthen you with power through his Spirit in your inner being." (NKJV)

182. Ephesians 6:16 "Above all, taking the shield of faith with which you will be able to quench all the fiery darts of the wicked one." (NKJV); "Ways that Evil Spirits Attach Human Beings", Long and Strickler, Let Jesus Heal Your Hidden Wounds, 146-147.

183. "Think of demons as analogous to bacteria or viruses." Long and Strickler, Let Jesus Heal Your Hidden Wounds, 148.

184. The most common is daimonizonmai, which means "to be demonized" or "to be as a demon" (Matthew 8:16, 28; 9:32; 12:22; Mark 1:32,34; 5:15; Luke 8:38; Long and Strickler, Let Jesus Heal Your Hidden Wounds, 146.

185. "If the person sexually abusing the child is demonized, then the demons may move through the abuser into the person. This is more likely when there has been actual sexual penetration. Human beings are made in the image of God, so sexual intercourse is not just a physical act. It touches the soul and gives evil spirits an entry point"; Long and Strickler, Let Jesus Heal Your Hidden Wounds, 148.

186. "The Formation of Vortex Memories" Long and Strickler, Let Jesus Heal Your Hidden Wounds, 112-122.

187. Colossians 2:5 "And having disarmed the powers and authorities, he made a public spectacle of them, triumphing over them by the cross." (NKJV)

188. "We are ministering to people, not demons. Deliverance is really part of the ministry of healing, and everything we say to the people we are trying to help should shine forth with

love.", Deliverance from Evil Spirits:A Practical Manual (Grand Rapids, MI:Chosen Books, 2009). 12

189. "Condemnation is reserved only for the demonic realm, not for the broken persons who come to us for help."; Ibid.

190. "Signs and Symptoms of the Involvement of Evil Spirits (#1-6)"; Long and Strickler, Let Jesus Heal Your Hidden Wounds, 154.

191. Ibid.

192. "The Formation of Vortex Memories"; Long and Strickler, Let Jesus Heal Your Hidden Wounds, 112-122.

193. "Ways Evil Spirits Attach Human Beings" Long and Strickler, Let Jesus Heal Your Hidden Wounds, 146-149.

194. Proverbs 25:2 "It is the glory of God to conceal a matter, But the glory of kings is to search out a matter." (NKJV)

195. Genesis 1:31 "God saw all that he had made, and it was very good. And there was evening, and there was morning—the sixth day." (NKJV)

196. David Crowder Band, Everything Glorious, song, Sixstepsrecord, 2007.

197. Romans 8:28 "And we know that in all things God works for the good of those who love him, who[a] have been called according to his purpose."(NKJV)

198. Dr. Kristina L. Chalfin, Adjunct Professor of Spiritual Formation, Regent University, School of Divinity

199. Exodus 34:6-7 6 And the LORD passed before him and proclaimed, "The LORD, the LORD God, merciful and gracious, longsuffering, and abounding in goodness and truth, 7 keeping mercy for thousands, forgiving iniquity and transgression and sin, by no means clearing the guilty, visiting the iniquity of the fathers upon the children and the children's children to the third and the fourth generation." (NKJV)

200. Deuteronomy 7:9 "Therefore know that the LORD your God, He is God, the faithful God who keeps covenant and mercy for a thousand generations with those who love Him and keep His commandments; (NKJV)

201. Isaiah 53:5 "But He was wounded for our transgressions, He was bruised for our iniquities; The chastisement for our peace was upon Him, And by His stripes we are healed." (NKJV)

202. Isaiah 61:1"The Spirit of the Lord GOD is upon me, Because the LORD has anointed me to preach good tidings to the poor; He has sent me to heal the brokenhearted, to proclaim liberty to the captives, and the opening of the prison to those who are bound." (NKJV)

203. Colossians 1:9 "For this reason we also, since the day we heard it, do not cease to pray for you, and to ask that you may be filled with the knowledge of His will in all wisdom and spiritual understanding." (NKJV)

204. 1 John 4:8 "He who does not love does not know God, for God is love." (NKJV)

205. 1 Corinthians 13:9 "For we know in part and we prophesy in part." (NKJV)

206. Psalm 26:2 "Examine me, O LORD, and prove me; Try my mind and my heart." (NKJV)

207. Acts 21:10-11 "10 And as we stayed many days, a certain prophet named Agabus came down from Judea. 11 When he had come to us, he took Paul's belt, bound his own hands and feet, and said, 'Thus says the Holy Spirit, 'So shall the Jews at Jerusalem bind the man who owns this belt, and deliver him into the hands of the Gentiles.''" (NKJV)

208. Acts 21:12 "12 Now when we heard these things, both we and those from that place pleaded with him not to go up to Jerusalem." (NKJV)

209. Acts 21:13 1"3 Then Paul answered, 'What do you mean by weeping and breaking my heart? For I am ready not only to be bound, but also to die at Jerusalem for the name of the Lord Jesus.'" (NKJV)

210. Acts 26:32 "Then Agrippa said to Festus, 'This man might have been set free if he had not appealed to Caesar.'" (NKJV)

211. John 15:26 "But when the Helper comes, whom I shall send to you from the Father, the Spirit of truth who proceeds from the Father, He will testify of me." (NKJV)

212. Proverbs 1:7 "The fear of the LORD is the beginning of knowledge, But fools despise wisdom and instruction."; John 16:13 "However, when He, the Spirit of truth, has come, He will guide you into all truth; for He will not speak on His own authority, but whatever He hears He will speak; and He will tell you things to come." (NKJV)

213. Matthew 4:1:11

214. Luke 4:4 But Jesus answered him, saying, "It is written, 'Man shall not live by bread alone, but by every word of God. (NKJV)

215. Luke 4:6-7 6 And the devil said to Him, "All this authority I will give You, and their glory; for this has been delivered to me, and I give it to whomever I wish. 7 Therefore, if You will worship before me, all will be Yours." (NKJV)

216. Luke 4:9-10 "Then he brought Him to Jerusalem, set Him on the pinnacle of the temple, and said to Him, 'If You are the Son of God, throw Yourself down from here. For it is written: "He shall give His angels charge over you, to keep you."'"

217. Acts 16:16-19

218. Acts 16:17 "This girl followed Paul and us, and cried out, saying, 'These men are the servants of the Most High God, who proclaim to us the way of salvation.'" (NKJV)

219. Acts 16:18 "And this she did for many days. But Paul, greatly annoyed, turned and said to the spirit, 'I command you in the name of Jesus Christ to come out of her.' And he came out that very hour." (NKJV)

220. 1 Corinthians 14:3 But he who prophesies speaks edification and exhortation and comfort to men. (NKJV)

221. 1 John 4:1 "Beloved, do not believe every spirit, but test the spirits, whether they are of God; because many false prophets have gone out into the world."(NKJV)

222. John 3:34 "Jesus said to them, 'My food is to do the will of Him who sent Me, and to finish His work.'" (NKJV)

223. John 15:5 "I am the vine, you are the branches. He who abides in Me, and I in him, bears much fruit; for without Me you can do nothing." (NKJV)

224. Psalm 51:2 "Wash me thoroughly from my iniquity, And cleanse me from my sin." (NKJV)

225. Romans 9:32 "Why? Because they did not seek it by faith, but as it were, by the works of the law, For they stumbled at that stumbling stone." (NKJV)

226. Romans 3:23 "For all have sinned and fall short of the glory of God." (NKJV)

227. Matthew 17:20 "So Jesus said to them, 'Because of your unbelief;[a] for assuredly, I say to you, if you have faith as a mustard seed, you will say to this mountain, "Move from here to there," and it will move; and nothing will be impossible for you.'" (NKJV)

228. Hebrews 12:6 "For whom the LORD loves He chastens, And scourges every son whom He receives." (NKJV)

229. Ephesian 1:5 "Having predestined us to adoption as sons by Jesus Christ to Himself, according to the good pleasure of His will." (NKJV)

230. Ephesians 3:20 "Now to him who is able to do immeasurably more than all we ask or imagine, according to his power that is at work within us" (NKJV)

231. Psalm 18:32 "It is God who arms me with strength, And makes my way perfect." (NKJV)

232. Galatians 2:16 "Knowing that a man is not justified by the works of the law but by faith in Jesus Christ, even we have believed in Christ Jesus, that we might be justified by faith in Christ and not by the works of the law; for by the works of the law no flesh shall be justified." (NKJV)

233. Ephesians 2:8 "For by grace you have been saved through faith, and that not of yourselves; it is the gift of God"; Acts 15:11 "But we believe that through the grace of the Lord Jesus Christ[a] we shall be saved in the same manner as they." (NKJV)

234. John 3:16 "For God so loved the world that He gave His only begotten Son, that whoever believes in Him should not perish but have everlasting life."; Ephesian 1:5 "Having predestined us to adoption as sons by Jesus Christ to Himself, according to the good pleasure of His will." (NKJV)

235. Ephesians 1:13 "In Him you also trusted, after you heard the word of truth, the gospel of your salvation; in whom also, having believed, you were sealed with the Holy Spirit of promise."; Ephesians 1:18 "The eyes of your understanding being enlightened; that you may know what is the hope of His calling, what are the riches of the glory of His inheritance in the saints." (NKJV)

236. Philippians 4:13 "I can do all things through Christ[a] who strengthens me."; 2 Corinthians 12:9 "And He said to me, 'My grace is sufficient for you, for My strength is made perfect in weakness.' Therefore, most gladly I will rather boast in my infirmities, that the power of

Christ may rest upon me."; Philippians 2:8 "And being found in appearance as a man, He humbled Himself and became obedient to the point of death, even the death of the cross." (NKJV)

237. Ephesians 3:9 "And to make all see what is the fellowship of the mystery, which from the beginning of the ages has been hidden in God who created all things through Jesus Christ.";2 Corinthians 5:15 "And He died for all, that those who live should live no longer for themselves, but for Him who died for them and rose again."; Romans 1:16 "For I am not ashamed of the gospel of Christ for it is the power of God to salvation for everyone who believes, for the Jew first and also for the Greek."; Galatians 4:7 "Therefore you are no longer a slave but a son, and if a son, then an heir of[a] God through Christ." (NKJV)

238. 1 Colossians 1:27 "To them God willed to make known what are the riches of the glory of this mystery among the Gentiles: which is Christ in you, the hope of glory."; Ephesians 3:17 "That Christ may dwell in your hearts through faith; that you, being rooted and grounded in love." (NKJV)

239. Hebrews 11:1 "Now faith is the substance of things hoped for, the evidence of things not seen." (NKJV)

240. Romans 10:17 "So then faith comes by hearing, and hearing by the word of God." (NKJV)

241. John 15:5 "I am the vine, you are the branches. He who abides in Me, and I in him, bears much fruit; for without Me you can do nothing." (NKJV)

242. John 1:12 "But as many as received Him, to them He gave the right to become children of God, to those who believe in His name."; Mark 10:27 "But Jesus looked at them and said, 'With men it is impossible, but not with God; for with God all things are possible.'" (NKJV)

243. Psalm 84:2 "My soul longs, yes, even faints for the courts of the Lord; My heart and my flesh cry out for the living God." (NKJV)

244. Ephesians 3:20 "Now to Him who is able to do exceedingly abundantly above all that we ask or think, according to the power that works in us." (NKJV)

245. Romans 5:8 "But God demonstrates His own love toward us, in that while we were still sinners, Christ died for us."; 1 John 4:16 "And we have known and believed the love that God has for us. God is love, and he who abides in love abides in God, and God in him." (NKJV)

246. 1 Peter 1:21 "Who through Him believe in God, who raised Him from the dead and gave Him glory, so that your faith and hope are in God."; Ephesians 2:10 "For we are God's handiwork, created in Christ Jesus to do good works, which God prepared in advance for us to do."; Ephesians 1:6 "To the praise of the glory of His grace, by which He made us accepted in the Beloved."; Colossians1:14 "In whom we have redemption through His blood, the forgiveness of sins." (NKJV)

247. Romans 8:1 "There is therefore now no condemnation to those who are in Christ Jesus,[a] who do not walk according to the flesh, but according to the Spirit."; Romans 8:31 "What then shall we say to these things? If God is for us, who can be against us?" (NKJV)

248. Psalm 139:14 "I will praise You, for I am fearfully and wonderfully made; Marvelous are Your works, And that my soul knows very well."; 2 Timothy 1:9 "Who has saved us and called us with a holy calling, not according to our works, but according to His own purpose and grace which was given to us in Christ Jesus before time began." (NKJV)

249. Romans 8:37 "Yet in all these things we are more than conquerors through Him who loved us."; Romans 2:8-9 "For by grace you have been saved through faith, and that not of yourselves; it is the gift of God, 9 not of works, lest anyone should boast." (NKJV)

250. Philippians 1:6 "Being confident of this very thing, that He who has begun a good work in you will complete it until the day of Jesus Christ." (NKJV)

251. Genesis 37:12-36 Joseph was betrayed and sold into slavery by his brother; Genesis 39:7-23 Joseph was unjustly thrown into prison.

252. Genesis 39:3-4:21-23 God showed Joseph mercy and favor, and prospered everything he did.

253. James 1:13 "When tempted, no one should say, 'God is tempting me.' For God cannot be tempted by evil, nor does he tempt anyone."; John 10:10 "The thief does not come except to steal, and to kill, and to destroy. I have come that they may have life, and that they may have it more abundantly." (NKJV)

254. Isaiah 61:3 "And provide for those who grieve in Zion— to bestow on them a crown of

beauty instead of ashes, the oil of joy instead of mourning, and a garment of praise instead of a spirit of despair. They will be called oaks of righteousness, a planting of the Lord for the display of his splendor." (NKJV)

255. John 15:7 "If you remain in me and my words remain in you, ask whatever you wish, and it will be done for you." (NIV)

256. John 14:13 "And whatever you ask in My name, that I will do, that the Father may be glorified in the Son." (NKJV)

257. Mark 9:23 "Jesus said to him, 'If you can believe, all things are possible to him who believes.'" (NKJV)

258. Romans 8:28 "And we know that all things work together for good to those who love God, to those who are called according to HIS purpose."

259. Hebrews 11:1 "Now faith is the substance of things hoped for, the evidence of things not seen."

260. Hebrews 11:13 "These all died in faith, not having received the promises, but having seen them afar off were assured of them, embraced them and confessed that they were strangers and pilgrims on the earth."

261. My friend Shawne called herself a blessing counter and even wrote a poem about it. Read, "The Blessing Counter and Her Poem" at BarbaraKoob.com.

262. Galatians 2:20 "I have been crucified with Christ; it is no longer I who live, but Christ lives in me; and the life which I now live in the flesh I live by faith in the Son of God, who loved me and gave Himself for me."

263. Psalm 4:8 "I will both lie down in peace, and sleep; For You alone, O LORD, make me dwell in safety." (NKJV)

264. I Peter 5:8-9 "Be sober, be vigilant; because your adversary the devil walks about like a roaring lion, seeking whom he may devour. Resist him, steadfast in the faith, knowing that the same sufferings are experienced by your brotherhood in the world." (NKJV)

265. Matthew 6:15 "But if you do not forgive men their trespasses, neither will your Father forgive your trespasses." (NKJV)

266. 1 Corinthians 3:10 "According to the grace of God which was given to me, as a wise master builder I have laid the foundation, and another builds on it. But let each one take heed how he builds on it." (NKJV)

267. Ephesians 2:6-8 "and raised us up together, and made us sit together in the heavenly places in Christ Jesus, 7 that in the ages to come He might show the exceeding riches of His grace in His kindness toward us in Christ Jesus. 8 For by grace you have been saved through faith, and that not of yourselves; it is the gift of God." (NKJV)

268. Luke17:1 "Then He said to the disciples, 'It is impossible that no offenses should come, but woe to him through whom they do come!'" (NKJV)

269. Titus 3:4-5 "But when the kindness and the love of God our Savior toward man appeared, 5 not by works of righteousness which we have done, but according to His mercy He saved us, through the washing of regeneration and renewing of the Holy Spirit."

270. Romans 2:4 "Or do you despise the riches of His goodness, forbearance, and longsuffering, not knowing that the goodness of God leads you to repentance?" (NKJV)

271. Matthew 6:14-15 "For if you forgive men their trespasses, your heavenly Father will also forgive you. But if you do not forgive men their trespasses, neither will your Father forgive your trespasses."; John 8:36 "Therefore if the Son makes you free, you shall be free indeed." (NKJV)

272. Ephesians 1:5-7 "Having predestined us to adoption as sons by Jesus Christ to Himself, according to the good pleasure of His will, 6 to the praise of the glory of His grace, by which He made us accepted in the Beloved. 7 In Him we have redemption through His blood, the forgiveness of sins, according to the riches of His grace." (NKJV)

273. Psalms 31:14-15 "But as for me, I trust in You, O LORD; I say, "You are my God." My times are in Your hand; Deliver me from the hand of my enemies, And from those who persecute me." (NKJV)

274. Philippians 2:5-9 "5 Let this mind be in you which was also in Christ Jesus, 6 who, being in the form of God, did not consider it robbery to be equal with God, 7 but made Himself of no reputation, taking the form of a bondservant, and coming in the likeness of men. 8 And

being found in appearance as a man, He humbled Himself and became obedient to the point of death, even the death of the cross. 9 Therefore God also has highly exalted Him and given Him the name which is above every name." (NKJV)

275. Sunnyside is the romantic homestead of American author Washington Irving located in Tarrytown, NC. He is best known for his short stories of Rip Van Winkle and The Legend of Sleepy Hollow. The Franklin D. Roosevelt National Historic Site, in Hyde Park, NY contains "Springwood", the lifelong home of American's only 4-term President. Also included on this 300-acre site is the Franklin D. Roosevelt Presidential Library and Museum, operated by the National Archives, as well as grounds, gardens and trails.

276. Romans 8:28 "And we know that all things work together for good to those who love God, to those who are the called according to His purpose." (NKJV)

277. John 10:27 "My sheep hear My voice, and I know them, and they follow Me." (NKJV)

278. 1 Corinthians 14:3 "But he who prophesies speaks edification and exhortation and comfort to men. (NKJV)

279. Genesis 9:13-15 13I set My rainbow in the cloud, and it shall be for the sign of the covenant between Me and the earth. 14 It shall be, when I bring a cloud over the earth, that the rainbow shall be seen in the cloud; 15 and I will remember My covenant which is between Me and you and every living creature of all flesh; the waters shall never again become a flood to destroy all flesh." (NKJV)

280. Ephesians 1:21-23 "21 Far above all principality and power and might and dominion, and every name that is named, not only in this age but also in that which is to come.22 And He put all things under His feet, and gave Him to be head over all things to the church, 23 which is His body, the fullness of Him who fills all in all." (NKJV)

281. Barbara Koob, "The Sign of the Red Cardinal" at http://barbarakoob.com/the-sign-of-the-red-cardinal/

282. Mark 15:33 "Now when the sixth hour had come, there was darkness over the whole land until the ninth hour." (NKJV)

283. Matthew 27:51 "Then, behold, the veil of the temple was torn in two from top to bottom; and the earth quaked, and the rocks were split." (NKJV)

284. Matthew 27:52-53 "And the graves were opened; and many bodies of the saints who had fallen asleep were raised; 53 and coming out of the graves after His resurrection, they went into the holy city and appeared to many." (NKJV)

285. Psalm 135:9 He sent signs and wonders into the midst of you, O Egypt, upon Pharaoh and all his servants.; Acts 2:22 "Men of Israel, hear these words: Jesus of Nazareth, a Man attested by God to you by miracles, wonders, and signs which God did through Him in your midst, as you yourselves also know— (NKJV)

286. Charles Capps and Annette Capps, Angels: Knowing Their Purpose, Releasing Their Power (La Habra, CA: Charles Capps Ministries, 1954).; Hebrews 1:14 "Are they not all ministering spirits sent forth to minister for those who will inherit salvation?" (NKJV)

287. One refers to beginning and united. Eight refers to putting off the old; hence, a new beginning. And twelve refers to becoming a committed mature disciple of Christ as Jesus had twelve disciples.

288. Intrauterine insemination (IUI) is a fertility treatment that involves placing sperm inside a woman's uterus to facilitate fertilization. The goal of IUI is to increase the number of sperm that reach the fallopian tubes and subsequently increase the chance of fertilization. (American Pregnancy Association - http://americanpregnancy.org/infertility/intrauterine-insemination/). In Vitro Fertilization (IVF) is the process of fertilization by manually combining an egg and sperm in a laboratory dish, and then transferring the embryo to the uterus. (American Pregnancy Association - http://americanpregnancy.org/infertility/in-vitro-fertilization/)

289. Romans 8:37 "Yet in all these things we are more than conquerors through Him who loved us." (NKJV)

290. Luke 1:37 For with God nothing will be impossible. (NKJV)

291. Psalm 37:4 "Delight yourself also in the LORD, And He shall give you the desires of your heart." (NKJV)

292. Genesis 37:5-11

293. Genesis 37:12-36
294. Genesis 39:7-20
295. Matthew 20:20 "Not so with you. Instead, whoever wants to become great among you must be your servant." (NIV)
296. Matthew 20:27 "And whoever desires to be first among you, let him be your slave—" (NKJV)
297. Genesis 39:2-6, Genesis 39:21-23 God's Favor for Joseph
298. Luke 2:52 "And Jesus increased in wisdom and stature, and in favor with God and men." (NKJV)
299. Genesis 40: 9-15
300. Genesis 40:9-15
301. Genesis 40:8 "'We both had dreams,' they answered, 'but there is no one to interpret them.' Then Joseph said to them, 'Do not interpretations belong to God? Tell me your dreams.'" (NIV)
302. Genesis 40:14-15
303. Romans 10:9 "That if you confess with your mouth the Lord Jesus and believe in your heart that God has raised Him from the dead, you will be saved." (NKJV)
304. Genesis 41:8 "Now it came to pass in the morning that his spirit was troubled, and he sent and called for all the magicians of Egypt and all its wise men. And Pharaoh told them his dreams, but there was no one who could interpret them for Pharaoh." (NKJV)
305. Genesis 41:12 "Now there was a young Hebrew man with us there, a servant of the captain of the guard. And we told him, and he interpreted our dreams for us; to each man he interpreted according to his own dream." (NKJV)
306. Genesis 41:16 "So Joseph answered Pharaoh, saying, 'It is not in me; God will give Pharaoh an answer of peace.'" (NKJV)
307. Genesis 41:25-32; Genesis 41:33-36
308. Genesis 41:37 "So the advice was good in the eyes of Pharaoh and in the eyes of all his servants. And Pharaoh said to his servants, 'Can we find such a one as this, a man in whom is the Spirit of God?'" (NKJV); Genesis 41:39-44
309. John 3:16-17 "For God so loved the world that He gave His only begotten Son, that whoever believes in Him should not perish but have everlasting life. 17 For God did not send His Son into the world to condemn the world, but that the world through Him might be saved."; John 14:13 "And whatever you ask in My name, that I will do, that the Father may be glorified in the Son." (NKJV)
310. Matthew 6:8-10 "Therefore do not be like them. For your Father knows the things you have need of before you ask Him. In this manner, therefore, pray: Our Father in heaven, Hallowed by Your name. Your kingdom come. Your will be done. On earth as it is in heaven."
311. Loved Retreats are an encounter weekend with Father-God, an opportunity to enter into His presence and experience your connections with Him as He reminds you just how much He loves you. These retreats are held through The Connecting Point Ministry which can be found at www.connectingpointloved.com
312. Hebrews 12:5 "And have you completely forgotten this word of encouragement that addresses you as a father addresses his son? It says, 'My son, do not make light of the Lord's discipline, and do not lose heart when he rebukes you.'" (NKJV)
313. Hebrews 12:6 "Because the Lord disciplines the one he loves, and he chastens everyone he accepts as his son." (NKJV)
314. Acts 2:21 "And it shall come to pass That whoever calls on the name of the LORD Shall be saved." (NKJV)
315. John 14:26 "But the Helper, the Holy Spirit, whom the Father will send in My name, He will teach you all things, and bring to your remembrance all things that I said to you." (NKJV)
316. Romans 3:23 "For all have sinned and fall short of the glory of God." (NKJV)
317. Genesis 3:23-24 "Therefore the LORD God sent him out of the garden of Eden to till the ground from which he was taken. 24 So He drove out the man; and He placed cherubim at the east of the garden of Eden, and a flaming sword which turned every way, to guard the way to the tree of life." (NKJV)
318. Romans 5:8 "But God demonstrates His own love toward us, in that while we were still sinners, Christ died for us." (NKJV)

319. Hebrews 9:22 "And according to the law almost all things are purified with blood, and without shedding of blood there is no remission." (NKJV)

320. John 3:16 "For God so loved the world that He gave His only begotten Son, that whoever believes in Him should not perish but have everlasting life." (NKJV)

321. 1 John 4:8 "He who does not love does not know God, for God is love."; Hebrews 12:23 "To the general assembly and church of the firstborn who are registered in heaven, to God the Judge of all, to the spirits of just men made perfect." (NKJV)

322. Romans 10:9 "That if you confess with your mouth the Lord Jesus and believe in your heart that God has raised Him from the dead, you will be saved." (NKJV)

323. John 3:16-17 "For God so loved the world that He gave His only begotten Son, that whoever believes in Him should not perish but have everlasting life. For God did not send His Son into the world to condemn the world, but that the world through Him might be saved."; John 3:18-19 "He who believes in Him is not condemned; but he who does not believe is condemned already, because he has not believed in the name of the only begotten Son of God. And this is the condemnation, that the light has come into the world, and men loved darkness rather than light, because their deeds were evil." (NKJV)

324. Ephesians 1:5-6 "Having predestined us to adoption as sons by Jesus Christ to Himself, according to the good pleasure of His will, 6 to the praise of the glory of His grace, by which He made us accepted in the Beloved."; Ephesians 1:18 "The eyes of your understanding] being enlightened; that you may know what is the hope of His calling, what are the riches of the glory of His inheritance in the saints." (NKJV)

325. Colossians 1:27 "To them God willed to make known what are the riches of the glory of this mystery among the Gentiles: which] is Christ in you, the hope of glory." (NKJV)

326. 1 Corinthians 2:13 "These things we also speak, not in words which man's wisdom teaches but which the Holy] Spirit teaches, comparing spiritual things with spiritual." (NKJV)

327. Genesis 3:7-8 "Before the fall in the Garden of Eden, Adam and Eve walked and talked with God." (Genesis 3:7-8)

328. John 14:6 "Jesus said to him, 'I am the way, the truth, and the life. No one comes to the Father except through Me.'" (NKJV)

329. Romans 5:15 "But the free gift is not like the offense. For if by the one man's offense many died, much more the grace of God and the gift by the grace of the one Man, Jesus Christ, abounded to many." (NKJV)

330. John 14:16 "And I will pray the Father, and He will give you another Helper, that He may abide with you forever— "; Hebrews 13:5 "Let your conduct be without covetousness; be content with such things as you have. For He Himself has said, 'I will never leave you nor forsake you.'" (NKJV)

331. 1 Corinthians 12:4-11 The Nine Supernatural Gifts of the Spirit are: a word of wisdom, a word of knowledge, and gifts of faith, healing, miracles, prophecy, tongues, interpretation of tongues and discerning of spirits.

332. Luke 11:11 "If a son asks for bread from any father among you, will he give him a stone? Or if he asks for a fish, will he give him a serpent instead of a fish?"; Luke 11:13 "If you then, being evil, know how to give good gifts to your children, how much more will your heavenly Father give the Holy Spirit to those who ask Him!" (NKJV)

333. John 4:10 "Jesus answered and said to her, 'If you knew the gift of God, and who it is who says to you, "Give Me a drink," you would have asked Him, and He would have given you living water.'" (NKJV)

334. John 11:22 "But even now I know that whatever You ask of God, God will give You." (NKJV)

335. 1 Corinthians 15:31 "I affirm, by the boasting in you which I have in Christ Jesus our Lord, I die daily." (NKJV)

336. Jeremiah 29:11 "For I know the thoughts that I think toward you, says the LORD, thoughts of peace and not of evil, to give you a future and a hope." (NKJV)

337. Proverbs 16:9 "A man's heart plans his way, But the LORD directs his steps." (NKJV)

338. 2 Corinthians 12:9 "And He said to me, 'My grace is sufficient for you, for My strength is made perfect in weakness.' Therefore, most gladly I will rather boast in my infirmities, that the power of Christ may rest upon me."

339. 2 Corinthians 12:10 "Therefore I take pleasure in infirmities, in reproaches, in needs, in persecutions, in distresses, for Christ's sake. For when I am weak, then I am strong." (NKJV)

340. 1 Peter 5:8 "Be sober, be vigilant; because your adversary the devil walks about like a roaring lion, seeking whom he may devour." (NKJV)

341. Romans 8:28 "And we know that all things work together for good to those who love God, to those who are the called according to His purpose." (NKJV)

342. 1 Corinthians 1:5-7 "That you were enriched in everything by Him in all utterance and all knowledge, even as the testimony of Christ was confirmed in you, so that you come short in no gift, eagerly waiting for the revelation of our Lord Jesus Christ."(NKJV)

343. John 15:7 "If you abide in Me, and My words abide in you, you will ask what you desire, and it shall be done for you." (NKJV)

About the Author

Barbara Koob is an ordinary woman who has learned to hope and dream with purpose. A biblical dreamer with a passion for prayer, she is desperate for God to splash His blessings on others so that they can welcome God, receive His healing touch, and step out into their destiny. She writes, speaks, teaches, and mentors people on prayer, healing and biblical dream interpretation.

Formally mentored in healing prayer, Barb attended the Presbyterian Reformed Ministries International (PRMI) Dunamis Institute and God's unique Dream University to both receive healing and pray for the sick. In addition, she is a graduate of PRMI's Advanced Healing and Deliverance program, and has served as the Prayer Director for the Hope Chapel Apex Women's Ministry.

Happily married to the man of her dreams, Barb lives with her teenage sweetheart and a cuddly cockapoo named Sunshine in North Carolina. They have been blessed with a beautiful daughter who is now a young woman embarking on discovering her own God-given purpose. You can find Barb on her website at BarbaraKoob.com where she journals about life as a real Barbie doll on her road to freedom.